U Hazards
Handbook

...de to the effects

...new technology

London Hazards
Centre

By Ursula Huws for the LONDON HAZARDS CENTRE

Contents

Acknowledgements

After the London Hazards Centre opened in 1984 it became apparent that a significant part of its work would involve responding to requests for information about the health effects of working with new technology, particularly the hazards of VDU work.

The few publications then available gave some information about these hazards, but none met all VDU workers' needs. Indeed, some of these publications seemed more concerned with reassuring and placating workers than with providing honest answers to their queries, or explanations of why their health was affected.

The Centre recognised the need for a single publication that considered the implications for employment, health and safety of the widespread introduction of VDUs into different types of workplace and how to organise for change.

I would like to thank Claire-Marie Fortin, who made a very important and useful contribution to this publication, including writing most of the introduction, the chapter on eye hazards and some valuable material on stress.

Thanks too to the overworked staff of the London Hazards Centre collective for their useful and often thought-provoking comments on the first draft, their help in chasing up references and the friendly welcome which unfailingly awaited me and my daughter in their office. I am especially grateful to Maggie Alexander, who steered the book through production in record-breaking time.

Thanks are also due to the hundreds of VDU workers I have met over the past ten years or so, as colleagues in the various offices where I have worked, as users of the Leeds Trade Union and Community Resource and Information Centre, as participants in surveys, and as attendants at conferences and day-schools. Without their experiences of VDU work, and their analysis of what can be done to minimise the hazards, this book could not have been written.

Finally, I would like to thank Richard Belfield for his helpful comments on the sections of the book which deal with the effects of radiation, and Chris Jones for his insights into ways of thinking about technology.

Ursula Huws
March 1987

– 1 –

Introduction

'Computer drives out women
As if it were a friend of women
It drives out women

Computer is an enemy of women
Though it glitters and looks clean
It makes a woman cry

Oh computer,
Women have long been waiting for you,
Hoping that you will help us to have more free time
And yet you, computer,
You have only helped us to shed more tears'[1]

This poem comes from high-tech Japan. It was written, we are told, 'like a murmur on a notebook' by an isolated office worker, but it expresses such a widespread feeling about the effects of computerised work systems that it has been passed on by word of mouth and is now very popular among women workers throughout Japan.

The sentiments in it are very similar to those of the hundreds of VDU operators, men and women, who inundated the London Hazards Centre with calls after the Centre was mentioned as a source of advice about the hazards of VDUs on a Thames Television 'Help!' programme in October 1984.

They were suffering from a range of bodily disorders including headaches, eyestrain, muscular problems, inflamed tendons, skin rashes, and disturbed body rhythms. And many were worried that there might be other effects, less easy to see or measure, such as dangers to their unborn children, changes in blood pressure or long-term damage to their eyesight.

Yet the popular image of this new technology is a positive one. The advent of the cheap microcomputer is usually seen as one of the great landmarks in the unstoppable march of progress, and progress, so we are generally informed, is making the world a better place for all. Computerisation is supposed to take the strain out of traditional chores, making work easier and quicker. It also helps us do without all those dirty old mechanical machines with their dangerous moving parts, giving us a cleaner and safer working environment. How can this image be squared with the reality of the workers' experiences reported to the London Hazards Centre?

In fact, these two, very different, images of new technology are not as hard to reconcile as they might appear at first glance. Historically, the introduction of new technologies has often been associated with new hazards for workers. Although we have been taught that the industrial revolution was a great step forward for humankind, we are all also familiar with horrific descriptions of accidents in the textile mills of the 18th and 19th centuries, where workers, often young children, might be dragged into unguarded machines by their hair and the loss of limbs was an everyday occurrence. Less well known are the health hazards of factory and put-out work in the textiles and clothing industries, which were described in the 19th century,[2] as including 'enervation, exhaustion, debility, loss of appetite, pains in the shoulders, back and hips, but especially . . . weeping, smarting eyes which soon become short-sighted', symptoms which are remarkably similar to those experienced by many VDU operators. On one side of the coin we find increased efficiency, higher productivity, cheap consumer goods, and new wealth for the factory owners; on the other, new hazards for the workers.

Mounting international concern about the safety of VDUs is now leading to an increasingly widespread view that the second, computer-based, industrial revolution also has its dark underside.

There are several parallels. The factory owners of the 18th and 19th centuries were fighting a cut-throat battle with one another for markets and profits. There were major advantages for those manufacturers who could lower their costs and speed up their production, as well as controlling the increasing militancy of their workforce. This drove them to pour resources into the development of ever more powerful machinery. The direct benefits of such innovation to the factory owners were obvious. The mechanisation of spinning, weaving and other forms of manufacturing brought about impressive increases in the amount a single worker could produce. In addition, machines provided the means of replacing highly skilled workers with cheaper labour, whose bargaining power and organised strength were weaker.

Successive waves of technological development, such as assembly line production and continuous processing, have followed a similar pattern. Companies have continued to seek technological routes to

This worker is responsible for the entire biscuit production and packing line. Alone, she oversees the processing of thousands of biscuits an hour.

Maggie Murray/Format

higher productivity to improve profitability and try to stay ahead of their competitors.

Although the basic motivation behind the present wave of innovation – the development of microelectronics – is not new, what does set it apart from previous technological developments is that it is being applied to a much wider spectrum of jobs. VDUs are now present, not just in factories, but in virtually every other type of workplace too: in warehouses, banks, supermarkets, offices small and large, travel agencies, schools, hospitals, mines, farms, garages, design studios, police stations, homes. . . They are used by large organisations like the armed forces, the government and transnational corporations and by small ones like accountants' or solicitors' practices, employment agencies or advice centres. The cheapness, adaptability and flexibility of computer systems has provided management with new ways of boosting productivity, reducing the need for highly skilled workers and applying factory-like machine controls outside the factory.

It is easy enough to blame the machines themselves for deteriorating working conditions. In the tradition of the Luddite hand weavers of the last century, who smashed the machines which threatened their livelihoods, we may find it easier to focus attention on the technology itself rather than on the social conditions which surround its use.

In reality the machines are not to blame. They do not set work quotas, plan redundancies or construct job definitions. There is no inherent reason why a computer must record the number of keystrokes a data entry operator makes in an hour, or how many minutes a telephone operator spends in the loo. Many of the physical problems suffered by VDU workers *could* be alleviated by proper design and planning and some investment in appropriate equipment.

To deal effectively with the hazards of VDUs, it is essential to combine a knowledge of the machines with an understanding of the social forces which shape the way the technology is being used. We must explore such questions as: Who is introducing the new technology? For what purpose? Why now? What do they expect to gain? What might be lost in the process? What are the effects on those of us who have to use the VDUs? And, most importantly, what can we do about it, as workers, parents, consumers and members of our own particular communities?

–2–

Why new technology is being introduced

In the 18th and 19th centuries employers introduced new technologies into their factories because they brought concrete advantages in the form of cheaper goods, faster production with fewer workers, lower skill requirements and greater control of the workforce. In the same way, the new information technology which has been entering our workplaces in quantity since the mid-1970s is also being introduced because it brings tangible benefits to employers.

The first and most obvious of these is that it can help them to reduce labour costs by cutting down on the number of staff required to do a particular job. The precise increase in productivity varies according to what type of work is being done, how sophisticated the technology is and how the work is organised. Job loss is sometimes masked by an expansion in the amount of business carried out by the organisation, or a growth in part-time working, but the tendency is always in the same direction – fewer workers producing more.

In the Grattons mail-order warehouse in Bradford, for instance, full-time staff were reduced from 1,000 to 550 and part-timers from 100 to 50 over a period of a few months when a new computerised system for dealing with orders was introduced in 1979, despite an increase in the volume of business.[3]

Williams and Glyn's Bank, in a report to BIFU, the Banking, Finance and Insurance Union, after purchasing eight word processors, said that:

> 'These machines have so far directly saved two staff and avoided the recruitment of a further three and a half staff (therefore each word processor replaces three quarters of a typist). It is anticipated that four more machines will be purchased in the near future with a further saving of three staff.' (BIFU's parentheses)[4]

Multiplied many times throughout an organisation, productivity increases like these represent a substantial saving for management. For workers, they tend to mean growing insecurity of employment.

It should be noted that such job loss does not necessarily mean actual redundancy for individual workers. A smaller workforce is often brought about by the process known as 'natural wastage', whereby jobs are simply not replaced if someone leaves.

Another advantage of new technology from the employer's point of view is that it can greatly increase the speed and accuracy of work. No longer need typists stop to look up the spelling of a word in a dictionary – the machine can do it for them. No longer need shop assistants spend hours counting boxes to take stock of the contents of a shop – with fully automated checkouts, stock-taking is a simple matter of pressing a few keys. A similar story can be told wherever computerised systems have been installed, from balancing account books to designing aircraft.

For the workers concerned, unfortunately, increasing speed can often lead to greater pressure of work and more monotony while the development of machine-checked accuracy may simply mean that hard-earned skills have lost their value.

Computerised information systems can also benefit employers in another way: by greatly increasing the amount of information available to management about individual workers, and by tightening its monitoring and control of the workforce.

Indeed, to some, this is the main advantage of new technology. In the words of Franco di Benedetti, managing director of Olivetti:

> 'Information technology is basically a technology of coordination and control of the labour force, the white collar workers Taylorian organisation does not cover.'[5]

In using the term 'Taylorian' he is referring to the 'scientific management' techniques developed in the 19th century by Taylor, the man who introduced the stopwatch to the factory floor. Taylorism demands that every movement involved in every task is carefully analysed and measured so that jobs can be broken down and simplified and the last millimetre of productivity extracted from every worker. Before the advent of the computer, many non-manual jobs were not susceptible to this type of measurement and control.

A typical advertisement in a retailing magazine for computerised cash registers promises 'checkout which is 50% faster and 100% more efficient'. It goes on to offer managers detailed information about their staff through its time and attendance system:

> 'At (the manager's) in-store terminal such daily information is obtained as the name, employee number, department, job title, work status (whether full or part-time) and the union affiliation of each employee currently in the store. He also sees the time that each employee has arrived for work that morning, the number of hours worked all week and the length of coffee breaks.'

It is not surprising that these advantages to employers often translate into disadvantages for workers. The fact that in many parts of the world the programs, or parts of programs, which monitor workers' performance are known as 'spies' speaks for itself. High levels of scrutiny by management are associated with high stress levels, low job satisfaction and lack of self-esteem.

New technology can bring still further benefits to employers. One of the effects of introducing it is to make it much easier to casualise employment, in other words to reduce the number of 'core' full-time permanent jobs within an organisation and get as much of the work as possible done on a casual, temporary or outwork basis. The new technology contributes to this tendency in several ways.

Firstly, it makes work much more routine and easy to measure. This makes it simpler to break up a complex work process into several separate parts which can then be put out to subcontractors. The computerisation of offices has been accompanied by a boom in subcontracting, to both large and small organisations, of services ranging from accountancy to advertising, from data entry to design.

Secondly, the telecommunications technology which makes it possible to link computers up remotely, combined with computerisation and machine monitoring, has made it possible to move jobs around geographically in ways that were not possible before. This has resulted in a transfer of some types of work out of city-centre offices into smaller suburban or regional offices, into people's homes, resulting in new forms of white-collar homeworking[6]; and even offshore, to the 'electronic sweatshops' of the developing world where women work in shifts round the clock keying in data for US-based transnational companies over satellite links[7].

Most of these forms of casual work, whether they consist of 'temping', working for small subcontracting firms or homeworking, are associated with less job security, lower wages, fewer benefits and much lower levels of unionisation than permanent jobs based at the employer's main premises.

The shifting of some types of office work offshore has started to create an international division of labour in white-collar work, similar to the international division of labour which has grown up over the past twenty years in manufacturing industry, whereby employers can transfer work from one country to another at their convenience.

A final effect of introducing information technology is, in some types of workplace, to change working hours. For managements that have invested in new computerised systems, there is an incentive to 'get their money's worth' out of them by having them used as much as possible, and this has led to the introduction of 'twilight' or Saturday morning shifts in a number of industries which were previously strictly nine-to-five.

Sometimes, the extension of hours is not done by introducing shift work but by asking staff to 'volunteer' for extra duties.

'The Yorkshire Bank's implementation of cashier terminals was welcomed in branches which had been short staffed and working frequent overtime as it reduced cashing up at the day's end by 15 to 30 minutes. Within six months the bank announced it was to open an extra half hour per day (to 4 p.m.) at all those and only those branches which had cashier terminals.

'National Westminster has recently announced a full personal service on Saturday mornings: in-bank ATMs (automatic telling machines) to draw and deposit cash plus senior clerical, administrative and management staff to advise. Staff not volunteering still have to process the additional work in normal hours.'[8]

Where on-line computerised systems operated by customers have been introduced, such as automatic cash dispensers in banks, it is necessary to have backroom staff servicing them 24 hours a day, and night shifts have been brought in. If the work involves communicating with other computers at a distance over the telephone lines, then evening and weekend working is even more valuable from the employer's point of view: it makes it possible to take advantage of cheap off-peak telephone charges.

Taken together, these changes mean that a substantial proportion of white-collar workers are now working the 'unsocial' hours more usually associated with factories or with service work in hospitals or transport. Needless to say, these unsocial hours also bring disadvantages to those who must work them: disrupted body rhythms increase susceptibility to a number of complaints such as digestive and circulatory disorders, and strains on family and social life.

Greater speed and accuracy, higher productivity, lower wage bills, tighter control over the workforce, lower overheads and the chance to spread working hours: taken together, these give the new technology an irresistible appeal to most employers. However they also have serious drawbacks for most workers who have to cope with enormous upheavals in their working patterns and live each day with the consequences.

– 3 –

The context in which new technology is being introduced

To understand the effects of new technology on work it is not enough simply to look at what happens in any particular workplace. No employer operates in a vacuum. The decisions made within any single organisation are a reflection of, and a response to, much broader economic, political and social changes taking place in the world.

Similarly, individual workers do not exist simply as workers. Who they are and what they do outside the workplace influences what job they get and how they are treated at work. Whether you are male or female, Black or white, old or young; whether or not you have children or other dependants; what class your parents and grandparents were; where you live; what education you had; whether or not you have a physical or mental disability; whether you are heterosexual, lesbian or gay; what language you speak and what accent you speak it with. Any of these factors can influence the work opportunities open to you, and social changes which affect people in any of these capacities may also change their position in the workforce.

It is necessary therefore to take a brief look at the broader context in which information technology is being introduced if we are to make sense of many of its effects on individual workers and their bodies.

Perhaps the most significant question to ask is why the present wave of technological innovation began at the historical moment that it did, in the mid-1970s. There is no particularly good technical reason why it should have been at this moment that there was a sudden interest in developing new computerised work systems. The computer had been around for at least twenty years, and so had the capability for linking computers to each other through landlines or over the telephone grid. Admittedly, the technology was rapidly becoming smaller, cheaper, and with higher capacity, but this, it could be argued, was largely a result of the new interest in developing commercial applications for this originally military technology rather than the cause of that interest.

The answer to this question is economic rather than technological. In the early 1970s, the world was plunged into a major economic crisis.

Companies could no longer rely on continuing growth to boost their profits but were forced into increasingly cut-throat competition with each other to stay in business at all. Profits could not come from selling more goods because the markets were shrinking, and they could not come from raising prices, because competition was so keen. There was only one way most companies could stay in business and produce the profits their shareholders demanded: by cutting costs. The race was on to find ways to reduce the numbers of staff, bring down wage levels and increase efficiency. The prize was economic survival and the means, in great measure, was new technology. A bonus, for many large companies, was being in at the birth of the new 'sunrise' industries manufacturing this new technology which were to become increasingly important in the world economy.

These developments were not confined to private companies. The recession also produced a monetary crisis for governments. With falling tax revenues and companies becoming increasingly ruthless in their refusal to contribute to the social costs of running a country, governments too became increasingly keen to cut costs, and looked to the technology to help them reduce their wage bills in much the same way. The British Government, like most others in the developed world, began a massive programme of cutbacks in public services.

Needless to say, these developments led to a huge increase in unemployment, so that at a time when the need for the payment of social benefits and the provision of social services had never been greater, they were in shorter supply than ever before since the foundation of the welfare state. Unemployment benefit and social security payments went down in real terms, while services like school dinners, nurseries, health care, day and residential care for people with disabilities and the elderly, and transport services deteriorated.

This has had a number of effects apart from simply causing hardship for millions of people. It has reduced the general level of health among the unemployed and their dependants and it has also drastically reduced the choices available to all working people. The threat of unemployment is enough to persuade most people to accept poorer working conditions and lower grade jobs than they would contemplate during a period of economic boom. Their reduced bargaining power as workers has prevented them from fighting worsening conditions, allowed dangerous working practices to proliferate unchecked and in some cases enabled employers to scrap trade union agreements altogether.

This tendency has been reinforced by political and legislative developments. A series of anti-trade union laws each more severe than the last has reduced workers' bargaining power still further, while legislation passed by the Labour Government in the early 1970s to provide some rights for workers has been amended or dismantled by the Conservatives so that it now provides little real protection. Workers in small firms have been particularly penalised, with the withdrawal of several rights, including the right to paid maternity leave. If they are under 21, workers are now also deprived of the right to a minimum wage fixed by a Wages Council. Both wages inspectors and health and safety inspectors have been reduced in numbers to such an extent that the chances of a law-breaking employer being found out are now minimal.

Women have been especially hard hit by these developments. During the 1960s and 1970s they entered the workforce in increasing numbers, making up four workers out of every ten by 1980. In some types of employment, such as shop and office work, this proportion is even higher. Large sectors of the economy now depend on women's work to keep them going. However, the cutbacks in social services have made it increasingly difficult for women to combine their role as a carer in the home with going out to work, and many have been forced into low-paid part-time jobs, temporary work or work near their home to survive. They are thus more likely than men to work for small, unorganised workplaces, and therefore generally receive fewer benefits and have less job security.

These material factors reducing employment choices for women have been accompanied by other, less tangible pressures not to compete with men on the open job market. There has been a strong drive to get women back into the home which has taken several different forms.

Many Government pronouncements have emphasised the value of the family, and an attitude has been encouraged which holds parents responsible for their children's behaviour, and blames mothers who go out to work for delinquency. Recent childcare literature, typified in many of Penelope Leach's books, emphasises the importance of bonding between mother and child and suggests that the child will suffer irreparably if separated from her for any length of time.

'Community care' is also the current watchword for care of the elderly and people with physical or mental disabilities. There is some justice in the criticisms levelled by the community care lobby at the vast and impersonal institutions in which these people have been confined in the past. However the Government has not responded to these criticisms by creating smaller, friendlier, more democratically run facilities. Its aim has been to 'reintegrate patients into the community' without providing any resources. In many cases the mentally ill, the physically disabled and the elderly have simply been dumped back into their families' homes to be looked after by women without payment or support.

That this rhetoric about strengthening and reuniting the family, reducing the state provision of social services and lowering the divorce rate should be circulating at precisely the same time as the widespread introduction of new technology seems at first sight to be merely a coincidence. In fact, however, the two issues are believed to be closely connected by a wide range of people including many politicians and the companies which manufacture the equipment.

Here, for instance, is Shirley Williams, a prominent politician in the Social Democratic Party:

'Microelectronics offers the opportunity of reuniting the family.'[9]

This was a view with which several members of the Conservative government concurred when announcing their plans for the development of cable networks to upgrade Britain's telecommunications infrastructure in 1983.

A year later, a similar point was made by the organisers of a conference of planners debating the future of Britain's housing stock. Not only, was it stated, would information technology revive family unity and 'restore the headship factor' to family life, but it would also free industry and commerce from the necessity to '"carry" unskilled labour in the factories and commercial centres of tomorrow'[10].

Even inside the computer industry, the family turns out to be a cause for concern. Mike Aldrich is managing director of ROCC Computers, formerly Rediffusion computers, part of the enormous British Electric Traction group. His company has a major stake in videotex, one of the technologies which marries computing and telecommunications to make 'remote working' possible, and in a book written by him to publicise the product, long passages are devoted to discussions of the family. First, he bemoans the loss of the Christian ethic of marriage 'till death us do part' and deplores the rising divorce rate. Then he goes on to say that:

'The growth of transient marriage and one-parent families is the counterpoint to the decline of the extended family and the gradual withering of family responsibility for the old, the sick, the handicapped and the disabled. They have all become the responsibility of the State in the main because home-based family society could not cope.'

However, all is not lost, because:

'If the underlying economic trends were anti-family in the past, perhaps the future offers better prospects for our basic unit of social organisation because of trends in our working lives. In 1981, 60% of the total US labour expense was consumed by office workers. The total size of this workforce dedicated to working with logical goods or paperwork continued to grow...We have to face the fact that our society has changed from being blue collar to being white collar. This may change our attitude to work. It is not possible to deliver a steel mill to a cottage each day for the worker to use, but it is possible to deliver electronic paperwork to the cottage everyday. With the array of telecommunications products and services becoming available at ever reducing costs in real terms, the burden of change must be towards home-centring our lives rather than town or city-centring as at present for work as we know it.'[11]

The mysterious connection between new technology and the family is at last revealed. By making it possible to shift information processing work away from central workplaces it enables new forms of homeworking to be created, returning women to their roles as unpaid cooks, cleaners and carers in the household while keeping their labour available for an economy which has increasingly become dependent on it. This possibility offers enormous advantages to employers, who are saved the costs of office overheads and gain a much more pliable and less organised workforce while retaining the services of their women workers. It is also attractive to a government which wishes to keep public expenditure on such items as transport, childcare and facilities for the elderly and disabled at a minimum. For women, however, it holds few advantages, since it reduces choice still further. It is likely to lead to isolation, deteriorating wages and conditions, and the stress of trying to do two jobs at once – the paid and the unpaid.

Accompanying this hardening of attitudes on women's right to work has come an upsurge in racism. Black people have often become the scapegoats for high unemployment levels and deteriorating services. They are blamed if they have a job, for taking what it is said should belong to a white person, and are blamed if they are unemployed for 'scrounging'. Subjected to increasingly violent levels of racial harassment both at work and in the community and suffering much higher unemployment than whites, Black people have been driven into the worst-paid, least secure and most dangerous jobs. The establishment's encouragement of the racist attitudes of many white workers has produced a divided workforce, enabling employers to introduce changes detrimental to both Black and white workers.

All these features have contributed to the creation of a new climate for workers and people seeking work. It is a climate in which there is much less certainty than in the past that a job will remain secure or that agreements reached in the past about how it should be carried out will be honoured.

This has affected the bargaining position of workers, placing unions on the defensive and making it very difficult to raise positive demands. Theoretically, the new technology could be used to bring great improvements to working life: to remove hazards, to reduce the boring and repetitive aspects of many jobs and make them more creative, to shorten working hours and improve the quality of services to the public. In practice, the trade unions have their hands full responding to management and government initiatives which threaten to make these things worse.

Regaining the initiative for workers will involve changing the political climate and challenging the supremacy of profit. It will involve transforming the current value system to insist on the overriding importance of the basic human rights to health, freedom of choice and an income which guarantees a decent standard of living.

– 4 –

How new technology changes jobs

Chapter 2 looked at some of the reasons why employers are introducing new information technology into their workplaces, and showed that some of the advantages of new technology to the employers become disadvantages when seen from the workers' point of view. This chapter examines workers' experience of new technology in more detail, and outlines some of the main changes which computerisation typically brings.

Work tends to become more repetitive and monotonous

Before a work task can be automated, a process of work study has to take place. This involves a step-by-step breakdown of everything the worker does during the course of carrying out the task. Once all these steps have been measured and counted, they are analysed by a systems analyst. The next stage is carried out by a programmer, who translates this analysis into a set of instructions which the computer can understand, creating a program which actually incorporates much of the knowledge which the workers previously carried in their heads, whether consciously or unconsciously.

Of course, if the work which you do is reasonably standard, such as copy-typing or book-keeping, then your job will not need to be studied individually, but can be automated using a standard off-the-peg program, or 'software package' as it is often known. Nevertheless, this program will incorporate many of the things which you or your predecessor previously carried out on your own initiative.

The effect of this process is to standardise the way that the task is carried out, leaving much less room for individual choice or flexibility. This makes the work more routine and repetitive.

Breaking down the work into its component parts like this also encourages managers to separate the tasks, giving some to some individuals and some to others. Individual workers are therefore more likely to become specialists, doing the same task repeatedly all day, instead of developing an all-round knowledge of several different aspects of the job. In one typical American office:

> 'The jobs of a group of secretaries were broken down into five subtasks when word processing equipment was brought in. One to type all day, one to enter data all day, one to take it out, and so on. Now, each woman must complete a "tour of duty" in each "subtask" before she can be considered for advancement. In other words, she has to be promoted four times just to get back to where she started!'[12]

This change is already beginning to show in the recruitment practices of some organisations. In banks, for instance, the traditional career structure whereby everyone was recruited at the lowest grade and worked their way up has broken down. Now a 'two-tier' entry system is becoming the norm, with high-flyers (usually men) recruited at a higher 'career' grade while the lower grades have become dead-end jobs, generally filled by women, consisting of a single repetitive task and with little prospect of learning new skills.

The more repetitive and monotonous a job, the more likely it is to lead to physical and mental stress, and therefore adversely affect the health of the person who has to carry it out.

Jobs are more closely monitored and controlled

Another source of stress for VDU workers is having their work closely monitored and controlled. A work monitoring program is a standard part of the software of most data entry systems and of many word processing and other computer-related functions, and managers have come to take their existence for granted.

When a study was carried out of the Greater London Council's data entry staff in 1983, high levels of stress were discovered among the keyboard operators, whose work was closely monitored and who were obliged to meet set productivity targets in order to progress to higher gradings, and therefore higher rates of pay[13]. Their manager was asked why this group of workers had been singled out for monitoring when no other group of white-collar workers in the organisation was either monitored or paid according to performance. His reply was, 'It's a standard part of the software'. In other words, the technology is used in this way, even by organisations attempting to achieve equal opportunities policies and develop less exploitative ways of working, simply because it is there. Suspicion of keyboard operators and a desire to control them has been designed into the technology itself.

In many cases, of course, managers relish using this capability and see it as an important tool to keep productivity high. Here is one

**High levels of stress are common in data entry keyboard operators who are
required to meet set productivity targets.** *Jenny Matthews/Format*

American manager of an offshore office in Kingston, Jamaica:

> 'When a worker turns on a machine, she must sign on with her identification
> number. The machine monitors the productivity level in keystrokes per
> hour. So, if she goes for a break, she must turn off the machine . . . Some
> workers think they are being smart and fooling us by leaving the machine
> on when they go to the bathroom, but we can tell when they try to do this,
> too, because their recorded productivity drops, since they've been gone
> from the terminal.'[14]

Some systems have gone even further. Sometimes a woman may
decide that today she's just had enough. No matter how much bonus
payment she might lose, she's simply not going to push herself any
further and will work at a slower pace for a while. To get round this
response, a French hire purchase company has begun using a system
which exploits women's loyalty to their fellow workers. Instead of
basing the bonus payment on individual productivity, workers are
divided into small groups, and rewarded on the basis of the group's
productivity (although individual workers' records are still kept by
management)[15]. A woman who slackens is thus made to feel that she's
letting down her colleagues. Such a system can also become a means
of getting workers to police each other, perhaps even setting the faster
ones against their less productive workmates.

It is no accident that all these examples concern women. The lower
grades of keyboarding work are almost exclusively female. In Britain,

for example, over 98 per cent of typists are women. However, many of their managers are men. This adds another dimension to the control structure in the computerised workplace. Not only is it control by managers over workers; it is also very often control by men over women, using technological systems which have, by and large, been designed by men.

This creates particular problems for women who try to strike back and regain some control over their own work. They may be subjected to sexual harassment and ridicule as well as more formal means of discipline.

In addition, it creates a situation where there is unlikely to be any understanding of the stress to which women are already subject through their double role as paid workers and unpaid carers. This can interact with the tension caused by constant management policing at work to create an intolerable degree of stress.

To show how universal this pattern is, the next example comes from Japan, where 80 per cent of jobs were eliminated in one office of the Tokyo Postal Savings Bureau when it was automated. The remaining 520 workers have been reorganised so that most now spend half their day as terminal operators in 'letter printing rooms' where they are closely watched by supervisors who record who talks to whom and when, and all visits to the toilet. The machines monitor the workers' speed, accuracy and attendance and they are constantly being urged to work faster. One woman said:

> 'At work, even though I am dead tired, I am constantly being pressed to go faster. As soon as my day is over, I have to rush to the day-care centre to pick up my child; then I must rush home and make him his tea and give him a quick bath; then I find myself telling him to hurry up and get to bed. I have become obsessed with rushing and hurrying about, because I am pressured so much at work. I am so tired at work that I feel like going straight to bed as soon as I get home. The computerisation at work has made a mess of my whole life.'[16]

Work involves fewer skills

The same Japanese office also provides an example of the way in which skill requirements change when new technology is introduced. As in other Eastern countries, before the advent of the microcomputer, most Japanese book-keepers were still using an abacus to add, subtract, multiply and divide. Now they have been reduced to key-punch operators. One experienced worker commented:

> 'In the past, being able to use an abacus was the most important skill a worker could have. But now, just how much key punching can be done? The computer can discover your errors, and worse yet, it can record them.

There seems to be no place in a system like this for a middle-aged or older worker like me.'[17]

All over the world, in many different types of workplace men and women have made similar discoveries: that their skills and qualifications, often learned the hard way through long apprenticeships, attendance at night school and hours of practice, have become out of date and well-nigh useless.

In warehouses, for instance, workers once needed to be skilled fork-lift truck drivers and have good memories to locate goods. New electronic warehousing simply involves sitting at a desk terminal, directing automatic units to the right location and removing the required item by remote control.

Similarly, typists needed good spelling and grammar, and a knowledge of a variety of different forms of address and document layout. They were also expected to know a wide range of 'tricks of the trade', such as how to feed stapled documents into a typewriter, how to prevent small cards or labels from slipping when they are typed, how to deal with stencils and so on. They might also have been expected to take down dictation in shorthand, to be familiar with the office filing system, to be able to use duplicating machines and a variety of other things. Now, the most important requirement is the mere ability to type. There are computer programs to check spelling and grammar, and standard layouts for letters, including banks of standard paragraphs. Printing is done by pushing a few keys on the keyboard and the filing cabinet has been replaced by the computer disc. As for shorthand, it is now rarely used except by journalists and specialist reporters of court, conference or parliamentary proceedings, having been replaced by the cassette recorder for most purposes.

Likewise in the printing industry the skills of the linotype operator, who needed a detailed knowledge of typefaces and typesizes, the ability to remember their positions on a vast keyboard and to estimate accurately the space they would take up, have been supplanted by the skills of the copy-typist using a QWERTY keyboard.

In shops, there is no longer any need for the skills of estimating the quantities and types of foods required when stock-keeping. Each item sold can be recorded at the checkout using electronic scanning of bar-codes or by requiring the cashier to enter a reference number, so that a replacement can be ordered automatically.

In the clothing industry, cutters used to be an elite. Their skills involved a knowledge of the behaviour of different types of cloth, precise accuracy and considerable mathematical ability to estimate how the maximum number of pieces could be fitted into the minimum length of cloth, skills which were only acquired through a long apprenticeship. Now, computerised cutting has become the norm. Working out how the pieces can be fitted most economically into the cloth is done remotely at a VDU screen, where the operator can juggle around miniature outlines of the desired shapes until none overlap. Training takes six weeks.

Such examples could be multiplied many times. Suffice it to say that the loss of skills, and the sense of personal worthlessness which it engenders can become an additional source of stress to VDU workers, and hence affect their general state of health.

Work involves less moving about and changing of position

Many of these examples also demonstrate another way in which new technology changes jobs – by cutting down on most types of physical movement. There are no more drives around in a fork-lift truck for the warehouse worker, nor trips to the filing cabinet or duplicator for the typist. The printer no longer has to carry trays of type around the printshop nor does the shop worker need to walk up and down the shelves.

Workers can now control machines and processes throughout the shopfloor without moving from their computerised consoles.   *Jenny Matthews/Format*

Even more dramatic is the case of the railway worker who used to have to walk an entire length of railway line to check on the quality of the track. Now it is checked at a screen by someone sitting miles away in an office.

Work becomes exclusively keyboard and screen-based

All these and many other varieties of bodily movement have been reduced to a single type of action: sitting immobilised before a screen, with only the eyes and fingers engaged in movement. This restriction of movement leads to a wide range of health problems, many of which have no immediately obvious connection with the eyes or fingers.

Work involves less interaction with other people

Less moving about, of course, also means less chance of bumping into other workmates and exchanging a friendly word. But the introduction of new technology does not just cut down on informal chat between workers; built into its design is the ability to cut out the sort of contact with other people which used to be part of the job.

We have already seen how human supervisors are being partly replaced by machine monitoring, so that work can be checked and analysed somewhere quite different from where it is being carried out. The ease with which computers can be connected up with each other by telecommunications links also makes it possible for many other sorts of information to be 'read' remotely. For instance a document which requires editing or proof-reading can be 'delivered' to the worker concerned without either party leaving his or her workstation, which could be at the next desk, in another room or on the other side of the world.

Not only does this increase the amount of time spent at the screen, and cut down on 'natural breaks' in the work, but it also contributes to isolation and loss of job satisfaction. Another side effect is to make it much more difficult for workers to compare notes with each other, discover common grievances and organise for change. Perhaps this is the reason why managements frequently go to great lengths to use new technology to separate workers from each other even when there is no very good technical or organisational reason for doing so.

Job security is reduced

The effect of the standardisation and routinisation of work which results from automation, and the lowering of skill requirements, is to make individual workers more expendable. This makes people feel less secure in their jobs which in turn makes them more likely to accept lower wages and poorer working conditions than they might demand if they felt their unique skills and knowledge gave them some value to their employers, and therefore some leverage for negotiation.

This may lead to a lowering of safety standards within the organisation, agreeing to fewer or shorter rest breaks, accepting substandard equipment, not insisting on proper maintenance or a number of other factors which could seriously affect health and safety at the workplace.

So this, in addition to the other changes brought by new technology discussed in this chapter, can either directly or indirectly become a threat to VDU workers' health.

Taking all these changes into account, it becomes clear that new technology brings with it fundamental changes in the *design of jobs* which can damage the physical or mental health of workers.

VDUs also bring other hazards to their users, related to the *design of the technology.* These are examined in greater detail later in this book.

– 5 –

New technology and you

All work involves the use of your body in some way or another. Even 'non-manual' work requires you to use your hands for such things as holding pens or telephones, turning knobs, pressing switches or the keys of a cash register, typewriter or keyboard. Your whole arm may be involved in operating machinery such as photocopiers, printing machines, guillotines, staplers, and the rest of your body in activities involving moving around the workplace. Eyes are required to read, check and make precise judgements about accuracy, and ears to take in information over the telephone, from a recording or in person, and to register whether machines are performing properly.

Since the industrial revolution, many manual jobs have required workers to overwork some parts of their bodies, causing stress and physical damage. Some of the occupational illnesses which have resulted have become well known. Few are surprised to discover, for instance, that a lathe operator has a 'frozen shoulder' or that a textile worker has 'cloth ears', having been deafened by the noise of the looms.

So-called non-manual work, however, has generally involved a more balanced range of physical movement. Although many office workers have been required to sit all day (as have a large number of assembly-line workers), because of the low level of automation in offices, shops and other 'white-collar' workplaces, their jobs have generally involved quite a wide range of movements and varied tasks for the eyes and ears to carry out.

The introduction of new information technology has changed this. Millions of workers are involved, from thousands of workplaces in scores of different industries. Their job titles differ widely but, from their bodies' point of view, a single universal way of working has now been introduced. From the huge variety of different tools and machinery which made up the way these workers carried out their jobs in the past, one dominant form has emerged: the television-like screen attached to a keyboard which in Britain is most often known as a VDU. It is on these devices that workers' attention must be focused for a growing proportion of their working lives as evermore information is computerised, and evermore work involves putting that information in, taking it out, analysing or checking it. The screen and keyboard are the meeting place between the computer and the worker. Because the machine never varies, neither can the worker's bodily response. The eyes and fingers of a VDU worker have become trapped in a pattern of intensive and repetitive activity.

What is a VDU?

Although the technology is more or less standard, with minor variations, the name is not, and you may come across a variety of different terms for it. Sometimes these reflect the status of the operator; sometimes varying usages between different countries, different types of organisation or different manufacturers.

If the VDU is on the desk of a senior executive or technical officer (generally male) it is often referred to as an 'intelligent terminal'. Sometimes, too, it may be called a 'remote terminal', especially if it is some distance away from the main computer to which it is connected.

More junior staff (usually women) will often find the VDUs with which they work referred to as their 'work stations', although strictly speaking this term refers to the desk, chair and everything else surrounding the VDU as well as the machine itself.

Others may find the technology described in terms of what it does, for instance it may be called a 'word processor' a 'microcomputer' (or 'micro'), a 'typesetter', a 'counter teller', an 'EFTPOS' machine (electronic funds transfer at the point of sale) or 'CAD' (computer-aided design) terminal.

In some organisations, especially those where several different types of VDU are in operation, they are called by their brand names – the 'Wang', the 'IBM', the 'Rank Xerox' and so on, or even by the type of software, or program, which they use, for instance the 'displaywriter' or the 'database'.

Finally, there are names for VDUs which refer only to the visual display aspect of their use – the 'video', the 'monitor' or 'visual monitor', the 'screen', the 'television' or the 'CRT' (or cathode ray tube). The term visual display unit, or VDU for short, strictly falls into this category, but it has been adopted in this book because it is so widely used in Britain, in preference to the more accurate term 'video display terminal' (or VDT for short) which is generally used in the rest of the English-speaking world.

Whatever name it goes by, the hardware of a VDU – the actual physical equipment – generally consists of the same basic ingredients: a keyboard, for putting information into the computer; a processing unit for processing the information (this may be on the operator's desk, perhaps attached to a disc drive, or it may be some distance away, forming part of a central mainframe computer installation); and a television-like screen for showing what information is being taken out of the computer, or for seeing what is going in. Another accessory which may or may not form part of the operator's individual work-station is a printer, which, like the screen, is also a way of seeing what information is being taken out of the computer, but this time in a more permanent form. Alongside these you may also find other items of new equipment which can be attached to it or run in parallel, for instance modems, telex terminals or electronic switchboards.

When you are operating a VDU, the important points of contact are those between your eyes and the screen and your hands and the keyboard, although many other parts of your body are brought into play to sustain this interaction – your arms which support your hands, your neck which holds your head so that your eyes can see the screen, your legs and back which are forced into a particular posture to hold them in position and so on.

The screen

Compared with traditional technologies, the most startling innovation which the body of the VDU operator has to cope with is the screen. Eyes which are accustomed to looking at things at varying distances, and of differing shades of brightness, are now obliged to stare straight from a fixed distance of about eighteen inches at this bright screen. Instead of looking down at a document laid flat on a desk or lap to read, they must look across at a vertical image.

The screen is backed with fluorescent radioactive powder, which is being bombarded at very high speed by electron particles. These electrons are fired from an electron gun at the back of the cathode ray tube which projects behind the screen. To power the gun, 4,000 volts of electricity – about seventeen times the energy used for most household appliances – are required.

The beam is directed by powerful magnets to the back of the screen which it scans in a rapid continuous motion, visiting every spot several times a second to 'refresh' the fluorescent powder, making it glow to produce the bright characters which you can read on the screen. If you switch off a VDU in a dark room, you can see the power of this fluorescent effect in the glow which lingers on the screen long after the supply of current has been cut off.

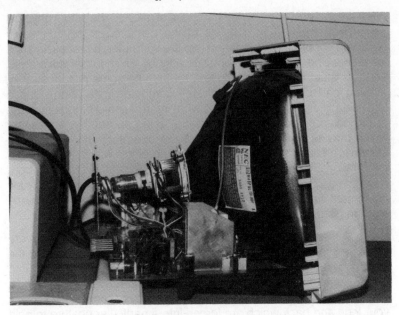

Picture of a VDU with the rear casing removed to show the internal components.

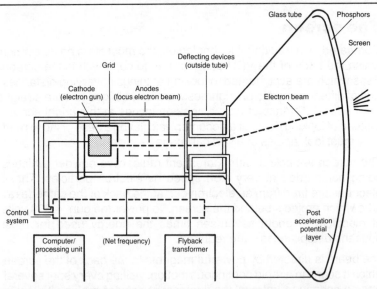

Diagram showing the principle of how a VDU works. The electron gun (the cathode) generates electrons. The electron beam is channelled along the cathode ray tube by the anodes. The beam is then deflected onto the fluorescent screen. This excites the phosphors that make up the fluorescent coating of the screen causing them to glow.

Looking at the screen is rather like staring into a very high-voltage light bulb in which the filament, instead of diffusing light in all directions, is concentrating it all in one, intensely bright, fast-moving beam. As one commentator remarked, in the Canadian *Environmental Health Review*, 'Looking directly into the cathode ray tube seems unnecessarily primitive with today's technological capability.'[18]

Indeed, if the operator has no control over the timing of breaks, and has to gaze continuously at a bright light-source for seven or eight hours a day, VDU work could be compared with the 'bright light torture' of prisoners under interrogation, familiar to most people in a dramatised form from 1950s spy movies.

The retina at the back of your eye, which is subjected to this bombardment of light, is one of the most sensitive organs in your body. In evolutionary terms, the retina is a small bit of brain tissue which has become light-sensitive, developed a lens over itself and found a hole in the skull to look through. All your eyes' movements are controlled by a delicate network of muscles. Working in harmony with each other, these muscles guide your eyes through an incredible range of precise operations without conscious effort. They enable your eyes to switch rapidly from object to object backwards and forwards or up and down, to 'cross' and 'uncross' so that near or distant objects can be brought into focus, to adjust the size of the opening of the pupils to let in just the right amount of light according to the brightness of what is being looked at, to squeeze and flatten the lens so that light rays are focused correctly on the retina, to track a moving target smoothly, or to compensate for unusual body positions.

Under normal conditions, all these muscles are given frequent opportunities to relax. Any given set of them might work very hard for short periods, if for instance you were walking in and out of bright sunlight through some trees, looking for a dropped needle on a patterned carpet or watching a tennis match, but it is unusual for all of them to be engaged at once or for a long period of time. Working at a VDU, they are almost all under continuous tension. Your eyes are focusing on bright, flickering, light, at a fixed, short distance, scanning backwards and forwards across the screen and also sometimes from a piece of paper to the screen. If there are reflections on the screen, you may also unconsciously be holding your head at a peculiar angle to avoid the glare and decipher the characters behind the reflection. Your eyes muscles may then have to work even harder to compensate for this.

After several hours of such stress, it is not surprising that these muscles, like any other muscles in the body forced to hold the same position for long periods, begin to send out chemical distress signals to the rest of the body, which may be experienced as pain or in some other physical way. Some of these effects are described in greater detail in the chapter on *eyes* which begins on page 39 of this book.

The keyboard

The computer keyboard's impact on your body is less dramatic, but it too can cause major problems. To operate it, most of your body must be held still in a rigid posture while your fingers, and the tendons which control their movements, move very rapidly in repetitious, though precise, up and down and sideways motions. Most traditional keyboard machines necessitate frequent short breaks in this pattern for changes of movement, for instance to insert a new sheet of paper, return the carriage or check back on what has already been produced. However the computer keyboard typically produces a pattern of non-stop finger movement.

Returning the carriage, starting a new page, doing a mathematical calculation, activating the printer, scrolling back, checking the contents of another file – even checking the date – can all be done directly via the keyboard, and hence involve your fingers in locating and pressing keys. Where breaks are built into the system, for instance if there is a delay in loading a program, or searching a data-file, these are of an unpredictable length so, instead of relaxing, you generally find yourself waiting in a tense posture, with hands poised over the keyboard in expectation of the next step, and eyes fixed in anticipation on the screen. The injuries to shoulders, neck, arms and hands caused by this repetitive strain are also the subject of a chapter of this book, which begins on page 50. The broader effects of stress are described in the chapter on general health beginning on page 84.

Other hazards

Stresses to eyes and fingers are not the only hazards of VDUs, merely the most direct and obvious ways in which this new technology affects the functioning of our bodies. When it comes to examining the overall effects of VDUs on our health, they represent the tip of an iceberg.

Some other predictable hazards are risks to hearing from unacceptably high noise levels, particularly from printers (described on pages 66–69), and the danger of accidents resulting from electrical faults, trailing cables and so on. Ventilation and temperature may also be affected by the presence of computer equipment in the working environment.

Less easy to detect and more controversial are the unseen hazards of radiation.

Radiation

Since VDUs were first introduced, there has been speculation that they might emit damaging levels of radiation, so much so that in the mid-1970s several trade unions were advising their members to wear film badges, of the type worn by workers in nuclear power stations, to measure the doses they had been exposed to[19].

Since then, numerous tests have been done to measure the radiation from VDUs and it has been widely reported that the levels of ionising radiation – the type which can be measured by these badges and is generally associated with nuclear fall-out or medical X-rays – are very low, well below most officially recommended standards for safe exposure.

On the face of it, this seems good enough evidence to allay any fears that radiation from VDUs could be a hazard to VDU operators. Unfortunately, things are not so simple.

Many people imagine radiation to be a single, invisible type of 'ray', which, though deadly, can be accurately measured. We are used to seeing images on the television of people with ticking geiger counters measuring the radioactivity of rocks, clothes or whatever and we assume that this is a simple process. Either there is no radiation or there is some present, in which case we can find out how strong, and therefore how dangerous, it might be.

In fact the reality is much more complex. Radiation is a word used to describe electrical and magnetic energy travelling in the form of waves. These waves differ enormously in frequency (how many go past a given point in every second) and cover a wide spectrum from the very high frequency 'hard X-rays' or 'gamma rays' of nuclear fall-out to the extremely low frequencies given off by electrical appliances operating at high voltages. The types of radiation which are higher in frequency than visible light are called ionising radiation because they have the ability to disrupt the normal electrical balance of an atom by displacing one of its electrons, thus converting it into an ion with an electrical charge. The types which are visible or lower in frequency than visible light are non-ionising. Table 1 summarises the main types of radiation, with examples of what might produce them, whether they are present in VDUs and some of their known hazards.

These different types of radiation require different methods of measurement. In the case of extremely low frequency radiation, there are few methods of accurate measurement yet developed, since the electrical instruments used to measure emissions can themselves interfere with and distort the fields which they are measuring[20].

Table 1: Types of radiation and associated hazards

NON-IONISING RADIATION							IONISING RADIATION		
extremely low frequencies	very low frequencies	radio frequencies	micro-waves	infra red	visible light	ultra violet	soft X-rays	hard X-rays	gamma rays
eg high voltage lines, food mixers	eg navigation equipment	eg radio, CB, TV	eg micro-wave ovens, radar	eg sun, heatlamp	eg sun, candle light	eg sun, striplight	eg TV, medical X-ray	eg nuclear fall-out	
emitted by VDUs									
possible reproductive hazards							reproductive hazards		
			cataracts						
						skin cancer	many cancers		
possible general effects on health							severe general health effects		
									death

Very little is known about the biological effects of most of these forms of radiation, and such research as has been done has often made the issues seem even more complicated than was originally thought by suggesting that the effects may be confined to very specific frequencies, or that they may vary according to the exact shape of the wave-forms. There is evidence that the biological effects of low frequency radiation are much greater if the waves are 'pulsed', that is if the energy travels in batches, or 'bleeps', rather than as a continuous stream.

The low frequency radiation from the flyback transformer of a VDU is pulsed. When the electron beam is moved from side to side 15,000 to 20,000 times a second, a pulsed very low frequency (VLF) field is emitted, and when it is moved vertically 60 times a second, a pulsed extremely low frequency (ELF) field is produced. The waves also have a characteristic shape, described as 'sawtooth'.

As can be seen in table 1, VDUs are also known to emit radiation of all other types apart from 'hard' X-rays and gamma rays.

'Soft' X-rays

A considerable amount of X-radiation is generated inside the cathode ray tube of a VDU. The tube face (the screen) is designed to filter this out so that it does not leave the tube. However it is still quite possible for X-radiation to be emitted from the screen because of manufacturing defects, machine failure, improper maintenance, or simply the age of the equipment. Some X-radiation may also be released from the rear of the terminal.

Most of the tests which have been carried out on VDUs have detected some X-radiation, although this has always been below official safety limits. Some critics have, however, argued that this does not necessarily give VDUs a clean bill of health as far as X-rays are concerned. They point out that most of the tests have been carried out in laboratory conditions on new models supplied by the manufacturers. VDU operators, in contrast, are likely to be working on older machines in rooms where there is a higher ambient level of radiation (in other words where some radiation is already present in the atmosphere), and often several VDUs are being operated at once. This exposes workers to higher levels of X-radiation than the test results would suggest. They also make the point that recommended 'safe' levels of radiation in Western countries may in fact be too high.

The effects of X-radiation are cumulative. That is, the longer you spend exposed to them the greater the build-up of effects on your body. So little is known about the effects of such a build-up over a lifetime that it is sometimes argued that there can be no safe level of radiation. As the trade union APEX has pointed out, even if current safety standards are accepted, a full-time VDU operator will come perilously close to the maximum permitted dose on some types of VDU:

> 'X-radiation tests conducted by NIOSH (The US National Institute for Occupational Safety and Health) since 1977 found maximum levels of between 0.25 mr/hr (millirems per hour) * and 0.3 mr/hr emitted from VDUs. While this is below the 0.5 mr/hr standard, a continuous dose of 0.3 mr/hr over a working year would be equivalent to 450 mr. The X-ray exposure standard for the general public is 500 mr/yr.'[21]

* The new unit used in assessing the effect of radiation on health or *dose equivalent* is the sievert (Sv).

1 sievert = 100 rem; 0.001 millisievert = 1 millirem

Ultra-violet radiation

VDUs emit ultra-violet radiation along with visible light from their screens. At its higher frequencies, ultra-violet can be ionising. This type of radiation, commonly received from sunlight in hot climates, has been implicated as a cause of skin cancer.

The fact that ultra-violet radiation can cause cancer is proof that it can mutate cells, which could be a contributory factor in other types of cancer or in altering the normal development of cells in a foetus.

Infra-red radiation

All electronic products which increase in temperature emit infra-red, or thermal, radiation and VDUs are no exception. The heating of tissues which results makes people who have been exposed to it more susceptible to other types of damage, for instance from ionising radiation. At high levels – for instance in foundries – infra-red radiation can cause cataracts.

Too much heat can also, of course, be a major source of discomfort to VDU operators, causing drowsiness and irritability. When work is already tiring or stressful, excessive heat can make matters even worse.

Microwaves

Along with other types of radio-frequency radiation, microwaves are emitted by the sweep oscillator circuits at the back of the cathode ray tube in a VDU, and are therefore measured at their strongest near the flyback transformer at the rear, rather than in front of the screen. This would suggest that those most at risk from microwave radiation are people who work in rooms where there are several other VDUs also in operation, alongside or backing onto their own workstation.

A simple test for radio-frequency radiation is to hold a transistor radio tuned to a VHF station near your VDU. As you move it around, you can tell where the emissions are strongest by listening to the interference to the sound. The devices used by builders to detect where mains cables are hidden in walls will give similar results.

Microwaves are known to cause cataracts in people who have been exposed to them (see pages 48–49). They can also affect conception, pregnancy and birth. These effects are described in greater detail in the chapter on the subject, on pages 70 to 83. The effects of microwave radiation on general health are discussed on pages 95 to 98. However, as with X-rays, the important question is at what level these effects begin to occur. Recommended standards for exposure to radio-frequency radiation are complicated, with variations depending on the specific frequencies concerned. It appears from the literature that microwave emissions from VDUs have, when they have been measured, fallen well within Western recommended limits. Nevertheless, to conclude that this means that there are no dangers to VDU operators from microwave radiation might be over-optimistic. Many of the same question-marks which hang over the issue of X-radiation also apply to microwaves.

To those who are sceptical about the hazards of microwaves it should be pointed out that in the Soviet Union, where much more research has been done on the 'non-thermal' effects of radio-frequency radiation than in the West, standards are 1,000 times stricter than in Britain or the United States.

Other radio-frequency radiation including ELF and VLF

Radio-frequency radiation, including very low frequency (VLF) radiation and extremely low frequency (ELF) radiation is emitted from the flyback transformer of the cathode ray tube at the back of a VDU because of the very high voltage which it produces. There is nothing very remarkable about the existence of these low frequency fields in themselves. In our electric-powered society we are frequently exposed to such fields, which are emitted by most electrical appliances, even those which operate on ordinary mains voltages, such as food-mixers, electric drills, electric blankets and so on. They are also to be found in the vicinity of high- voltage electric power lines.

The low frequency (30 kHz (kilohertz) – 300 kHz) and very low frequency (3 kHz – 30 kHz) bandwidths are in fact responsible for the greatest emissions of radiation from VDUs[22]. However there is some disagreement about what the exact levels are, since few reliable means have yet been devised for measuring them, because the instruments used for this purpose are themselves electrical and can interfere with the signals they are supposed to be measuring.

The exact effects of these fields on the human body have, however, been the subject of considerable controversy in recent years.

One debate has focused on the effects of living near high-voltage power lines. Despite anecdotes from farmers whose animals graze under them, which tell of high rates of miscarriage and still-births, little research has been done on the effects on human reproduction. Some research has indicated that living near these power lines is associated with an increased incidence of depression, abnormally high suicide rates, increases in general susceptibility to illness as well as childhood and adult cancers (caused, it is thought, by suppression of the mechanism by which the body normally resists cancer). Workers subjected to electrical fields as part of their job are also more likely to suffer from leukaemia[23].

In the Soviet Union, ELF radiation has been shown to cause bone deformation in the foetuses of rats and rabbits[24].

Animal experiments in Spain and Sweden have also produced disturbing new evidence of reproductive hazards resulting from this type of radiation. This is discussed on pages 78 to 80 in the chapter on conception, pregnancy and birth.

Bill Guy, a scientist who tested radiation from VDUs for IBM, is reported to have been 'shocked' at the strength of the electric fields he measured and recommended that older VDUs should be shielded to prevent emissions of radiation which might have harmful biological effects[25]. On finding that someone who touched the case of a VDU would be exposed to electric fields of between 30 and 100 kilovolts per metre, he wrote that:

> 'The localised (electric) fields at the surface of an unshielded cover of a VDT nearest the flyback transformer can reach extremely high values. Since these fields have a capability of inducing much greater currents in an exposed user of the device than the relatively low magnetic field emissions it certainly is desirable to shield the cover of the VDT. Since such shielding is relatively inexpensive the benefit to cost ratio is large. Such shielding is generally present in newer models of VDTs to satisfy (US Government Federal Communication Commission) requirements for reducing electromagnetic interference.'[26]

The effect which concerned him was the thermal effect of the high current induced in the people in contact with the VDU – the danger that their bodies might in effect be 'cooked' by the radiation without their knowledge.

Other commentators believe that it is the non-thermal effects (effects which are not connected with producing heat) of low frequency radiation, or 'electrical pollution' as it has been called, which have the most harmful effects on people's bodies. One theory is that these effects vary according to their precise frequencies, with certain frequencies being very much more harmful than others. This is explained by the fact that people's bodies are themselves electrical systems. For instance, our brains give out electrical signals which can be picked up by electroencephalographs (EEGs), best known as 'alpha' or 'beta' waves. Our muscles give out signals which doctors measure with electromyographs and our hearts signals which are measured by electrocardiographs or magnetocardiographs. Electricity is crucial to the working of our nervous systems for transmitting the information around our bodies which is necessary to keep us alive and fully functioning.

These systems are very poorly understood, but some of the electrical impulses can be measured, for instance heart signals are normally between 0.2 and 100 Hz in frequency while brain signals range from less than 5 Hz in a state of deep sleep to 30 Hz in highly active states such as anxiety, surprise, fear or hunger. It has been suggested that pulsed fields which coincide with these natural biological frequencies can have highly disturbing effects on the functioning of the human body. Sometimes these effects may be beneficial, for instance in the medical use of pulsed fields of approximately 100 Hz to speed up the healing of broken bones. Others may well be harmful. A prime suspect is the 50-60 Hz pulsed field emitted by high voltage power lines and many electrical appliances including VDUs[27].

There is a further discussion of the effects of low frequency radiation on general health on pages 96 to 98.

With such disagreement and so little hard information among the experts, it is difficult to come to any firm conclusions about low frequency radiation. Perhaps the only conclusion on which all might agree is that insufficient research has been done to prove that it is *not* dangerous. With the present state of knowledge, it cannot be ruled out as a possible work hazard.

Static electrical fields

Even more speculative than the effects of radiation is the possibility that a further health hazard to VDU workers might be caused by the high positive electrical charge in the atmosphere in most rooms where VDUs are used.

These electrical fields differ from radiation because the electrical energy does not travel in waves, but is 'static' – hence the name static electricity.

High positive electric charges affect the balance of ions (electrically charged particles) in the atmosphere causing too many positively charged ions and not enough negative ones. Some commentators believe that this can impair health.

VDUs carry a positive electrostatic charge on the surface of the screen. It has been calculated that someone sitting 18 inches away from a VDU screen is experiencing a positive charge of 150 volts per square inch, compared with a charge of 3 volts experienced under normal conditions in the atmosphere[28]. You can in fact feel this if you run your hand (which can also carry a positive charge) over the screen of a VDU when it is switched on. Most people experience a noticeable tingle in the palm.

In addition to the fields emanating from the screen, the atmosphere in which VDUs are used is also likely to have a high positive charge, because of such things as the metal-frame structure of many office buildings, air-conditioning, air-carried central heating, and carpets and curtains made of artificial fibres. In addition, VDUs deplete the surrounding atmosphere of negative ions. People too can carry positive charges, a charge which builds up to high levels if it cannot be conducted away to earth because you are wearing rubber or plastic-soled shoes (from this point of view, hob-nailed boots would be the most suitable office-wear!). Positive charges are also produced by friction, especially such things as rubbing surfaces with silicon or cellulose-based polish.

Most people have experienced the effects of this in the sort of mild electric shock felt when, for instance, a metal door-handle is touched after walking across a carpeted room in rubber-soled shoes. However few are aware that their bodies might be affected in other ways.

One result of this high positive charge is that the number of ions (charged electrical particles) in the air goes down, particularly the number of negatively charged ions, so that what is left is air with a small concentration of positive ions, and virtually no negative ones.

Almost nothing is known of how these ions affect living creatures, but a body of evidence is building up to show that, somehow, they do. It seems to be the case that living things need ions. In Russia, scientists tried to raise small animals such as mice, rats, guinea-pigs and rabbits, in air with no ions at all and they all died within days, and similar experiments with plants have produced stunted growth. It appears that air with more positive than negative ions is generally harmful and that air with more negative than positive ions is generally beneficial in its effects.

Not all the imbalances between positive and negative ions are caused by the artificial human environments of the 20th century. Some can occur naturally, for instance high positive charges are produced by friction, and therefore occur when there are dry, dust-raising winds blowing or before thunderstorms. They are also produced around the time of the full moon, when the negatively charged moon is closer to the earth than at other times and therefore pushes the (also negatively charged) outer face of the earth's ionosphere further down, bringing its positively charged inner face nearer to the earth and releasing more positive ions than usual into the air which surrounds us. Large numbers of negative ions are to be found by the sea and near waterfalls.

Folklore gives us many examples of the bad effects of these high positive charges – increases in suicides, mental hospital admissions, and the onset of labour during the full moon; anger, irritability and migraines before a thunderstorm; illness, both physical and mental, and unexplained violence when the 'witches winds' (like the French Mistral, the Swiss Foehn, the Israeli Sharav or the Chinook on the north American west coast) are blowing. In some countries, when these winds blow, surgeons avoid operating because there is a greater risk of haemorrhaging during these times, and the fact that the Mistral was blowing has even been accepted as a valid defence in murder trials.

It is also a familiar belief that people feel better and more sexually aroused near the sea, beside waterfalls, and after a rain-shower or its artificial equivalent, a bathroom shower.

Most of the studies on the effects of positive and negative ions which have a bearing on our subject have been done on these naturally occurring phenomena, in particular the so-called 'witches winds'[29].

One of the effects of too many positive ions compared with negative ones is to stimulate the body to produce more serotonin, a little-understood substance, a neuro-hormone which helps control bleeding and seems to play an important part in the working of the brain, perhaps by transmitting impulses between nerve cells.

Like adrenaline, which is also a neuro-hormone, serotonin seems to be produced as a bodily response to stress. Colloquially, serotonin has been described as a 'downer', whereas adrenaline is an 'upper' in its effects.

Some research suggests that high levels of serotonin may be destructive to pregnancy, and that ion levels may influence fertility and reproduction in ways which have yet to be explored. This is discussed separately in the chapter on the subject on pages 70 to 83 of this book. The possible effects of ion levels on general health are looked at on pages 98 to 100.

It must be emphasised that the effects of high positive electrical charges, or a shortage of negative ions on the body, have not been widely studied, and most of the evidence contains a good deal of speculation. The firmest claims we have come across which suggest that too many positively charged ions in the atmosphere cause ill-health are made by people with a vested interest in selling negative ionisers and should therefore be treated with some caution. Nevertheless, they cannot be dismissed until more research has been done on the subject.

'Synergistic' effects

The research shows that a VDU can affect the health of its users in a number of different ways. However these effects are not necessarily experienced separately. A VDU operator feeling tired or under stress, for instance, will probably have no way of telling whether this has been caused by eyestrain, from staring at the screen; by muscular stress in the fingers, wrist or forearm; by a shortage of negative ions in the atmosphere or by any other of a variety of causes. The human body is a single organism and it is impossible to isolate one aspect of how it works and study it separately. Anything wrong with one part will influence the whole. Although for convenience, many of the hazards of VDUs are examined separately in this book, it would be a mistake to assume that their effects are isolated from each other.

Just as one disease can make your body more susceptible to contracting another, so the existence of one hazard can affect the body's ability to respond to another. Sometimes the combined effects of several different hazards can produce a condition which is much more serious than you would expect from simply adding them all together. This situation, where the whole is greater than or different from the sum of its parts, is known as a 'synergistic' effect, in other words the effect of several different hazards 'acting together', which is the literal meaning of the word.

In considering the synergistic effects of VDU work, it is important to take into account not only the physical properties of the VDU described in this chapter, but also the effects of new technology on work organisation and working conditions described in chapter 4. We must also remember that new technology is being introduced in a social context in which many people's health is already being adversely affected.

Poverty, anxiety, fear of harassment and worsening public services all take their toll, leaving people with high levels of stress, a stress which is particularly acute for women attempting to combine paid work with the care of dependants. In addition, more and more workers are turning up for work when they are ill, because of fear of dismissal or, if they are temporary staff or other casual workers, because they are not eligible for sick pay.

Bodies which are already straining to resist this bombardment may be weakened in their ability to withstand the additional hazards of VDUs before they have even entered the workplace. This background should be borne in mind when reading the ensuing chapters of this book, which examine in greater detail how VDU work specifically affects particular parts of your body.

– 6 –

Your eyes

Of all the hazards of working at a VDU, eye trouble is perhaps the best known. In the few years since VDUs have been in general use, this hazard has become so well known as to be almost taken for granted. In a typical optician's office in the centre of London, the receptionist asks first-time callers why they wish to make an appointment to have their eyes tested. If they answer that they have had a bit of trouble focusing lately, or that they've been getting headaches, she says, 'Work on one of those VDUs then, do you? Well, what do you expect?'. To an enquirer who asks her to explain, she might add, 'Oh they all get that. We get them in here every day'.

Most people who have worked for prolonged periods with a VDU or had regular contact with people who do are well aware of the existence of 'VDU eyestrain' and this impression is borne out by a number of studies which have reported a wide range of eye and vision problems which affect VDU operators more than other groups of workers.

These include:

▲ the sensation commonly described as 'eyestrain'

▲ burning or tender eyes

▲ reddened, watering eyes

▲ blurred vision or difficulty in focusing

▲ double vision

▲ grittiness, dryness or aching of the eyes

▲ the need to get prescriptions for glasses changed more often

▲ coloured after-images after using the screen (e.g. seeing floating red or orange blobs or seeing everything white imbued with a pink tinge after working at a screen)

▲ a feeling of heaviness in the eyes

▲ headaches just above the eyes

▲ cataracts

Here are some typical results of such studies:

Table 2: Percentage of VDU operators suffering visual problems

Date	Study	VDU work		Non-VDU work	
		light use	heavy use	profes-sional	clerical
1977	Swedish Board of Occupational Safety & Health	77% (all)		—	
1978	Cakir et al	68%	85%	—	
1980	NIOSH	60%	91%	35%	60%
1982	Canadian Labour Congress	65%	87%	46%	64%
Table modified from Marvin Dainoff, **VDU Work Task Categories**					

Other surveys have reached similar results, including those by Smith and colleagues (two studies, in 1980 and 1981), Elias and colleagues (in 1980), and Coe and colleagues (in 1980).[30]

Elias and colleagues found that vision-related problems were higher among off-line operators doing repetitive keyboard-and-screen work in banking centres than among VDU workers doing more creative question-and-answer work in a publishing and a pharmaceutical company, suggesting that the intensity and repetitiveness of the work may be an important factor. Coe and colleagues reached similar conclusions when they found that VDU operators were more likely to suffer from hot, heavy, tired and aching eyes than non-screen-based workers and that both blurred vision and migraine were commoner for VDU workers involved in input and editing work than for those in more creative work. Full-time workers suffered noticeably more than part-timers from these effects.

These findings were also supported by a major study of 3,819 VDU operators in Britain by Jennifer Evans published in *Health and Safety at Work* in 1985. She found that 70.3 per cent of operators suffered from eyestrain and 43.8 per cent from irritated eyes. This eyestrain became worse in direct proportion to the amount of time spent each day at a VDU, as shown in table 3[31]:

Table 3: Relationship between eyestrain and time spent at VDU

Hours spent at VDU	Percentage experiencing eyestrain
1–2	63.9%
2–4	72.7%
4–6	76.7%
`6–8	80.4%
Source: Evans J, *Health and Safety at Work* (November 1985)	

This researcher also discovered that women were more likely than men to experience eyestrain. Perhaps the explanation for this is that women are likely to be doing the most routine and intensive jobs.

Taken together, these results produce a fairly clear picture. We can see that all of the types of work studied cause some visual strain, but that this varies according to the type of work, with clerical workers more severely affected than professional or technical workers. However work involving the use of VDUs produces considerably more eyestrain than even the most hazardous of the non-VDU types of work, and this eyestrain becomes progressively worse, the longer the time spent at the screen. In addition, work which is more machine-paced and intensive, such as data input, is more stressful than more creative work in which the VDU operator has a fair amount of control over the pace of work, such as 'question and answer' or 'dialogue' work.

This much is clear from the evidence. Within this broad pattern, however, there are wide variations. The extent to which individual VDU workers are likely to suffer from eye trouble will depend on a number of factors including the state of their eyes, the design of the office, the design of the workstation, the nature of the work and the frequency of breaks.

It has been estimated that about one person in three in the general population has some eyesight trouble which has not yet been diagnosed or corrected. Some opticians argue that most of the difficulties resulting from working with VDUs can be put down to such undiagnosed visual problems, which only become noticeable to the worker after working at a screen. It is their opinion that proper eye-testing before the worker begins VDU work, and the prescription of the correct spectacles or contact lenses can eliminate such problems.

Others are not so confident. They point out that no studies have been carried out to measure the long-term effects of VDU work on eyesight, and without such evidence it is impossible to say whether prolonged exposure is damaging or not.

In recent years, considerable scientific effort has been put into attempts to prove that VDUs are harmless to eyesight. In the United States, for instance, the National Research Council's Committee on Vision set up a Panel on the Impact of Video Viewing on the Vision of Workers, whose members were drawn from the councils of the National Academy of Sciences, the National Academy of Engineering and the Institute of Medicine. Much of their report, published in 1983, consists of criticism of research already carried out which suggests that VDU work might cause eye problems. This existing evidence is mostly dismissed as being either 'circumstantial' or 'inadequately controlled'. The implication is that the only way to prove beyond doubt that eyestrain actually exists is to find two large groups of workers, one working at VDUs and the other not, in which *all* other factors are identical. They must be equally tired, equally under pressure from their supervisors, suffer equally from headaches, from job dissatisfaction and so on. The thought that there might be some connection between these factors and eyestrain does not appear to have crossed the minds of these distinguished experts. Reading their report gives the impression that anyone who is concerned that VDUs are not entirely safe and healthy for their users is ignorant, unscientific, and probably hysterical.

However, tucked away at the back of this report is a page and a half which strikes a very different note. Entitled 'dissent' it is by Lawrence W. Stark, a member of the panel who is professor of physiological optics and engineeering science at the University of California and professor of neurology (neuro-ophthalmology) at the University of California Medical Centre. He is also the author of a standard work on neurological control systems and has published over 200 scientific articles. His dissent makes interesting reading. As well as criticising the very narrow brief of the panel, and its failure to consider issues of policy, he says that:

> 'My own review of the literature substantiated the opinion that visual fatigue is not a well-defined physiological or clinical entity, but this scientifically accurate statement cannot negate the fact that most of us feel fatigue at various times. Indeed, many of us, finding ourselves at a given moment without sufficient motivation to go on, have halted tasks as a result of fatigue. I believe that many highly motivated VDT users suffer from ocular discomfort and visual fatigue beyond that appropriate to a normal workplace.

> 'Implicit in the appearance of video display terminals on the marketplace for office and clerical work is the manufacturers' claim that adequate legibility can be obtained from these terminals. I believe this not to be true. I have never seen a video display terminal that was nearly as legible as the ordinary pieces of typewritten paper or copied reports that circulate in our paper world. We all prefer to look down with easy convergence on reading matter – a book, a sheet of typewritten material or handwritten correspondence. No VDTs provide robust enough contrast to enable this "natural" position for the tube face . . . Also consideration must be given to the length of time spent at a task and the possible inflexibility of a job requiring reading from the face of a VDT for an 8-hour day.'[32]

Professor Stark is unusual among his kind in that he obviously has the insight to be able to imagine himself at a VDU workstation and to picture the world from that viewpoint. This commonsense approach immediately leads him to the view shared by most people who have either worked at a VDU themselves for some time, or listened to people who have. This view is one that does not accuse VDU workers of suffering from some sort of collective hallucination or hysteria, but believes them when they make statements such as these:

> 'I get tired and hot eyes after prolonged VDU use and afterwards white articles have a pink tinge.'

> 'I have headaches with a burning sensation from the eyes to the back of the head. I feel dazed, bleary-eyed, weak and depressed.'

> 'Sometimes it comes on after I've finished work. Yesterday, after picking my daughter up from nursery, I was rushing round the supermarket looking for a particular item on the shelves when suddenly I couldn't focus at all. My eyeballs felt swollen and blurred shapes seemed to be swimming in front of my eyes. I knew it would be another evening when I couldn't watch the telly or read.'

'It starts with things looking blurred, and a dull throbbing in the eyes. If I don't take a break then a splitting headache will develop.'[33]

Although many managements deny that such problems exist, some of the practices they adopt suggest that in reality they are well aware of them.

At the Japanese Airlines reservations office in Tokyo, for instance, complaints of visual fatigue became common after the installation of a new IBM computerised booking system, which was soon nicknamed 'the controller' by the 1,000 computer operators who had to use it. In fact when an independent survey was done among the whole staff it was discovered that 80 per cent of computer terminal operators suffered from eye troubles, compared with an average of 20 per cent in the office as a whole. However most of the remedial measures taken by the management did nothing to address the real cause of the problem. They included discouraging workers from engaging in any spare-time activities which might strain their eyes, such as reading books, watching TV or knitting; and painting the walls orange, so that the pinkish after-image about which the operators had been complaining would become invisible![34]

It is abundantly clear that VDUs do affect people's eyes in a variety of ways. It is also true that little is known about exactly how these effects are caused.

The eye is a complex organ which operates through the coordinated activity of several muscles. Each of these muscles responds instantaneously to the situation, with no conscious effort at all. The types of movement involved include:

Scanning movements

One set of external muscles moves the eye in a rapid scanning movement, known as a saccade, from one object to another. This type of movement is involved in such processes as reading, and is thus greatly used in VDU operation. It has been estimated that reading a VDU display requires approximately four saccades per second. These movements have been shown to be affected by fatigue, although there is some dispute about whether what is actually happening is fatigue of the eye muscles or fatigue of the central nervous system which controls them.

There is also another type of scanning movement, used for slowly tracking a moving target, which is controlled by a different set of external eye muscles and works in close coordination with the rapid scanning type of movement. This ability has also been shown to deteriorate with overuse.

Studies have also shown that both poor lighting and badly designed typography can lessen the efficiency of these types of movement in reading. Given the poor standard of lighting in many offices and the crudity of most VDU typefaces compared with those used in print, many of which have evolved over centuries, it is likely that these are additional causes of strain for most VDU operators.

Blinking

Blinking is the eye's natural windscreen wiper. It stimulates tear production and washes out contaminants.

Some studies have found that the blink rate goes down among VDU operators, leading to greater dryness and irritation of the eye. If contaminants are not removed effectively by the blinking reflex then infections can result.

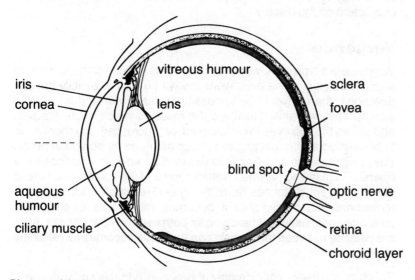

Diagram of the human eye (shown in cross section).

Accommodation

Accommodation is a word used for the action of the muscles which tighten and relax the lens of the eye to allow accurate focusing to take place. The range of accommodation becomes gradually smaller throughout our lives, so that by the time we reach the age of forty we cannot focus on things as near or as far away as a child can. In order for accommodation to take place, the eye relies on several signs, which trigger it into action. One of the most important of these is blur. If a blurred image is registered, then an error signal is sent out to the muscles, which continue to squeeze or relax the lens until they receive a message that the image is now sharp. If an operator is using a poorly designed VDU which produces a constantly blurred image, then this process cannot function properly, and looking becomes an uncomfortable activity.

There have been a lot of studies of accommodation and fatigue among people working with VDUs, ranging from air traffic controllers to telephonists, most of which show a marked deterioration in the speed at which operators can change their focus between far and near objects after they have spent time at a VDU screen.

These muscles are particularly likely to become stressed if there are reflected images on a screen and the operator's eyes are forced continually to focus and refocus on the reflected images and on the characters on the display.

Vergence

Vergence is a type of movement which works in close conjunction with accommodation. If the eyes were always pointed in exactly parallel directions, then it would be impossible to see near and far objects exactly. This movement involves the muscles which rotate the eye, and allows the two eyes to be 'crossed' or 'uncrossed', in other words to be pointed at different angles to keep near and far objects in range. These movements are often involved in VDU work, for instance if the operator is glancing between written copy and the screen when these are at different distances from the eyes. Research on this type of movement has shown that it becomes much less efficient with prolonged use, making it harder to fix both eyes on near objects. Also, the balance between the muscles on each eye becomes increasingly uneven.

This function varies considerably between individuals and with age. It is also easily disrupted by drugs and tiredness. Some commentators think that continual vergence movement is the greatest single cause of eyestrain.

Pupil size

The muscles controlling the pupil regulate the amount of light allowed into the eye. If the eyes are obliged to look at bright light, such as the light from the fluorescent tubes which illuminate many workplaces and which all too often appears as reflected glare on VDU screens, then the pupils constrict, or shrink the size of the opening at the front of the eye.

If the pupil is constricted the depth of focus is also affected, so this type of movement has to work in close cooperation with accommodation and vergence movements for the eye to function effectively.

One study showed that the set of muscles controlling pupil size had to work especially hard when shifting between looking at dark characters on a light background and light ones on a dark background. This is precisely what many VDU operators have to do all day when they shift their eyes between handwritten or typed copy on white paper to light coloured characters on a dark screen.

Constricted pupils can also result from boredom, the opposite of the process by which pupils tend to dilate, or open up, when people are interested or excited. One study of directory enquiry operators using microfiche readers and telephone books found very high levels of pupillary constriction. This could have been due to a combination of the visual intensiveness of their work and its extremely boring and repetitive nature[35].

Because it forces them alternately to tighten and relax very rapidly, it is these muscles too which are affected by flicker. At high speeds the eye does not register the flicker of a bright light, but if it flickers at less than sixty times a second, slow enough for the eye to register it and attempt to respond, acute discomfort can be experienced. This is why the so-called character refresh rate of a VDU is important. This is the speed at which the beam inside the cathode ray tube revisits, or 'refreshes', the fluorescent phosphors which coat the back of the screen to make the characters on it glow. Flickering becomes a greater problem with old units in which the phosphor coating has begun to break down with age.

Epilepsy

In certain types of epilepsy, known as photosensitive epilepsy, the flickering of a VDU screen can trigger an epileptic fit in a susceptible person either working at a VDU screen or within visual range of one. The condition is comparatively rare, suffered by one person in 5-10,000. Half of these have their first attack in front of a TV set, usually in their early teens. Occasionally, sufferers may not know that they have the condition until a first attack is brought on through exposure to a flickering VDU screen. Nobody suffering from photosensitive epilepsy should be obliged to work in the same room as a VDU screen against their wishes. However epilepsy sufferers should not be barred from VDU work either. They are the best judges of their own work requirements and, with care, the risks can be substantially reduced. Factors which increase the risk of triggering an epileptic fit are: a large screen, large amounts of bright text, prolonged viewing at close range, particularly when the screen is viewed at an angle or a neighbouring screen can be seen from the corner of the eye, and a flicker rate between 25 and 50 cycles per second (Hertz or Hz)[36].

Cataracts

Another eye problem which appears to be connected with VDU use is cataracts, a loss of transparency in the lens of the eye causing dimness of vision. There is still considerable dispute about the extent to which cataracts can be caused by the microwave radiation which VDUs are known to emit. According to the Ontario Public Service Employees Union:

'Radiant energy cataracts have been reported among VDU operators in both Canada and the US. All of these cataracts were diagnosed as occurring on the posterior of the lens capsule – a sign of radiant energy damage. The victims were too young to have developed ageing cataracts and their medical background did not reveal exposure to radiant energy other than their use of VDUs.'[37]

Dr Milton Zaret has been studying cataracts in workers exposed to microwaves since 1964 and specifically among VDU operators since the mid-1970s. In numerous publications he has catalogued particular cases and pointed out the ways in which microwave-induced cataracts are different in form from those due to other factors[38].

The general literature on what has become known as 'electrical pollution' also gives many examples of cases where cataracts have been observed among radar operators or workers regularly exposed to microwaves. Battocletti, for instance, cites 19 separate studies on the subject between 1943 and 1974[39].

Such findings are contested by the US Government's health and safety organisation, NIOSH. However no evidence has been put forward to demonstrate that long-term exposure to VDUs does *not* cause cataracts and the British Health and Safety Executive keeps an open mind on the issue, merely noting that it is a matter of controversy[40]. Until such evidence is produced, there are serious grounds for concern.

The possible risk of developing cataracts, combined with the other eye hazards faced by VDU operators, is a strong reason for regular eye-tests for anyone who has to work with a screen, so that problems can be picked up as early as possible.

However, eye tests in themselves are no substitute for safe work organisation. The best action to take to prevent eye problems is frequent rest and variety of movement. Even if you do not experience the symptoms of eyestrain, if the eye-muscles are not given the chance to rest but are required to hold a fixed position, or to move rapidly, for long periods of time then – like any other muscles subjected to stress – they begin to send distress signals to the rest of the body, leading to the general stress reaction which is discussed more fully later in this book, on pages 87 to 95.

Minimising hazards to eyes from such stress may involve redesigning many aspects of jobs, workstations and the office environment, to remove known hazards and give workers a greater degree of control. Some of these changes, together with other measures which can help to protect your eyes, are described in the final sections of this book.

– 7 –

Your hands, wrists, arms, shoulders, neck and back

In Osaka, Japan, a study was recently carried out of the health of 20,000 working women, in an attempt to find out which were the most serious work hazards in each industry and occupation. From factories to banks, one condition stood out as by far the most common: stiff shoulders.

In the banking and insurance industries, in which nearly all work is white-collar and many jobs involve keyboarding and screen work, the highest complaint was 'very stiff shoulders' suffered by 58.7 per cent of the women in the survey, surpassing even 'eye fatigue', at 45.7 per cent, as the number one hazard in these sectors.

When the figures were analysed according to the women's occupations rather than the industries in which they worked, there were similar results. 59.8 per cent of VDU operators and typists suffered from stiff shoulders, which was also the most important complaint among telephone operators.

So prevalent is this problem in Japan that the combination of stiffness in the shoulders with stiffness and pain in the upper arms and neck has become known as 'key-punch disease' and, after a protracted struggle by some of the women workers affected, is now officially recognised as an industrial disease entitling the sufferer to compensation. One woman, employed by Mitsumi Electric to key in data from payment vouchers, describes how it feels:

> 'At work, I would get a heavy feeling in my arms, and they would become numbed with pain. My shoulders would become extremely stiff and there would be a tightening from the lower part of my neck all the way to the back of my head. My head would develop a strange heaviness to it. It was just as if I had a weight attached to the back of my head pulling me down from behind. Because of this, when I walked I would feel as if I was falling backwards. There was a feeling of pressure in my neck. I felt as if something was caught in my throat, so even breathing became uncomfortable. My shoulders would smart with pain. It was like a weight on both shoulders.'[41]

She put the severity of her condition down to the fact that she was not just having to key in information, as she had done in her previous job, but also having to read small, hard-to-decipher characters from the VDU screen at the same time.

Japan is not the only country where such effects have been noted. Neither are stiff shoulders the only problems of this sort to affect VDU operators. They are just one of a group of painful conditions affecting the muscles and tendons of the upper limbs and torso, often known as musculoskeletal disorders, which are becoming increasingly common among white-collar workers throughout the world. Injuries like these have been affecting manual workers for centuries.

Doctors recognise several distinct types of injury in this group, each known by a different medical name. Several also have popular names which, as well as the 'key-puncher's disease' already referred to, include such terms as 'typist's cramp', 'writer's cramp', 'frozen shoulder', 'cotton twister's arm', 'mother's shoulder', 'process worker's arm', 'washer-woman's wrist' and, in Australia in the 1960s and early 1970s, 'ethnic wrist'.

Such names tell their own story. These conditions are the result of continuous strain on the muscles and/or tendons caused by monotonous work performed under pressure, mostly in the sort of jobs in which women and Black people are to be found.

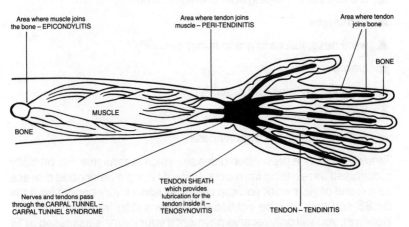

Diagram of the human arm showing where strain injuries are likely to occur.

Diseases in this group are often known as repetition strain injuries. This term is in some ways deceptive, suggesting as it does that repetitive movement is the sole cause of injury. There is no denying that having to make the same movement over and over again does put the muscles and tendons under tremendous strain. However it is equally, if not more, stressful to have to hold them in the same tense position for long periods, a type of strain which is known as 'static load'. The last chapter described how your eyes can become strained both from the need to scan backwards and forwards at speed and from the need to hold the same focus for a long time. It is a similar story with the muscles and tendons of the rest of your body. They can be injured, sometimes permanently, both by being forced to move and by being forced to keep still. To avoid confusion, the term we use here to describe the diseases which result is 'strain injuries'.

The main types of strain injury affecting the hands, wrists, arms, neck and shoulders are as follows:

Tenosynovitis

Tenosynovitis, or 'teno' as it is sometimes called, is an inflammation of the sheath surrounding the tendons, usually the tendons of the hand and wrist. Its symptoms include:

▲ pain on the back of the wrist and forearm, typically a dull ache when the limb is at rest, becoming acute when it is moved

▲ swelling, sometimes accompanied by throbbing

▲ a crackling or rasping sound when moved

▲ numbness

▲ weakness, failure to grasp things securely

▲ cramp

▲ tingling, like 'pins and needles'

▲ 'shooting' pains

▲ stiffness, tightness or heaviness

Tenosynovitis is a prescribed disease, which means that it is officially recognised as resulting from work. If you develop a prescribed disease as a result of your work you can claim industrial injury benefit from the DHSS and may also be entitled to compensation from the employer. However, you will only receive payment if your injury is assessed at 14 per cent or greater disability. Tenosynovitis is in fact the second commonest prescribed disease in the United Kingdom[42]. More information on prescribed diseases can be found on pages 186 to 187.

If use of the affected wrist is not stopped as soon as the symptoms of tenosynovitis appear, then the tendon and tendon sheaths can become permanently damaged, leaving you incapacitated and in pain for life.

In the early stages, numbness, tingling or pain during movement are usually the first symptoms to be felt. Work should be stopped at this stage. Once the condition has become severe, cure is increasingly difficult and permanent injury may have set in. Although numerous treatments have been attempted, few appear to work, and some of the more drastic, such as surgery to remove the pain, are reported to do more harm than good, and have left some sufferers with a permanent disability[43].

Complete rest is the best cure. When inflammation is present, this can often be helped by hot-and-cold treatment several times a day, massaging with oil to improve circulation in the area and then wrapping in wet crepe bandages or applying a cold compress to cool it down.

It is infinitely better, of course, to ensure that tenosynovitis never develops in the first place, by slowing down the pace of work, redesigning the workstation and giving operators the freedom to change position and take breaks as frequently as their bodily comfort requires.

Tendinitis

While tenosynovitis is the name given to inflammation of the sheath surrounding the tendons, tendinitis is an inflammation of the tendons themselves. If such inflammation is allowed to persist, it can cause a thickening of the tendon, leading it eventually to lock. The symptoms of tendinitis are similar to those of tenosynovitis and include pain, tenderness, restriction of movement and locking. While it is most common in the hands and wrists, tendinitis can also cause shoulders to lock in some circumstances.

Like tenosynovitis, tendinitis may be caused by keyboard work, and the two diseases are often found together. However tendinitis alone is not a prescribed disease.

'Trigger finger' is a type of tendinitis. As its name suggest, this is a condition where it becomes difficult to straighten a finger after it has been bent. It is caused by the thickening of the tendons in the finger which prevents easy movement. It can be caused by long periods of repetitive movement or by the use of power tools.

Peritendinitis

Peritendinitis is inflammation of the area surrounding the tendons and their sheath, including the place where tendons and muscles join. It is often found in conjunction with tenosynovitis and tendinitis but is not, on its own, a prescribed disease.

Bursitis

Bursitis is inflammation of a bursa, the sac of fluid over a bone which allows easy movement of the tendons. Bursitis is caused by prolonged, repeated pressure, or repeated jolts to the joint. Jolting of this sort can be caused by keyboard work, particularly if the keyboard is being struck too hard. This often happens with badly designed keyboards which do not give the user a clear indication that a key has been struck. It can also happen when operators are required to switch from one machine to another or are becoming used to an electronic keyboard after working with a manual or electric typewriter. Bursitis is a prescribed disease.

Epicondylitis

Epicondylitis is the term used for strain injuries in the region of the elbow joint, involving the area where the muscles which bend the fingers and wrist are attached to the bone and ligament just above the elbow.

Symptoms include pain, tenderness and swelling in or near the elbow, with the pain becoming especially acute if the hand is moved. The disease is often caused by repeatedly lifting objects with the hand facing downwards and the thumb and forefinger in a grasping position or by repeated twisting movements of the hand and forearm.

Lateral epicondylitis is the medical term for 'tennis elbow' which, despite its associations with sport, is usually found among people doing repetitive manual jobs. This is an inflammation of the elbow end of the humerus bone. The symptoms are pain and tenderness when fingers are moved with the elbow held away from the body[44].

Neither type of epicondylitis is a prescribed disease.

Carpal tunnel syndrome

The carpal tunnel is a small channel of fibrous tissue on the inner side of the wrist through which ten tendons and a nerve, the median nerve, pass. The name carpal tunnel syndrome is given to two distinct conditions, known as 'simple carpal tunnel syndrome' and 'secondary carpal tunnel syndrome' and it is extremely important to get a correct diagnosis.

Simple carpal tunnel syndrome involves the constriction of the median nerve due to the presence of fluid or thickening of the tissues. The symptoms are pain, loss of feeling in the palm and fingers and loss of ability to move the fingers freely, a condition which often becomes worse at night. For this condition an operation known as a carpal tunnel release operation is often recommended and is frequently successful in releasing the nerve.

Secondary carpal tunnel syndrome has very similar symptoms but is much more serious, since it also involves an inflammation of the tendons in the tunnel. This can often be produced as a secondary effect of tenosynovitis. When secondary carpal tunnel syndrome is present, a release operation brings no benefit and can actually make matters worse.

Secondary carpal tunnel syndrome is often produced by fast repetitive finger movements such as those used to operate a keyboard[45]. It is not a prescribed disease but is most often found in association with tenosynovitis, which is prescribed.

Dupuytren's contracture

In this disease, deposits of fibrous tissue on the tendon sheath of the palm and thumb cause a thickening and drawing together of the skin of the palm and hand. This can make the hand close up, and may eventually lead to a permanent bending of the hand[46].

Writer's cramp

Continuous repetitive movements of the hand or forearm can cause cramp, known as 'writer's cramp'. Perhaps because it has afflicted so many famous writers over the centuries, this is one of the best-known occupational diseases and is officially prescribed.

Ganglion

A ganglion is a round, hard swelling near a tendon, sheath or joint, containing a clear jelly-like substance which can often be released by bursting the ganglion, although sometimes minor surgery is required to get rid of the swelling. It is found most often on the back of the wrist and is often associated with the development of other strain injuries. It is believed to be caused by the strain resulting from precise, repetitive hand movements and is common among office workers[47]. Ganglions are often confused with sebaceous cysts.

A ganglion is not a prescribed disease.

Cervicobrachial disorders

There are a number of different strain injuries which affect the neck and shoulders, including 'tension neck' and humeral tendinitis. These are known collectively as cervicobrachial disorders or sometimes by other, more cumbersome names such as 'occupational neck and upper limb disorder due to constrained work' and 'cumulative trauma disorder (upper extremity)'. As well as the symptoms described at the beginning of this chapter, these injuries can cause pain in the neck and shoulders when at rest, stiffness in the neck and shoulders, headache arising from the neck, muscle tightness and tender spots in the muscles. Sometimes these symptoms become worse at night; sometimes they are aggravated by movement.

As with other strain injuries, one cause of these cervicobrachial disorders is repetitive movement. However the main culprit is static load. In VDU work, the neck and shoulder muscles and tendons are in constant use, not just to hold up the head but also to support the arms. If you are a typical keyboard operator you are holding your hands over the keyboard, with no support from below, for most of the working day. This puts a tremendous strain on these neck and shoulder muscles. When they are also having to hold your head in a rigid posture to see the screen properly, then this strain is even more intense. If they are not given enough opportunity to relax, injury sets in.

None of these cervicobrachial diseases are prescribed in Britain.

Muscle strain

As we have seen, muscles, as well as tendons, are placed under stress both by repetitive movements and by static load. The first sign that they are being pushed past their limit and require rest is a condition known as muscle fatigue, the symptoms of which are feelings of tiredness, weakness and sometimes stiffness, with movements becoming slower and less well coordinated. If these warning signs are ignored, and rest is not provided, they develop into muscle strain. Pain, tenderness, swelling and restriction of movement appear. This condition is sometimes known as non-specific repetition muscle strain and may be spread throughout the hand, arm and shoulder. Sometimes it becomes more localised and affects a particular muscle or group of muscles which could be anywhere from the neck to the hand.

Again, muscle strain is not a precribed disease.

Despite the clear connection between virtually all these types of strain injury and work involving concentrated or repetitive stresses on the muscles or tendons, only tenosynovitis, bursitis and writer's cramp are officially recognised as occupational diseases. If you want to find out more about claiming compensation, please turn to pages 186 – 187.

It seems likely that one of the reasons why it has been even more difficult than in the case of other types of industrial disease to get these strain injuries officially prescribed has been the fact that a majority of sufferers have been working class, female or Black, and that most doctors and lawyers in this country are middle class, male and white.

Strain injuries are often considered to be 'hysterical' or 'psychosomatic' and may frequently be blamed by employers or company doctors on out-of-work activities such as knitting. Women suffering from them often feel they are in a no-win situation. Once they have developed them, they are seriously incapacitated in their unpaid jobs as housewives and carers. As one tenosynovitis sufferer put it:

> 'You wouldn't believe the things it prevents you doing. You can't wash up, you can't turn a key in a lock, you can't pick the baby up, you can't push the buggy, you can't drive a car. It's agony just doing up a shoelace!'

Yet they are obliged to play down their domestic role if they want to get their illness taken seriously as resulting from their work. This makes it extremely difficult to negotiate changes to prevent it occurring again.

Another frequent problem is obtaining a correct diagnosis from your doctor. The London Hazards Centre has come across many cases where strain injuries have been diagnosed as arthritis or as rheumatism. In other cases, there is a reluctance to believe that any specific disease is present. One 38-year-old tenosynovitis sufferer told us:

> 'After three days of agony I decided I'd better go to the doctor. My right wrist was really swollen, and much redder than the left one. It was pretty obvious to most people who saw it that something was wrong. When I went in, I told him what the matter was and he said, "Well, you do have to expect a bit of wear and tear on the joints as you get older, you know". I asked him what it was and he said, "Oh, nothing serious". I asked him what I should do about it and he said "I can give you some pain-killers if you like, but you shouldn't really keep taking that sort of thing". It was as if he'd put me in the category "neurotic middle-aged mum" and I couldn't be trusted even to take aspirins without getting hooked on them. I said I thought it might have something to do with my work and he gave a laugh as if he was indulging me and said that it was conceivable, he supposed, and maybe I should get a new typewriter. He didn't take my job seriously or my bad wrist. He kept on writing the whole time he was talking to me. Not once did he even look at me, let alone examine my wrist.'[48]

Black workers also have a particularly hard time getting something done to prevent strain injuries. Many have little or no job security and this makes any negotiation with their employers extremely difficult. For those who do not speak English, additional problems are caused by the fact that training, information and advice about avoiding strain injuries is not made available in their own language.

Black workers are also less likely than whites to be taken seriously by doctors or lawyers. In Australia a study of Black tenosynovitis sufferers showed that by the time their doctors took the condition seriously it had already reached a stage when permanent damage had been done, and a life-long disability was unavoidable[49].

These difficulties have hidden the prevalence of strain injuries in both traditional and new types of work. Yet even the fragments of information we have about them show that they are common, and becoming more widespread, particularly among VDU operators. Often, more than one type of injury is present at once, blurring the boundaries between the neat medical categories outlined in the previous section.

In one typical workplace survey carried out at a computer centre in Bristol on the initiative of members of the CPSA (Civil and Public Services' Association), high levels of pain and numbness were discovered, as follows:

shoulders and neck	64% of keyboard operators
forearms	33% of keyboard operators
wrists	48% of keyboard operators
fingers	31% of keyboard operators[50]

In a survey of keyboard operators at the Greater London Council in 1983 it was discovered that 86 per cent of data entry operators and 60 per cent of word processor operators suffered from pain in the neck, shoulders, arms, or wrists. Eighty per cent of data entry operators also suffered from backache, as did 54 per cent of typists. Surprisingly at first sight, the level of backache was slightly lower among the word processor operators. This turned out to be because, unlike their colleagues, they had been issued with new, ergonomically designed chairs. In view of this, it was still high, at 46 per cent.[51]

Why is it that such injuries are so high among VDU workers?

As has already been mentioned, the particular bodily posture required to operate a VDU is highly conducive to strain. In order to remain comfortable, most people need to change their position every five minutes or so. However few workstations make this possible. Many operators are obliged to spend long hours in the same cramped position, with forearms held tense over a keyboard, hands awkwardly angled outwards, the lower back inadequately supported, knees held so that the muscles at the front and back of the legs are in tension, and

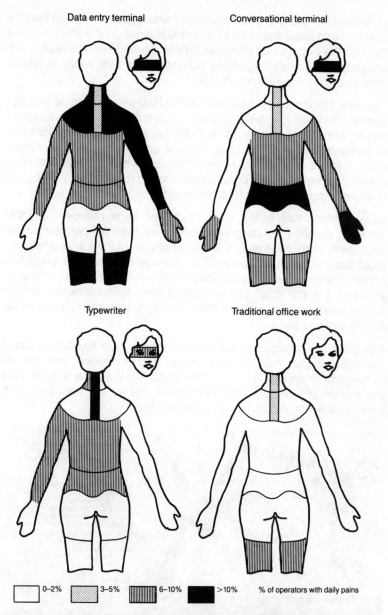

Data entry terminal

Conversational terminal

Typewriter

Traditional office work

0–2%	3–5%	6–10%	>10%

% of operators with daily pains

Diagram comparing the incidence of daily pains in different groups of office workers. The shading indicates the percentage of operators with pain and the location of the pain.

Diagram reproduced from: **Constrained postures in office workstations**, in *Ergonomics of workstation design*, ed Kvalseth T O, Butterworth (1983) quite possibly the head and neck tilted uncomfortably too so that the operator can avoid the glare of reflected images on the screen or see through the bottom half of bifocal lenses. Meanwhile, the fingers are obliged to make rapid repetitive movements and the wrists to flex so that keys can be struck accurately.

However, the working posture which VDU workers are forced to adopt cannot in itself be held entirely to blame. With well-designed equipment and furniture, a relaxed working pace and frequent opportunities to vary the body's movements, it would pose only a minor hazard. It becomes a major problem when the workstation is poorly designed and the pressures of the job require that the posture is sustained continuously for long periods.

Unfortunately, this is the daily reality for large numbers of VDU workers. In order to keep productivity as high as possible, most employers encourage precisely those features of VDU work which are most likely to lead to strain injuries. They go to enormous lengths to ensure that each worker produces the maximum possible number of keystrokes in the minimum amount of time, by penalising them for making mistakes or taking too many breaks and by giving bonuses for speed and accuracy.

It is generally recognised that a rate of more than 10,000 keyboard depressions per hour is hazardous, and increases the risk of developing strain injuries. This is the reason for the famous Australian trade union slogan 'Go safe; Go 10,000'. Yet we still frequently find announcements in company journals like this:

Ross Operators!

A CHANCE TO WIN A £1000 HOLIDAY VOUCHER

The Operator of the Year Keying Competition for 1986/87 will give ROCC operators the chance to win some really exciting prizes.

The winning operator will receive a holiday voucher to the value of £1000 with the runners-up receiving holiday vouchers to the value of £500 and £250 respectively. Your voucher could go towards a holiday of a lifetime! Imagine yourself on a sun drenched beach in Hawaii or the Seychelles, or even visiting the beautiful island of Bali!

Again the competition is only open to users with R-range and 2800 systems. Operators should have a MINIMUM speed of 20,000 key depressions per hour keying in alpha and numeric.

Details of the competition will be sent out to user sites in the AUTUMN, but in the meantime, I hope the senior computer personnel on our user sites will inform their operators about the fabulous prizes to be won.

The announcement is accompanied by a report of the presentation of prizes to the previous year's winner, who achieved a score of 27,686 keystrokes, *after* 100 had been deducted for every character incorrectly keyed.

Another issue of the same journal informs us that three previous winners of the competition (all with rates of over 25,000 keystrokes per hour) were employed at the same data preparation bureau in Bradford. An interview with their manager gives some insight into how this level of productivity is achieved:

> 'We are very selective in the staff we employ. We always look for . . . some evidence of keying rates before we recruit. We initially employ staff on a three-month basis. Out of a batch of six, perhaps two will fall by the wayside . . . Our operators are motivated by bonus rates . . . Bonuses can account for as much as half of their take home pay.'[53]

Bradford is a city of high unemployment, and it is not hard to imagine how stressful it must be to be obliged to take part in this race for productivity to keep your scarce job. Apart from the chance of winning a holiday in Bali, the work must provide few satisfactions. We are told in the same interview why the bureau prefers batch to online processing. Batch processing simply involves keying in data in a standard sequence, whereas online processing involves entering information in response to questions or cues which appear on the screen:

> 'Online data entry can often be substantially slower than batch. This is because . . . the question/response to data entry often requires time-consuming thought from the operator – this is avoided in batch systems by the set up procedure.'

These are jobs which have been reduced to the level achieved several decades ago in factories with the invention of the assembly line. Workers must be prevented from time-consuming thinking at all costs. Maximum productivity is achieved by reducing them simply to a pair of hands, to be kept in motion as continuously as possible.

Conditions like these, which are common and becoming more so in Britain at present, are obvious breeding grounds for strain injuries. However workers who can boast more interesting jobs than these should not be complacent. Strain injuries are widespread even in workplaces which are comparatively humane. They can only be eliminated by careful design of jobs, equipment and workplaces, taking full account of the needs of each individual worker.

Later sections of this book discuss some ideas for bringing these about.

– 8 –

Your skin

Some VDU operators experience skin trouble as a result of their work. Symptoms which have been reported include:

▲ a red rash on the face

▲ itching

▲ peeling

▲ raised spots or pimples

▲ a glowing sensation, rather like sunburn

Typically, these symptoms begin two to four hours after beginning work at a VDU with an itching sensation, sometimes described as 'like being brushed with a feather'. Later, a rash develops on the cheeks and chin and sometimes also the forehead, the tip of the nose and even the eyelids. The symptoms usually disappear overnight and do not appear at weekends and holidays.

Most of the scanty research so far carried out into these skin disorders has been in Scandinavia. At the University of Umea, Sweden, for instance, there was an investigation of a group of office workers at a paper mill, where nine out of fourteen VDU operators developed facial skin problems within a month of the terminals being installed. The investigator, Berndt Stenberg, could not establish the cause of these rashes, but concluded that the most likely explanation was that they were the result of a combination of very dry air and high levels of dust particles in the air. Filter screens installed on the VDUs to reduce the build-up of static electricity were initially successful in reducing the problem, but failed after six days[54].

The most usual theory is that this type of rash is a form of industrial contact dermatitis, caused by irritation from dust particles attracted to the VDU operator's skin by a build-up of static electricity[55].

A Norwegian researcher, Walter Cato Olson, found that, under high static field conditions, more than 10,000 particles per square

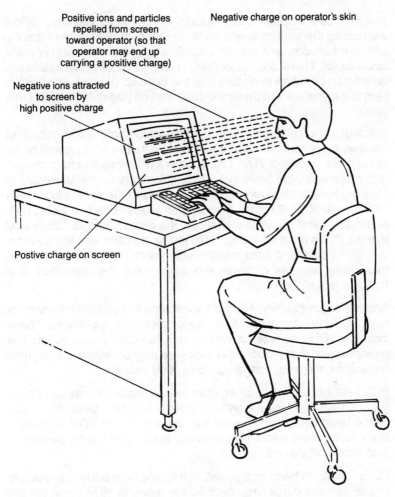

Positive ions and particles repelled from screen toward operator (so that operator may end up carrying a positive charge)

Negative charge on operator's skin

Negative ions attracted to screen by high positive charge

Postive charge on screen

Diagram showing how a VDU can affect the electrostatic charges carried by operators working on the screen.

millimetre can collect on an operator's face in an hour, compared with only 100 particles per square millimetre per hour when the field is eliminated[56].

Although only a minority of VDU operators suffer from this uncomfortable and unsightly form of dermatitis, many are affected by a build-up of static electricity in their workplace which is often experienced in the form of electric shocks when touching pieces of equipment. Management responses to workers' complaints about this problem can be ludicrous, including (in a local authority office) instructing the staff to buy a bottle of fabric conditioner to wipe the affected surfaces with and (in a bank) banning the wearing of nylon underwear! There are, of course, much more effective measures which can be taken to ensure that the build-up of static electricity is kept to a minimum and these are described on pages 153 – 155 of this book.

Although no cases have so far been reported, there is a possibility of another, more serious risk to the skin of operators working with some of the older models of VDU. This is the risk of skin cancer from contact with polychlorinated biphenyls (PCBs). A survey by the University of Oslo in Norway discovered that PCB levels in the air of offices with VDUs were 50 to 80 times greater than levels outdoors. Using both quantitative and qualitative analysis, the researchers demonstrated that the PCBs must have originated inside the office and were almost certainly emanating from electric equipment within the office. The most likely sources of these emissions were the capacitors and transformers of the VDUs[57].

Another paper published in the *Lancet* reported several instances of high PCB concentrations near indoor electrical appliances. These included VDUs as well as kitchen and laboratory equipment. The paper warned that indoor PCB exposure may be linked to malignant melanoma, the most dangerous form of skin cancer.

PCBs are hazardous in other ways too, for instance they can cause liver damage, and increase the amount of fat in the blood which can cause heart disease. However the greatest risk to VDU workers is likely to be from direct skin contact, which can cause dermatitis, chloracne and skin cancer.

PCBs have long been recognised as hazardous, and the manufacture of components containing them was stopped in 1977. However the manufacture of VDUs containing PCBs was only banned in June 1986 and it is quite possible that in the meanwhile some VDUs were produced using old components containing PCBs. The greatest danger is therefore from old (pre-1977) models, although the possibility cannot be ruled out that PCBs are present in some later VDUs as well.

When the VDUs are new, the hazard is insignificant, unless there is a manufacturing fault or the terminal is accidentally damaged, allowing some PCBs to leak out in the form of an oily or waxy liquid. However as they get older, the danger of leakage becomes greater.

The main risks of PCB-induced dermatitis or skin cancer would therefore be to operators working on very old, malfunctioning VDU terminals or to people carrying out maintenance on them, and it would be most likely to appear on parts of the skin, such as the fingertips, which had been in direct contact with the PCBs. Skin cancers on the face, arms or other exposed parts of the bodies of office workers are more likely to result from other causes, such as ultra-violet radiation. This is not to say that PCBs which reach the body through the air, for instance by being inhaled after they have become attached to dust particles, are completely safe. Air-borne PCBs are carcinogenic and could contribute to the development of other cancers[58].

Another possibility for which there is so far little evidence is that some VDU operators might develop dry skin, along with swelling of the face, brittle hair, a dull expression and lethargic, irrational behaviour, as a symptom of myxoedema, a condition that occurs when the thyroid gland does not produce enough of the hormone thyroxine. Women are seven times more likely than men to be affected by this disorder, which is commoner in middle age and can, if untreated, lead to permanent intellectual impairment.

Some commentators believe that myxoedema can be caused by the imbalance of ions in the atmosphere which is described on pages 98 to 100 of this book[59].

It should be emphasised, though, that we know of no direct evidence to link high levels of myxoedema with VDU operation. Nevertheless, the possibility should not be discounted out of hand when so little is known in this field. VDU operators who feel that they may be suffering from the symptoms of thyroid deficiency are advised to consult their doctors.

–9–

Your ears

Noise is not a hazard which usually springs to mind in association with new technology. Many workers have become so accustomed to a noisy environment that they are hardly aware on a conscious level that it is noisy. For instance, a typical office may be filled with the sounds of typing, telephones ringing, the opening and shutting of filing cabinets and other miscellaneous sounds varying from the rumble of traffic in the street outside to the hum of an air conditioning system. Shop workers may be obliged to listen to poorly amplified music, the clash of trolleys or the shouts of customers, while warehouse workers may be surrounded by the noises of fork-lift trucks, conveyor belts or goods being stacked.

Onto a background like this, the introduction of VDUs inevitably adds extra noise. In some cases this noise may not be very loud in itself, but when overlaid onto all the other sounds it can become like the proverbial last straw which broke the camel's back, pushing the overall noise level past the point where it can be tolerated. In other cases, the new noise may be loud enough to form a hazard in its own right even against a silent background.

A computer workstation can produce noise in a number of different ways:

▲ hum from the cooling fan in the processing unit

▲ ultrasound (at 15–18 kilohertz) from the VDU's flyback transformer

▲ clicking, tapping or sometimes, in cheap models, a tinny, rasping sound from the keyboard in use

▲ hum from the cooling fan of the printer

▲ noise from the printer in use

In some cases VDU operators are also expected to work with earphones. For instance customer service staff and telephone sales assistants generally receive the information about what to input or retrieve from their VDU over the telephone from their employer's customers. Many word processor operators have to key in data dictated onto audio cassettes or relayed to them via their employer's internal telephone network. Such workers are subjected not only to continuous noise, often with a high level of distortion or interference, but also intermittently to high-frequency sounds generated within the telephone system[60]. As well as creating a noise hazard, these earphones can also harbour bacteria which can cause ear infections.

Noise can affect the worker who is exposed to it in several different ways:

Deafness

As with eyesight, our hearing ability gradually deteriorates as we get older and the ear's nervous system becomes less sensitive. In particular we lose much of our sensitivity to high-pitched sounds. Few adults, for instance, can hear the squeaking of bats, although most children have no trouble hearing them clearly.

This natural hearing loss is not very great, however. Most deafness suffered by adults below retirement age, and which has not been caused by infection, drugs or accident, can be attributed to the effects of too much noise.

Exposure to excessive noise causes the destruction of nerve cells in the inner ear and a permanent and incurable loss of hearing, usually in the same frequency range as the sounds which caused the trouble.

If the damaged frequencies include speech frequencies, then this deafness can become a severe social handicap, excluding sufferers from the speech-based activities of the hearing world, ranging from everyday conversations to theatre, TV and radio programmes.

The question is, how is an 'excessive' level of noise to be defined? Sound is measured in decibels (dBA), a measure which rises logarithmically not arithmetically. Every increase of ten decibels represents a ten-fold increase in the intensity, or energy, of a sound, so that a vacuum cleaner, at 85 dBA, is putting out ten times as much energy as a typewriter at 75 dBA. An increase of three decibels roughly doubles the level of noise, so 93 dBA is twice as damaging as 90 dBA.

It is generally accepted that a continuous noise of about 80 dBA can strain the ear causing a decrease in hearing ability, and some countries have set maximum noise levels at or below this point, for instance in West Germany the legal maximum level for occupational noise is 70 dBA, while in the Netherlands it is 80dBA[61]. In Britain, however, there is still no legal maximum for most workplaces although the HSE Code of Practice for reducing the exposure of employed persons to noise states that:

'If exposure is continued for 8 hours in any one day, and is to a reasonably steady sound, the sound level should not exceed 90dBA.'[62]

This is backed up by the general duty in Section 2(2)(a) of the Health and Safety at Work Act to provide a safe workplace without risks to health.

Some unions have agreements covering much lower noise levels which can cause stress. In the civil service there is an agreement that in new buildings the general noise level (including traffic noise) should not exceed 65dBA with the windows open (or 55dBA with the windows closed) and that in older buildings action should be taken where the general level exceeds 60dBA with windows closed.

Factory inspectors and environmental health officers have the power to order noise abatement in any situation where noise is harmful, and can be controlled.

A typical daisywheel-type computer printer produces, when unshielded, about 75 dBA. If several printers are in use in a single office or where there are additional sources of noise, much higher levels are often found, which can lead to hearing damage. Particularly vulnerable to occupational deafness are audio typists or word processor operators who have to turn the volume up high to decipher unintelligible tapes or to make them audible over high levels of background noise.

Tinnitus

As well as causing loss of hearing, too much noise can also lead to tinnitus, a continual buzzing, hissing or ringing sound in the ear. This distressing condition generally begins as a temporary effect but can easily become permanent if the sufferer remains exposed to loud noise.

Pain

Pain, sometimes intense, can be caused to people with sensitive ears by certain high-pitched sounds. Similar effects on animals are put to practical use, with ultrasound being used, for instance, to scare seagulls away from football pitches. Although most people cannot hear the ultrasound emitted from the flyback transformer of a VDU, some older adults with particularly good hearing and most children and young adults can. For them, this forms an additional hazard, at best annoying and at worst intolerable[63].

Pain in the ears is also a symptom of ear infection, which may be caused by the use of earphones in which bacteria are breeding.

Stress

Even where noise is not loud enough to cause permanent deafness or tinnitus, it can be a major source of stress at work. This is discussed in more detail on pages 87 – 95.

Information about ways to make your workplace quieter and safer can be found on pages 155 – 156.

– 10 –

Having a baby

Perhaps the most controversial – and certainly the most alarming – effects of VDUs on their operators are those relating to conception, pregnancy and birth. Women working on VDUs have noticed:

▲ difficulty in conceiving a baby

▲ abnormally high rates of miscarriage

▲ abnormally high rates of still-births and complications at birth

▲ abnormally high numbers of babies with disabilities

Most public attention has focused on a series of 'clusters' of VDU operators who have had many more miscarriages or abnormal births than the average. These include:

1   At the Toronto Star newspaper in Ontario, Canada, 4 out of 7 infants born to a group of VDU operators within 1 year, 1979-80, had defects: 1 club foot, 1 cleft palate, 1 underdeveloped eye, 1 multiple heart abnormalities. Normally 3 per cent of live births in Ontario have defects.

2   At an Air Canada office in Montreal, Canada, 7 pregnant VDU operators out of 13 miscarried during a period of 2 years, 1979-81.

3   At the Defence Logistics Agency, a defence contracting office near Atlanta in the United States, there were 7 miscarriages and 3 birth defects out of 15 pregnancies in 1 year, 1979-80.

4   At Sears Roebuck in Dallas, also in the United States, 8 out of 12 pregnancies had adverse outcomes within a 14-month period in 1979-80: 1 premature baby which died of intercranial haemorrhage and 7 miscarriages.

5   In another North American office, at Pacific Northwest Bell, 3 pregnancies out of 3 had abnormal outcomes: 1 baby with Down's syndrome, 1 with spina bifida, and 1 still-birth.

6   At Toronto Old City Hall, in Ontario, Canada, 10 pregnancies out of

19 ended in miscarriage in 1980-81.

7   At the Solicitor General's office in Ottawa, Canada, 7 out of 8 pregnancies ended abnormally during 1979-82. There were 4 miscarriages, 1 premature birth and 2 babies born with respiratory diseases. All 7 women worked on VDUs. The eighth did not, and gave birth to a healthy baby.

8   In the accounts department of the Surrey Memorial Hospital in Vancouver, Canada, 5 out of 6 pregnancies had adverse outcomes: 2 miscarriages, 1 infant with a club foot and needing eye surgery, 1 premature birth, and 1 baby born with bronchitis. All the mothers were VDU operators working in the same room[64].

9   At a United Airlines office in the United States, there were 24 abnormal pregnancies out of 48 between 1979 and 1984, of which 15 ended in miscarriage, 2 in serious birth defects, 2 in premature births, 1 in a still-birth, 1 in neonatal death, and 3 involved other problems.

10 At Southern Bell's data processing centre in Atlanta in the United States, there were 6 miscarriages out of 15 pregnancies[65].

11 At a telephone company office in Alma, Michigan, also in the United States, 17 out of 32 pregnancies ended abnormally during a 16-month period[66].

12 In Britain, at a Department of Employment office in Runcorn, 20 pregancies between 1974 and 1982 ended abnormally. In a survey of 803 women there, the rate of abnormalities among VDU users was 20 per cent higher than for non-VDU users.

13 Also in the north west of England, at the offices of the Greater Manchester Fire Service, 8 pregnancies out of 10 were abnormal, with 2 miscarriages, 3 hospitalisations with high blood pressure, 4 threatened miscarriages, 4 emergency sections and problems at birth.

14 Further east, at an un-named bank in Grimsby, 5 pregnancies out of 5 between 1977 and 1978 were abnormal. There were 3 miscarriages, 1 still-birth and 1 baby born with deformities.

15 At the British Telecom data processing department in Bristol during 1983 and early 1984, 4 out of 5 first-time pregnancies ended in miscarriage[67].

16 At an un-named public library in Denmark, 8 out of 10 pregnancies among VDU operators between 1978 and 1984 ended in miscarriage[68].

In Japan, the General Council of Trades Unions carried out a survey of 13,000 VDU workers of whom 4,500 were women, including 250 who became pregnant or gave birth after working with VDUs. Of these, 91, more than 1 in 3, had abnormal pregnancies including 8 miscarriages, 8 premature births and 5 still-births. What was particularly interesting about this study was the fact that the researchers studied the amount of time spent at the screen by these women and discovered a close correlation with problem pregnancies. Two-thirds of the women who spent 6 hours or more a day at the screen reported problems, compared with just under half of those who spent 3-4 hours at the terminal and a quarter of those who spent less than 1 hour a day at the screen[69].

A Swedish study looked at 4,000 births between 1980 and 1983 among women working in social security offices. The researchers found 57 'significant malformations' among women working with VDUs compared with 9 among women with little or no exposure to VDUs. Among the 57 serious malformations there were 12 cases of cardiovascular (heart and blood system) malformations. There were no disabilities of this type among the babies born to women who did not work with VDUs[70]. A similar study carried out in Finland reported 13 birth defects among mothers working with VDUs, compared to 8 among those who were not exposed[71].

In both of these surveys, unlike the Japanese study, women who worked part-time with VDUs seemed slightly more at risk than full-time VDU operators. Some scientists have argued that this finding disproves any direct connection between the VDUs and the problem births. However there are a number of possible explanations, so far unresearched, which might account for this apparent discrepancy. For instance, none of the studies looked at unintended exposure. Women working for part of the day at a VDU may have spent the rest of their day at work sitting near a VDU operated by someone else, perhaps near the rear of it where many types of emission are at their maximum intensity. Another possibility is that part-time workers were under much greater stress than their full-time colleagues, being already burdened with heavy domestic responsibilities.

Set in the context of the millions of VDUs in use today, these figures may seem slight. But the total of human tragedy which lies behind them is incalculable, as anyone can testify who has suffered the heartbreak of losing a wanted baby or faced the unending struggle of bringing up a child with a disability in a discriminatory society.

More worrying still is the fact that they may well represent the tip of an iceberg. Most of these clusters did not come to light as a result of any systematic analysis of the statistics; in almost all cases, they emerged because groups of VDU operators happened to notice them, and felt strongly enough to bring them to public attention.

The reaction of the authorities has not, by and large, been one which helps to allay the worries of VDU operators who are considering becoming parents. In the United States, in Britain and elsewhere, government departments have joined with equipment manufacturers and employers' organisations in dismissing these clusters as chance occurrences. Their researchers have been quick to conduct studies demonstrating mathematically the likelihood of such clusters occurring by chance. For instance one American epidemiologist reckoned that statistical accident could result in 50 clusters like the Sears Roebuck one over a three-year period in the USA[72].

However, they have been remarkably slow to undertake any studies which investigate the fertility, miscarriage or abnormal birth rates of VDU operators and compare them with those in the population at large. Without such large-scale epidemiological studies, there can be no assurance that VDU operators have a fair chance of producing healthy babies, and real grounds for worry will remain.

In Britain, there has been one small glimmer of official recognition that pregnant women have a right to feel concern about the safety of their unborn baby in the presence of VDUs. In September 1984, an industrial tribunal in Scotland found that an Inverness library assistant, Hazel Johnstone, had been unfairly dismissed for insisting on being transferred to non-VDU work when pregnant. The tribunal decided that her fears about the possible health hazards involved were 'by no means ill-founded' and recommended that she be re-instated in her job. In fact her baby was born with anencephaly, a rare neural tube defect which prevents brain growth and occurs during the first 4-6 weeks of pregnancy, before the mother knows that she is pregnant[73].

Anencephaly is one of the birth defects which was found among babies born to mothers who had been exposed to radiation in the atomic explosions at Hiroshima and Nagasaki[74], although it can also result from other causes, such as acute mercury poisoning.

Anyone trying to arrive at a realistic assessment of the dangers to pregnancy of working with VDUs is faced with formidable obstacles.

For one thing, nobody knows the normal rates of infertility, miscarriage, still-birth and many types of infantile disability. Without this information it is, of course, impossible to say what constitutes an abnormal rate. No national registers are kept in most cases and record-keeping varies widely from one hospital to another, with few having the resources or the inclination to correlate abnormal pregnancies with the parents' occupations.

Estimates of the number of pregnancies which normally end in miscarriage vary considerably. In a study by Harlap and others it was predicted that 14.4 per cent of women seen one week after missing their periods would be likely to lose the baby before the 28th week of the pregnancy. Another researcher, Stickle, estimated that 32 per cent of all conceptions would result in miscarriage, still-birth or infant death, while Oakley estimated that a quarter of pregnancies would be lost after the fourth week. Roberts and Lave put the percentage of human conceptions likely to be lost before birth as high as 78 per cent, but this would, of course, include a high proportion of 'invisible' losses which took place before the mother was aware that she was pregnant. In another study, by Miller and others, which took a positive result to a chemical pregnancy test as a definite sign of pregnancy, 43 per cent of 197 women were judged to have lost their babies. However only 14 of these pregnancies ended in a medically recognised miscarriage. Fifty of them might never have been thought to have happened had it not been for the positive test results[75].

Trying to make sense of these varying figures is made even more difficult by the fact that some women do not report their pregnancies until they are well advanced, so that their miscarriages may go unrecorded, while in other cases planned abortions may appear in the records as miscarriages in areas where abortion is illegal or difficult to obtain.

The best that most experts can do is guess that a 'normal' rate of miscarriage is about 15-20 per cent after pregnancy has definitely been diagnosed.

Statistics on infertility are just as imprecise. Here it is 'guesstimated' that about 10 per cent of couples trying to conceive will fail. However little is known about how much of this is because the man is infertile, how much because the woman is infertile, or what might be attributed to other factors.

When it comes to statistics on babies born with disabilities, things become even more complicated. Not all disabilities are immediately obvious at birth, and, even when they are, they are not uniformly recorded, with variations depending on the nature and severity of the disability. There have been several well-publicised cases of individual doctors being prosecuted at the instigation of 'right-to-life' groups for allowing babies to die (or, as some would put it, failing to use high-tech methods artificially to keep them alive) when they have been born with severe multiple disabilities. These have highlighted the subjective nature of many such decisions and the scope for variations in the records which result. A child in one district hospital might be kept alive, and therefore appear on the records as a baby with a disability, while an identical case in another hospital where a different philosophy prevails could end up as a neo-natal death in the statistics and in reality.

Quite apart from these very considerable problems of deciding at what point a group of problem pregnancies becomes 'abnormal', there is another problem of which pregnancies to include in a study. Most commentators on the subject seem to forget that it takes two people to make a baby. To our knowledge, no research whatsoever has been done on the effects on conception or the health of the foetus which might be caused by the fact that the father works on a VDU.

This omission comes as no surprise to anyone familiar with the general literature on health and safety at work. When it comes to most health hazards, women are completely invisible in the majority of these books, all real workers being assumed to be men; that is, until the subject of reproduction comes up. Then, suddenly, all the men quit the stage and women make their star appearance in what is clearly seen to be their only appropriate role – as walking foetus-carriers. The safety of a future baby is such an emotive subject that other issues tend to be forgotten.

Many of the hazards to foetuses – such as lead or ionising radiation – are also known to be hazardous to adult men and women who are exposed to them. However these health problems have generally been 'solved' not by banning these hazards outright, or carefully controlling exposure to them, but by barring fertile women from working with them. Instead of removing the hazard, the foetus-carrier (actual or potential) is removed, leaving behind an all-male workforce in a hazardous environment.

In most cases no research has been done to find out whether this 'solution' even solves the problem of abnormal pregnancies resulting from the hazard. Since Victorian times it has been known that male lead workers run an increased risk of sterility, impotence and fathering babies with disabilities, yet all the publicity and the legal requirements relating to lead hazards still focus on mothers as the group which must be 'protected'. There has been some similar research on male anaesthetists, but again it is never publicised, and it is pregnant women who are presented as most at risk from radiation hazards. The vast majority of research on reproductive hazards relates exclusively to women.

One exception to this approach is a study in which large numbers of mice, both male and female, were exposed to radiation to see what effect this might have on causing genetic mutations and chromosome abnormalities in pregnancy. The results were surprising. When mothers were exposed, the effects were virtually undetectable. However when fathers were exposed it was estimated that for every million pregnancies there would be between 2 and 10 live-born malformed babies for every rad (a measure of radiation) of radiation, between 10 and 50 recognisable abortions and between 20 and 100 losses at an early stage in the pregnancy[76].

This is not quite as unexpected as might appear at first sight when you consider that sperm is in many ways much more vulnerable than ova, being nearer the surface of the body and continuously produced.

Quite apart from this, there is of course a 50 per cent chance that any damage to a foetus caused by faulty chromosomes will come from the father, since the father provides half of the genetic material from which the embryo is formed. It is estimated that 60 per cent of miscarriages in the first three months of pregnancy result from chromosomal damage, and a lower proportion in the second three months[77], when miscarriages are, in any case, much rarer. Chromosomal damage is also responsible for a number of abnormalities found at birth.

When damage is caused to the embryo in the womb, this very often takes place during the first few weeks of pregancy, sometimes even before the first period has been missed, and well before a woman can be sure that she is pregnant.

It is clear that if a definite link between VDUs and abnormal pregnancies were to be shown, then forbidding women known to be pregnant from working with them would not necessarily solve the problem. The only sure way would be to bar from this type of work anyone who was trying to become a parent, whether male or female – probably a substantial majority of all VDU workers.

Such a link has not yet been proven and it is impossible to state categorically that VDUs do cause abnormal pregnancies. However, the opposite has not been proved either, and it would be equally rash to assert that they do not. All that can be said with any confidence is that there has been a scandalous lack of research in this area, and that the difficulties of proof are immense.

In addition to the problems already outlined of defining what is an abnormal rate of infertility, miscarriage, still-birth, infant death or disability, there are also major difficulties to be overcome before it can be established how, if at all, VDU work produces these effects. There are currently several different theories as to the most likely cause of the clusters of unusual pregnancies which have been noted.

Chance

As already mentioned, the view most favoured by government departments, equipment manufacturers, employers' associations and other groups with a vested interest in the status quo is that they were caused entirely by chance. A similar line of argument was adopted by Sir Douglas Black when he concluded that the high rate of leukaemia among children living near the Sellafield nuclear reprocessing plant in Cumbria was due to a random freak of the statistics. His investigation had been set up, he argued, precisely because there was a high rate of leukaemia in the area; therefore any inquiry would undoubtedly find a high rate, but this could not be attributed to anything other than chance. All cases of leukaemia have to happen somewhere and the laws of probability suggest that some will occur in clusters. This was clearly one such case and the fact that it happened to occur in the most radioactive part of Britain was the merest coincidence.

This argument was quoted approvingly by the authors of a government paper seeking to discredit the findings of the survey into abnormal pregnancies among VDU operators carried out at Runcorn[78], and a similar line of reasoning has been followed in official reports on clusters of abnormal pregnancies in the USA and in Canada, often accompanied by complex mathematical tables drawing on probability theory. So far as they go, such arguments are hard to fault. It is difficult to make any meaningful discoveries without investigating much broader samples of people than those which appear in these small clusters. However not one of these inquiries has made any attempt to do this. The conclusion seems inescapable that their motives have been not so much to find out the truth about VDUs and pregnancies but to quieten public concern. Until serious studies are set up to investigate the effects on a broad section of the population then the 'chance' theory should be viewed with scepticism.

Radiation

Some of the reproductive hazards of radiation have already been touched on in chapter 5 on pages 29 – 35 of this book. They are summarised in table 1 on page 30.

There is no doubt at all that X-radiation in large doses can cause severe damage to the cells of living tissue. This can make people sterile or alter their genes so that a foetus they conceive is defective. This either causes the mother to miscarry or leads to the baby being born with disabilities. There is doubt about whether the X-radiation from VDUs is the likely cause of the unexplained clusters of abnormal pregnancies only because of the low levels at which it has been found to be emitted.

In the central part of the radiation spectrum, neither ultra-violet nor infra-red radiation has been associated with reproductive hazards, although both are hazardous in other ways.

It is the low end of the frequency range which has been the focus of most of the recent concern about risks to pregnancy from radiation emanating from VDUs.

Microwaves have been suspected to be a reproductive hazard for some time. At levels over 10 mW/cm^2 (milliwatts per square centimetre) they have been shown to cause still-births and deformities at birth in laboratory animals in a Polish study[79], while a similar study in the USA discovered damage to the testicles, debilitated or still-born offspring and changes in spermatogenesis (the process by which the body produces sperm) in experimental animals exposed to microwaves[80].

A Russian study of 31 male technicians who had been exposed to microwaves found significantly reduced sperm counts and sperm mobility and an increased proportion of abnormal sperm compared to an unexposed group. Seventy per cent of the technicians showed decreases in libido (the desire for sex) and problems with erection, ejaculation and orgasm[81].

Other studies have discovered a higher rate of malformations in children of US military personnel in an area with many microwave-emitting installations[82].

A study of women in Czechoslovakia working with microwave radiation reported a wide range of effects including changes in menstrual patterns, retarded development of foetuses, congenital deformities in newborn babies, increased miscarriage and decreased lactation (production of breast-milk)[83].

Microwaves are not the only form of radio-frequency radiation to affect reproduction. In the Soviet Union, ELF (extremely low frequency) radiation has been shown to cause bone deformation in the foetuses of rats and rabbits[84].

Since 1984, some even more disturbing findings about VLF (very low frequency) radiation have emerged. In that year, Dr Jose Delgado and his associates at the Centro Ramon y Cajal Hospital in Madrid, Spain, published a paper in the British *Journal of Anatomy* which described some experiments in which the development of chick embryos was altered, leading to deformities, as a result of being subjected to VLF fields. The significance of this research was that the effects were produced despite the fact that the fields were extremely weak, as much as 500 times weaker than the earth's natural magnetic field.

Where they differed from these fields, and from other fields to be found in the everyday environment, was in the fact that the fields were pulsed, and with waves of a very specific shape[85].

As it happens, the fields emitted by the flyback transformers of VDUs are also pulsed, and have a 'sawtooth' shape similar to those of the fields used in Dr Delgado's experiments, according to Richard Tell, a physicist with the US Environmental Protection Agency, and Professor Bill Guy, who carried out a study of VDU radiation for IBM[86]. However Guy did note that the waves emitted by a VDU included a tiny 'ripple' which was not present in Delgado's wave-forms, and neither of these experts has gone so far as to suggest that ELF radiation may be the cause of the clusters of abnormal pregnancies which have been noted. Delgado's experiments were initially treated with scepticism by some other scientists.

However in 1986 the results of some Swedish experiments forced them to reappraise this assessment. Researchers at the Karolinska Institute in Stockholm discovered that when pregnant mice were exposed to VDU-like pulsed magnetic fields, their foetuses developed nearly five times the rate of malformations of those which had not been exposed. A Polish study was also reported in which male rats exposed to television sets had testicles of a lower weight than unexposed rats[87].

The results of two other Scandinavian studies which had attempted to replicate Delgado's results were also disclosed. In one, at the University of Kuopio in Finland, it was found that a variety of different types of magnetic field could harm chick eggs, leading the researchers to conclude that it is not important whether or not the wave is pulsed, a finding which conflicts with Delgado's, although it does not contradict the idea that low frequency radiation can be dangerous to the development of a foetus[88].

The other experiment, carried out jointly by the University of Umea and the Swedish National Board of Occupational Safety and Health, involved exposing eggs to the same type of sawtooth magnetic field pulses as those used in the Karolinska Institute's experiments on mice. Here, the results were negative.

The issue is obviously still extremely controversial. However Dr Ricardo Edstrom, medical director of the Swedish National Board of Occupational Health is now on record as saying that 'we can no longer rule out the possibility that radiation could affect foetuses'.

If future research confirms a link between increased exposure to electromagnetic radiation and problems in pregnancy, then a recent development in 'anti-bugging' devices may be worrying. These devices have been produced to prevent people with equipment similar to TV detector vans from deciphering electromagnetic emissions from VDUs and 'reading' other companies' computers.

One manufacturer claims to have produced a data protecting device which works by creating an electromagnetic field around the VDU which corrupts the emitted data making it unintelligable to anyone trying to bug the system from outside. A *Guardian* review of this equipment[89] suggests that the emissions are similar to those of VDUs, which means that VDU operators working at VDUs with these devices attached may be exposed to an increased dose of electromagnetic radiation.

Static electrical fields

Even more speculative than the effects of radiation is the possibility that problem pregnancies might be caused by the high positive charge in the atmosphere in most rooms where VDUs are used.

Some of the possible effects of this on general health have already been discussed on pages 35 to 37, including the role that an overdose of positive ions may play in stimulating the body to produce excessive quantities of the neuro-hormone serotonin.

If the balance of ions in the air does affect pregnancy, then it is a change in the levels of this hormone which seems most likely to be responsible.

In Jerusalem, where studies had already been carried out on the relationship between the positively-charged Sharav wind, positive ions and the production of serotonin, some research was done on the effects of serotonin on pregnancy. First, it was discovered that pregnant rats aborted if injected with serotonin. Then 20 women who had asked for, and been given permission to seek, legal abortions were injected with serotonin and all miscarried. Attention was then turned to women who wanted to have babies but who had had a continuous series of miscarriages, described as 'habitual aborters'. They were treated with a serotonin-blocking drug. Over a period of ten years over a hundred women were treated in this way and almost all bore healthy babies. However in the mid-1960s the use of this serotonin-blocking drug was made illegal in Israel and the experiments came to an end[90].

If the positively charged atmospheres in which VDU operators work have the same effect of increasing serotonin, and if the results of this research are to be believed, then it seems quite possible that high serotonin levels could be a contributory factor, if not a major cause of the large numbers of miscarriages found in some of the clusters of

VDU operators quoted at the beginning of this chapter.

To our knowledge, no research has been done to test levels of serotonin among VDU operators, or levels of negative or positive ions in the offices where abnormal pregnancy clusters have been found. Research in these areas would be helpful. Perhaps it could shed some useful light on the problem. If not, it would at least eliminate one possibility.

We can speculate that if this did turn out to be part of the explanation for these abnormal pregnancy clusters (assuming, for the moment, that they really are abnormal) then it might also explain why most of the clusters have been found in regions like Canada, the United States and Scandinavia, where the winter air is very cold and dry, and therefore positively charged; and where there is a high standard of living and therefore a high likelihood that workplaces will be centrally-heated, carpeted and air-conditioned, producing a highly artificial environment, often in high-rise buildings. These are also very hygiene-conscious countries with high standards of cleanliness (the frequent use of vacuum cleaners, dusters, brooms etc. raises clouds of dust to which negative ions become attached, and are therefore removed from the atmosphere – letting the dirt lie, as happens in so many British workplaces, is actually beneficial when it comes to keeping the negative ion levels high!). Finally, they have cold winters, so that for a great part of the year many people, including, we might guess, a large proportion of VDU operators, spend virtually all of their time indoors, in these artificial, and positively charged, environments.

It must be emphasised, however, that this is speculation. We cannot know the true effects of these positive electric fields without a great deal more research.

In Italy, studies have been carried out on the effects of negative ions on fertility. Both male and female mice reached sexual maturity much more quickly in negatively ionised air and when mature the females were much more fertile than normal. R. Gualterotti, who carried out the research, commented that:

> 'Many authors have noted an increase in sexual activity in man as a result of exposure to aerions. This has been confirmed by a series of experiments on animals living in an environment of artificially negatively charged ionised air. Histological examination of testicles and ovaries of animals exposed to high concentrations of negative ions for ninety six hours shows a definite stimulation of the process of maturation of a large number of cells.'[91]

If, as this writer suggests, negative ions can make both men and women more fertile, then it seems quite possible that a lack of negative ions might have the reverse effect and be a contributory factor to the difficulty in conceiving which has been reported by many VDU operators.

Again, we cannot be sure whether or not this is the case until more research has been done on the subject.

Posture

It has sometimes been suggested that one of the causes of the abnormal pregnancy clusters is poor posture, caused by badly designed seating and workstations. Very little medical evidence has been given for this view, although it does have a certain appeal to common sense. It is certainly true that most VDU workstations are not designed in a way that allows the operator to relax and change position as often as is desirable.

For example, in one survey of its members by the trade union APEX, it was discovered that 66 per cent – two thirds – of VDU operators had chairs which were not adjustable while sitting on them[92].

The bodily tension, pain and discomfort caused by badly designed funiture are a hazard to all workers. Regardless of whether they contribute to miscarriages or birth defects, these difficulties become particularly acute during pregnancy, because of the extra size which has to be accommodated, because of the increased likelihood of backache and circulation problems, and because of the need to change position when the baby kicks or turns in the womb. These should be sufficient reasons to insist on well-designed and comfortable seating arrangements for all VDU operators, pregnant or not.

It seems unlikely that research findings will be produced in the near future to prove a definite link between bad posture and restricted movement and high rates of miscarriage. By its nature, this would be a difficult proposition to test and we know of no organisations seriously interested in carrying out such a study.

Needless to say, this is not a reason for VDU operators to put up with badly designed furniture. Poor seating can lead to backache, stress and a wide range of musculoskeletal problems described in chapter 7 which begins on page 50.

Stress

Another suspect in the search for a cause for the problem pregnancy clusters is stress. This subject is dealt with in greater detail in the next chapter of this book which deals with general health. As will be seen, stress is associated with an enormous and varied range of physical and psychological symptoms, from heart disease to asthma; from stomach ulcers to insomnia.

The effects of stress on reproduction have not been well studied, although it is known that stress reduces sperm counts and that anxiety can cause difficulties in conceiving a baby. Stress is also associated with sexual impotence in men[93].

With the present state of knowledge on the subject, it would be foolish to rule stress out as a contributory cause to difficulties in conceiving and successfully carrying a baby.

The problem of stress demonstrates in a particularly clear form the difficulty of looking at any of these possible reproductive hazards in isolation. Quite simply, the problem is this: that anything which is hazardous to a foetus is also likely to be hazardous to any other living being, male or female, child or adult.

Any attempt at a solution which restricts itself to 'protecting' the foetus will still leave at risk any VDU worker not known to be pregnant. The only effective health and safety policy is one which applies to all workers and their unborn children.

Synergistic effects

Before leaving the subject of reproductive problems, it is important to note that the full explanation of the pregnancy problems of VDU operators may not rest solely on chance, radiation, static fields, posture, stress or some other as yet undiscovered factor. It may be that the damage is caused by several or all of these acting together, with each one exacerbating the effects of the others. Even if none of these factors alone is sufficiently strong to affect a VDU operator's pregnancy – and this has yet to be proved – it is quite possible that mixed together they make a cocktail which is dangerous both to a developing foetus and its would-be parents.

– 11 –

General health

Quite apart from the specific effects of VDU work on operators' eyes, ears, skin, musculoskeletal systems and reproductive abilities, there have also been many reports of a general worsening of their health, both physical and mental. Complaints range over a wide area including:

▲ increases in colds, flu and other viral infections

▲ asthma, bronchitis, sinusitis and other respiratory disorders

▲ digestive upsets

▲ angina and other heart or circulatory problems

▲ migraine attacks

▲ irregular or painful periods

▲ depression, sometimes suicidal

▲ irritability

▲ exhaustion

▲ going off sex

▲ nausea, loss of appetite or compulsive eating

▲ insomnia

▲ increased dependence on alcohol, tobacco, tea, coffee, tranquillisers or 'pep' pills

▲ phobias

Obviously none of these complaints is peculiar to VDU operators, and it would be impossible to pin down VDUs as the only cause of them. Some VDU workers would be surprised to think that any of them were connected with their work, although many have noticed a link. Here are some comments from VDU operators who have contacted the London Hazards Centre:

'Peaks of illness appear to follow after peaks of work. It is very noticeable then that I am depressed and impatient with others trying to learn to use the machine (they have had no proper training either). I have been in pain with undiagnosed digestive problems for over a year.'

'I've used the machine for just over a year - frequently for eight hours a day without any breaks. During the last few months I have suffered from bouts of extreme dizziness to the point of feeling as if I'm about to pass out. This culminated in what I can only describe as a 'sort of fit' in the office. I was taken by ambulance to hospital and now have an appointment with a neurological consultant.'

'I've worked on a VDU for four years now and feel I've aged ten years! I feel constantly tired and only start to unwind on Sunday which gives me half a day's rest each week because I start to get keyed up again during Sunday evening.'

'Menstrual problems once stabilised for many years are now running havoc.'

'I am slightly concerned with the way my monthly period has totally ceased to occur.'

'I don't think I've ever been so ill in my life as last year - the first when I worked continuously on a VDU. I was on antibiotics for one reason or another more or less continuously for six months, and I'm still in constant pain from chronic sinusitis. I've also started getting blinding migraine-type headaches just before my period each month.'

Women who have contacted the London Hazards Centre about disturbances to their menstrual cycles include:

▲ A group of women, all members of the clerical section of the trade union SOGAT, who worked all day on VDUs in the same office. All shared the same symptoms of heavy, painful and irregular bleeding.

▲ A 29-year-old woman who experienced no menstrual problems before taking a job which involved spending 7½ hours a day on a VDU. Shortly after she started, she began to experience discomfort in her stomach for two or three days at the beginning of her period, widely varying (but always short) gaps between periods, and two days of extremely heavy flow in each period. This woman's problems were so severe that she gave up VDU work and began to take the contraceptive pill, multivitamins, vitamin A and the pain-killer ibuprofen in an attempt to control the pain and heavy bleeding, which still continue, although the gap between her periods has increased to a regular eighteen days.

▲ A 38-year-old woman whose periods stopped altogether about six months after starting work on a VDU. She spent all day at the screen.

▲   A woman who had previously experienced the symptoms of the premenstrual syndrome (PMS) before her periods and who found after taking up full-time VDU work that she had incapacitating PMS virtually all the time. The symptoms subsided each time she stopped doing VDU work.

▲   Thirteen young women workers in the Civil Service, mostly in their teens, who took part in a questionnaire survey which revealed that five of them had experienced changes in their menstrual cycles since beginning to work with VDUs. Of these, there was one woman whose periods had stopped altogether while three had developed the symptoms of PMS, of whom one had also started to have irregular periods.

▲   A group of women workers in a council housing benefits office who had developed new menstrual problems since joining the section. They worked constantly on VDUs and the office was overcrowded with no natural lighting or ventilation[94].

In most people's lives there are many possible causes of ill health: bad housing, adulterated food, polluted air, having too much housework to do, physical violence or the fear of it, worry about money or about the health or safety of loved ones, problems in relationships: the list is endless. Can the effects of working at a VDU really be isolated from these, and blamed as the major cause of these health problems? In many cases, the answer is almost certainly yes.

There is a body of evidence slowly building up that points to a higher incidence of many health problems among VDU operators than among other comparable groups of workers, ranging from angina pectoris to migraine.

However this is perhaps not the most useful way of viewing the problem. Rather, working at a VDU should be seen not as an *alternative* source of ill-health to these other factors, but as an *additional* health hazard. In the cases of some types of illness, VDU work may well be the final straw that breaks the body's resistance to an illness which has already been threatening health, and has been fended off with difficulty.

This argument holds true particularly in relation to the three most likely causes of general illness among VDU operators: stress, radiation and static electrical fields. Of these, stress is by far the most important and is therefore considered first.

Stress

Everyone believes they know what is meant by stress. However on investigation it turns out to be a very imprecise word, which means different things to different people. To some it has a purely physical meaning, describing the effect of putting a heavy load on a particular set of muscles in very much the same way as an engineer might talk of the stress on a steel girder. To others it describes the chemical reaction in the body which takes place when it is theatened in some way – the so-called 'fight or flight' response. To some psychologists it is a term used to describe a particular mental state, usually due to anxiety. Other people use the term more generally to describe how they feel when under pressure, for instance from too much work or too many competing demands on their time. The Penguin Medical Encyclopaedia is broader still, defining it as 'any influence that disturbs the natural equilibrium of the living body'[95], following the view of Hans Selye, the Canadian who 'discovered' stress in the 1950s.

All these different definitions are intimately bound up with each other. Stress seems to be a bodily condition which can be caused both by physical and by psychological factors, and whose effects can be both physical and psychological. The precise nature of the interaction between mental and physical states in the body is shrouded in mystery, but many of its causes, mechanisms and effects have now been studied. At the centre of the process lies the body's immediate response to what it perceives as a threat. One commentator has described it like this:

> 'The body prepares for action by first tensing the muscles, as we tense up in races when the starter says, "Get ready, get set," before he says, "Go!" At the same time the body mobilises its vital supporting activities to support the anticipated activity. The cardiovascular system reacts by shunting blood to the muscles for increased oxygen supply, the heart beats faster, the blood pressure rises, the stomach and intestines slow to stopping, and many of the body's secretions stop. All of the body's resources are mobilised for its lifesaving task.'[96]

Crucial to this reaction are a group of hormones called catecholamines, which include adrenaline. When the stress response is triggered, the body produces more of these. Adrenaline stimulates the heart, raises the blood pressure, releases glucose and increases its consumption, increases the circulation of blood in the muscles, relaxes the air passages and stimulates breathing, producing a sense of excitement. At the same time it inhibits digestion and excretion and reduces blood flow everywhere except in the heart, the brain and the muscles.

It is generally believed that this first reaction is followed by a more balanced state, during which the body tries to resist the stress.

However if the cause is not removed, or the problem solved, this eventually breaks down and the body succumbs to illness.

Different types of stress can exacerbate each other, so that for example if the body is recovering from the stress caused by a physical injury, then it is less able to resist infection; both conditions could in turn be aggravated by worry. Being ill is in itself a source of stress, so a person who has begun to be affected by stress is likely to enter into a downward spiral of further stress which generates further illness and so on.

We have already seen several of the forms of stress which VDU operators may be subjected to. They include:

Muscular stress

Eye muscles, fingers, hands, arms, shoulders, back, trunk and legs are all involved intensively in gazing at the screen, operating the keyboard or supporting the rest of the body in doing so. Both repetitive movements and static loads are involved, all of which create tension and place abnormal demands on the body's resources.

Environmental factors

Many VDU operators are exposed to stressful levels of noise. They may also be experiencing overcrowding, extremes of temperature, dryness, or atmospheric pollution (such as that caused by cigarette smoke or photocopier fumes).

Hardware and software design

The physical design of equipment which is awkward or uncomfortable to use can be an important cause of stress. So can poorly designed software which produces unpredictable delays in response times or unexpected errors. In one Swedish study, it was found that periods of breakdown, when computer terminals went off-line, were extremely stressful for the operators, even though they appeared to be providing a break from work. Scores for irritation, fatigue, feeling rushed and boredom shot up and there were increases in blood pressure, adrenaline secretion, and heart rate during these breakdowns[97].

Where a single VDU workstation is shared between several workers, machine breakdowns affect those in the queue as well as workers who are actually operating the machine at the time.

Job design factors

A great deal of stress is caused by the way in which jobs are designed. Monotony, lack of any chance to change either one's position or the type of work being done, piece rates, pressure to work fast to meet production targets and the knowledge that work is being closely monitored can each place the individual operator under strain. If the job includes several of these factors, this strain can quickly become intolerable. Despite increasing medical evidence of the stressful effects of forcing productivity levels ever higher, it seems that the pressure on data entry workers is increasing all the time. The US Data Entry Management Association reported in 1984 that there had been an 11 per cent increase in keystrokes per hour by data entry operators since 1980. The group urged managers to raise productivity still further, aiming for a standard of 12,000 keystrokes per hour – 20 per cent higher than the norm still prevailing in most offices[98]. The effect of this on VDU operators doing data entry work can be judged from such statements as:

'We're just robots. To our management the data entry staff are the lowest of the low. However fast you work, it's not fast enough.'

'Nobody gives a damn about us. We're hardly human as far as the other staff are concerned. We're just part of the machinery. If we were to break down and stop meeting our targets, we'd be straight out of that door, no matter how long we'd been working here.'

These workers were employed by a British local authority in the relatively easy-going public sector. Similar views were expressed by Rebecca Alford, a VDU operator working for the Equitable Life Assurance Company in Syracuse, New York, who gave evidence in 1984 to a US congressional subcommittee on VDU health and safety. She said that:

'The electronic monitoring is one of the most offensive and pernicious aspects of our work. We "clock on" at 7 a.m. and from then until the end of the day the VDT is counting every keystroke. At the end of the day, managers have a computer read-out from which productivity is determined and then averaged with subjective factors such as attitude to determine our rate of pay. Being watched, counted and paced by a machine makes it very difficult to take pride in your work. The lack of control over our jobs combines with demeaning, boring work, assembly-line conditions, safety and health risks to ourselves and our children and unsupportive bosses to result in a highly stressful situation for clericals at Equitable.'[99]

For many VDU operators the most important factor of all in this list is 'lack of control over our jobs'. Where the worker has some control, there is always the possibility of modifying some of the most stressful aspects of a job, of varying the order in which tasks are done, perhaps, of choosing to take a break to rest tired eyes or wrists, of swapping roles with a workmate for a while, or simply changing one's position.

Without control such things are impossible. Something which might begin as a minor irritant (perhaps an apparently trivial detail like a reflection in the corner of a screen, a low hum, an itch on one's foot or a mistake that recurs every time a certain combination of keys is pressed) becomes more and more annoying, to end up being experienced as a relentless pressure which the operator is powerless to do anything about. Such is the raw material of stress.

Factors connected with work expectations

Many VDU operators began their working lives at a time when office or craft work was relatively high-status, and carried good career prospects. For them it has been particularly hard to adjust to a situation where many of their hard-earned skills are worthless, where they no longer have any promotion prospects and where jobs now have little more social prestige than a factory assembly-line. They have also had to face the reality, shared with more recent entrants to white-collar work, that most of them are readily dispensible, with skills that can easily be picked up by even younger operators, with nimbler fingers and lower expectations. The knowledge that your job may not be secure is a major cause of stress.

Factors connected with power relations in the workplace

As has been seen, the introduction of new technology tends to produce a polarisation between the low-grade jobs of VDU operators (generally women and frequently Black people) and the high-grade jobs of managers, senior technicians and designers (generally white men). By removing intermediary layers of low-level managers and supervisors, this tends to increase the power of senior staff in relation to low-level operators and make it harder to challenge their decisions, while giving them more and more sophisticated electronic tools for surveillance and management. Many VDU operators thus have real cause to fear the arbitrary power of their managers – a major cause of stress, to which may be added a fear of sexual or racial harassment in some cases.

Outside factors

It must be remembered that these stresses are not being created in a vacuum. VDU operators are human beings already coping with many stressful experiences to survive in a recession-hit world. Most have families to worry about, household responsibilities to perform, unpredictable public transport systems or traffic conditions to negotiate to get to work on time and a host of other anxieties to preoccupy them. All of these render them more vulnerable to the stresses produced by their work.

What is the evidence that VDU operators are affected by these potential stress factors in their jobs?

Even before VDUs were widely introduced into offices, office work was known to be a particularly stressful form of work. When the US National Institute for Safety and Health (NIOSH) carried out a survey of 22,000 workers in 130 occupations in 1977, being a secretary emerged as the second most stressful occupation, exceeded only by that of labourer. Incidentally the same survey exploded the myth of 'executive stress'. The rate of coronary heart disease and of other stress-related diseases went *up* with every step *down* the occupational hierarchy, not the other way round as is generally assumed. The US National Heart, Lung and Blood Institute also found that women in clerical jobs are twice as likely to suffer from heart disease as any other group of working women, including full-time housewives[100].

VDUs have added another dimension to this. In a survey carried out in 1984 by the US National Center for Health Statistics, it was discovered that nearly 20 per cent of 278 VDU operators in North Carolina telephone companies reported clear symptoms of angina pectoris compared with 10.1 per cent of 218 clerical workers who did not use the machines. Angina pectoris is the name given to painful spasms in the chest caused by lack of oxygen to the heart muscle. The condition can lead to heart attacks at a later stage. The US national average incidence of angina is only about 3 per cent[101].

A study by researchers at Stockholm University found that a high degree of mechanisation is closely associated with increases in stress levels. In a study carried out amongst sawmill workers, those whose jobs were characterised by repetitiveness, physical constraint, machine regulation of work pace and high demands for continuous attention were compared with a control group who had more control over the pace of their work and worked under more flexible, less mechanised conditions. The first group (whose jobs shared many of the characteristics of VDU work) were found to be excreting much higher levels of catecholamines (adrenaline and nor-adrenaline) than the control group. These workers also suffered from psychosomatic illnesses more frequently than the control group and were absent from work more often[102].

Later, the same researchers turned their attention to VDU operators in a survey carried out at the Goteborg branch of Skandia, Scandinavia's largest insurance company. Seventy per cent of all the workers surveyed (who included some who were not VDU operators) considered that their work caused mental strain. When asked what caused this stress, 34 different factors were listed. The ten most important of these, listed in order of importance, were:

▲   too much work

▲   computer breakdowns

▲   not knowing how long a breakdown might last

▲   too many interruptions

▲   too many demands on one's attention

▲   work piling up during computer breakdowns

▲   phone calls which interrupt VDU work

▲   high noise levels

▲   the office environment makes it impossible to express feelings such as joy or anger

▲   clients' demands and lack of understanding

As can be seen, a high proportion of these are directly connected with VDU work. When the rate of adrenaline excretion was measured it was found that VDU workers were producing more than non-VDU workers and that higher levels persisted into the evening after work, rather than dropping to normal base-line rates as they did with the non-VDU workers. VDU workers also showed significantly higher levels on days when they were at work, compared with measurements taken when they had a day off at home, although for non-VDU workers there was no significant difference.

This seems to show that VDU workers are subjected to more stress at work and find it harder to 'unwind' in the evenings than other workers, even though they can relax on days off. When asked to rate their own moods, VDU workers showed higher levels of 'rush', 'effort', 'irritation' and 'fatigue' than non-VDU workers, both at work and in the evening after work. As with so many other VDU-related hazards, it was the data entry operators who suffered the most severe effects[103].

In a British survey of keyboard operators at the Greater London Council, 77 per cent of data entry operators and 68 per cent of word processor operators complained of stress[104]. A survey of VDU operators in the Canadian Civil Service produced similar findings, with 73.7 per cent reporting that their jobs were stressful[105].

In Japan, psychiatrist Takashi Sumioka has made a special study of nervous disorders among working women and concludes that a wide range of symptoms can be attributed to stress, and that these are becoming more widespread as a result of computerisation. In particular, he singles out four psychological conditions:

▲ Depression which is accompanied by accelerated heart-beat, body pain, weight loss, loss of appetite and insomnia.

▲ Anxiety neurosis, sporadic symptoms of which are terrible anxiety, irregular heart-beat and breathing, chest pains, perspiration, trembling and dizziness.

▲ Anthropophobia (fear of others). People who suffer from this illness become very tense and anxious when they are in the presence of others. Especially prevalent in Japan (perhaps because of overcrowded living and working conditions) this disease used to be confined to men but has been becoming increasingly common among women since the mid-1950s, when computers were first introduced into Japanese workplaces.

▲ Obsessive-compulsive neurosis. This neurosis causes restricted bodily movements and obsessive repetition of actions which often appear meaningless. There is also a general feeling that life has no meaning which leads to severe depression[106].

While Western specialists may not agree precisely with this diagnosis, many studies have reported similar symptoms among people who are chronically under stress.

There is a general agreement among the experts that stress can lead directly to a number of 'psychosomatic' illnesses, including skin diseases like psoriasis, eczema and acne; digestive disorders such as overeating, stomach ulcers, diarrhoea and colitis; asthma; migraine; high blood pressure, auricular arrhythmias (jerky heartbeat), peripheral vascular disease and other heart and circulatory diseases; and increased susceptibility to viruses (such as colds, flu and gastroenteritis) and secondary infections (such as bronchitis, tonsilitis, sinusitis, ear infections etc.).

Stress can also aggravate many other diseases which are already present in the body, causing them to flare up or worsen. One of the first of these to be observed was tuberculosis, but there are many others, including herpes, rheumatoid arthritis and epilepsy. According to Professor Cary Cooper, head of Organisational Psychology at the University of Manchester Institute of Science and Technology, breast cancer is also in this category. In a four-year study of 2,163 women screened for breast cancer a direct link between stress and cancer was found[107]. It is thought that the main mechanism involved is a suppression of the body's natural immune defence system caused by stress.

As well as physical illness, stress can also cause a bewildering range of psychological problems, including anxiety, depression, learning difficulties, inability to concentrate, sexual impotence, delinquent behaviour, inability to hold down a job, alcohol, smoking or drug abuse, inability to sustain good relationships and general bloody-mindedness.

To understand how such an enormous variety of physical and mental disorders can be created by what is apparently the same stimulus, we must see human beings in their entirety, as complex organisms in which many different systems are constantly interacting with each other, with an array of delicate mechanisms which check and balance these interactions to sustain the overall state of harmony which we call 'good health'. We can then imagine that, like a machine, when it is under stress, this organism is jarred and jolted and many of its parts are knocked out of balance.

Mechanisms which can cope quite well with an occasional 'abnormal' upset cannot stand up indefinitely to such pressure when it has become the daily norm. Sooner or later, something has to 'give', and what gives is likely to be the weakest point in the organism. What this point is will depend on a number of different factors: the age and sex of the person under stress, medical history, genetic make-up, the other hazards present in the workplace or home, the types of behaviour which are socially acceptable in their particular culture and so on. In electronics factories in Malaysia it sometimes takes the form of seeing the spirits of one's ancestors down the microscope and triggering an outbreak of mass hysteria which has been described as a 'subconscious strike'[108].

In some Western men it might become visible as physical violence or vandalism; in others as the more self-destructive forms of heavy drinking or depression. The only one of these options which is socially acceptable for women is depression, which is therefore a common female reaction to chronic stress, although some might react with physical symptoms such as an attack of migraine or asthma.

Victims of stress are often blamed for their own condition, and told to learn relaxation techniques or take up yoga as a way of dealing with it. While such techniques may have some effect in allaying the some of the symptoms of occupational stress, they cannot in themselves do anything to remove the cause except in those very rare cases where the people affected have total control of their working environment, their working conditions, the design of their jobs and the design of the equipment with which they work.

Tackling stress involves tackling the causes of stress, and this means giving the worker some control over these factors. Some strategies for doing this are discussed in the later chapters of this book.

Radiation

Just as there can be said to be a 'background level' of stress in most people's lives, there is also a background level of ionising radiation. Some of this has always been there, from naturally ocurring deposits of radioactive minerals in the soil and from the sun's radiation. Because of the destruction of the earth's ozone layer by the indiscriminate use of new technologies, background radiation from the sun is steadily increasing.

Since the end of the Second World War, artificially produced radiation has been added to this. Some has come from fallout from the atomic bombs dropped on Japan by the Americans, and from atmospheric and underground tests of new bombs carried out in the United States, the Pacific, Australia and Siberia by the governments of the USA, Britain, France, China, the USSR and possibly also of Israel and South Africa. Some has come from the mining of uranium and some from waste from nuclear power stations dumped on land and in the sea. Radiation has also been emitted directly into the air as the result of accidents. Finally, some ionising radiation has been released as a result of the medical use of radiation.

Because of the military origins of much of this radiation, its effects have not been well studied, and evidence that it might be hazardous is generally ignored or rubbished by the government departments concerned. Nevertheless, it cannot be denied that the effects of radiation are cumulative, and, while background levels continue to climb, any factor which increases the exposure of any group of people to radiation, however slight, must be viewed with some concern. Although the emissions of most types of radiation from VDUs are extremely low, they are detectable in many models, and it is possible that, to an individual who has already been exposed to a great deal of radiation from other sources, they could be a real hazard.

In a conservative estimate, the United Nations Scientific Committee on the Effects of Atomic Radiation reckoned that between 1972 and 1977 alone, as a result of nuclear testing, radiation doses to the population increased by about 2 per cent in the northern hemisphere and 6 per cent in the southern hemisphere. Between 1945 and 1963, it had increased much more, with an estimated average dose to each individual of about 1 milligray (equivalent to 100 millirad, old units) to the sex organs and about 2 milligray (equivalent to 200 millirad, old units) to the cells which line the bones. In the temperate zone of the northern hemisphere these values were about 50 per cent higher,

0 per cent lower in the temperate zone of the
here. This estimate *excludes* the effects of
on, which takes longer to reach people via the
ain, and any radiation from other sources[109].

independent overviews of the research on the effects
vels of radiation was published in 1985, under the title
Danger: Prognosis for a Radioactive Earth. Its author,
Rosa... ell, who is Director of Research at the International
Institute of Concern for Public Health in Toronto, Canada, describes
the effects of such radiation on the human body:

> 'Natural background radiation causes us to age gradually, and increasing
> that background exposure will accelerate the ageing process. The wear
> and tear caused by radiation results in the gradual accumulation of
> mistakes in the body's homeostatic mechanisms; for example, we may no
> longer be able to produce an antibody to counteract some environmental
> irritant, so we become "allergic"; or, we cannot produce usable natural
> insulins, so we become diabetic; or, our cells multiply without having sense
> enough to rest, and so we get a tumour . . .

> 'Nor is radiation damage limited to the subtle harm done to the person
> exposed. It can also injure the ovum and sperm cells from which all future
> generations derive. The damage may range from severe to mild. Severe
> damage usually results in infant or childhood death, sterility or
> institutionalisation of the victim. In these instances, the tragedy is seldom
> perpetuated since these victims seldom reproduce. With milder damage –
> such as asthma or allergies, juvenile diabetes, congenital heart defects
> and sense organ or motor dysfunctions – the individual can live a semi-
> normal life and perpetuate the damage in succeeding generations. During
> my research in Buffalo, New York, working on the analysis of the Tri-State
> Leukemia Survey, I discovered that such slightly damaged individuals are
> roughly twelve times as susceptible to radiation-related leukemia as are
> those of robust health.'[110]

Radiation as a cause of miscarriages and birth defects has already
been discussed (pages 77 – 80). However in addition to reporting how
these have increased as the world has become a more radioactive
place to live in, Bertell also lists a large range of other diseases which
can be caused by low levels of ionising radiation. They include
hypothyroidism, a deficiency in the production of hormones by the
thyroid gland which causes lethargy, loss of IQ and an increase in
weight; loss of immunity to infections; leukaemia and other cancers;
asthma; hypertension; arthritis; bronchial diseases; and diseases of
the heart, liver, pancreas or any other part of the body where
radioactive particles have lodged.

Some aspects of the effects of low frequency radiation have already
been discussed on pages 33 to 35. The thermal effects, although
serious where large doses of radiation are concerned, seem, from the
limited knowledge we have available, to be too mild to be a major

hazard to general health where VDUs are concerned, alt\
can cause discomfort.

It is possible, however, that some of the non-thermal effec\
radiation may constitute a health hazard to VDU operators, \
very little is known about how these work. Some animal expe\
have been carried out at the Brain Research Institute at the Un⸱ ⸱rsity of California. Here it was discovered that pulsed low-level radiation at various 'biological' frequencies (frequencies which coincide with those used by the body's own electrical systems) had marked effects on the behaviour of monkeys and cats. Some frequencies made them lethargic and sleepy, while others made them hyper-active.

In a human experiment, a low-frequency magnetic field was applied to people's heads together with a direct current field and ultrasound (which is also emitted by VDUs). The ultrasound was coupled to the heads of volunteers by a water-filled chamber. The volunteers reported small muscle quivers in their eyelids, tingling in their hands and some dizziness. These experiments were discontinued because it was thought that they might produce some permanent brain damage.

In Russia, research in this field has focused on studying people who have been exposed to large quantities of low frequency radiation. Several effects have been noted, some at very specific frequencies. There are changes in blood pressure, heart-rate and electrocardiograph readings; changes in the percentage of haemoglobin, the protein composition and the histamine content of blood; changes in carbohydrate metabolism leading to an increase of sugar levels in blood and urine and producing a 'pre-diabetic sugar curve'; loss of the sense of smell; and a variety of complaints such as listlessness, excitability, headache, drowsiness and fatigue. A less conclusive study linked microwave radiation to enlargement of the thyroid gland and increased absorption of radioactive iodine[111].

Many of these diseases are similar if not identical to those produced by stress and it may well be that one of the effects of low doses of radiation is to reduce the body's ability to cope with stress. Another way of looking at this might be to see radiation, particularly ionising radiation, as the producer of the weak spots in the body which 'give' when it is subjected to stress.

While these findings are extremely alarming, it should be emphasised that there are other major sources of ionising radiation in our environment such as medical X-rays and air, water and food which has been polluted by the by-products of the nuclear industry. VDUs may well make a contribution to our overall intake of radioactivity but they are by no means exclusively responsible for it. However this should not be used as an excuse to put off the search for safer alternatives to the cathode ray tube, nor to permit manufacturers to supply VDUs which are not shielded to minimise the emission of radiation. Even though there may be some circumstances, such as some medical uses of radiation, where the advantages of a small dose outweigh the disadvantages, there is *no* 'safe dose' of ionising radiation.

Static electrical fields

The so-called 'ion effect' has already been introduced on pages 35 to 37 of this book, and discussed in relation to pregnancy on pages 80 to 82. There is some evidence that the depletion of negative ions in the atmosphere caused by the strong positive charge emitted by a VDU screen can affect the general health of a VDU operator both physically and psychologically.

A cubic centimetre of air in a typical air-conditioned office contains only about 50 negative ions and 150 positive ones, compared with 1000 negative ions and 1200 positive ones in the equivalent amount of clean, outdoor, country air. Researchers from the Department of Human Biology and Health at the University of Surrey who took these measurements set up a series of experiments to test the effects of different quantities of ions on human performance and health. They devised a way of blowing ions into a room via the air conditioning system so that neither the people conducting the experiment nor the people being experimented on could tell whether it was switched on or not, to produce 'double-blind' conditions.

In the first experiments, they tested volunteers' skills and speed in a number of simple tasks involving accuracy and hand/eye coordination. When there was an excess of positive ions, there was no significant change from their performance under normal atmospheric conditions. However when the levels of negative ions were raised, there was a statistically significant improvement in four out of five tasks, which was particularly dramatic for mirror drawing. This showed a 28 per cent improvement while rotary pursuit (which involves following with the hand the movement of a rapidly and unevenly rotating light on a screen) was improved by 22 per cent.

Although this seems to show that, while a lot of positive ions have very little detectable effect on people's performances, negative ions do make them noticeably more effective, this effect was not universal. It was estimated that between two-thirds and three-quarters of the people in the experiment showed this improvement, with a higher proportion of women affected. It was also noted that the effects disappeared at high temperatures and seemed to be less pronounced if the air was humid.

The researchers then set up experiments to test the effects of high doses of negative ions on office workers, using the same 'double-blind' technique.

In one computer office where there were a large number of VDUs in operation, the ionisers were installed but not working for the first four weeks of the experiment. Then they were switched on for seven weeks. At the end of each week, the workers were asked a series of questions about their health, their comfort and their views about conditions in the office. During the weeks when the ionisers were on, there were significant improvements in the ratings of 'freshness', 'pleasantness', 'comfort' and 'good'. Workers also felt calmer and more alert. On the night shift, complaints of headaches came down from an average of 26.6 per cent to 6 per cent when the ionisers were on and there were also fewer complaints of dizziness and nausea[112].

Research elsewhere in the world has associated a lack of negative ions with a wide range of diseases including thrombosis, haemorrhage, asthma and bronchial diseases, difficulty in breathing, aching joints, migraines, insomnia and increased susceptibility to infections. It has also been connected with depression, lethargy, anxiety, tension, anger and irritability leading to increases in accidents, mental hospital admissions, suicides and crimes of violence. It is generally estimated that about a quarter of the population is not affected by changes in the ion levels, while a quarter is acutely affected, with the remaining half of the population experiencing moderate effects. Sometimes people's first reaction to a high dose of positive ions and a shortage of negative ones is a temporary sense of euphoria (thought by some to be due to the body's initial stress-like response of producing a spurt of adrenaline to cope with it) followed later by a negative reaction.

In contrast, an excess of negative ions is associated with feelings of calmness, alertness and wellbeing, with quicker recovery from exhausting exercise, more energy, more appetite, sounder sleep, a better ability to absorb vitamin C, fewer bodily aches and pains and fewer respiratory complaints. In one Israeli experiment, even babies cried less often and more quietly when left in a room with high levels of negative ions[113].

How does this effect work? The short answer to this question is that nobody really knows. The little research that has been done suggests that ions affect the body's hormonal system and may therefore be closely allied to the stress reaction. Certainly many of the symptoms of negative ion deprivation are similar to the effects of stress. Speculating freely, we can conjecture that negative ions may in some way help the body to withstand stress, including the sorts of stress produced in the body by its constant bombardment with low levels of radiation. After all, the ions in the ionosphere, the earth's upper atmosphere, have a very similar effect when they protect the earth from the deadly blast of the sun's radiation.

If this is indeed the case, and ions do in some not yet understood way provide the body with help in its fight to resist damage, then finding ways to increase the levels of ions in the atmosphere may well be beneficial. In an increasingly polluted and hostile environment, our bodies need all the help they can get. However this should not become a substitute for removing the causes of stress. To do so would be rather like arguing that you could stop it raining by putting up an umbrella. The best way to improve the general health of VDU operators is to ensure safe working methods and a safe working environment, and to give the workers themselves sufficient control over their working conditions to take the preventative action best suited to their own state of health and their own personal situation.

The remaining chapters of this book discuss some of the ways it is possible to work towards this goal.

– 12 –

What can be done? Organising for change

If you are a VDU worker who has suffered from any of the symptoms described in the previous chapters you will naturally want to do something to prevent them occurring again or becoming chronic. The question is, what? As with most other workplace health hazards the options boil down crudely to two: adapting the worker (yourself) or adapting the job (this includes not only your actual job but also your working conditions, the equipment you use and the environment you work in).

The first alternative, adapting the worker, does not in practice offer many possibilities to most VDU workers. You can, of course, leave the job, but that would quite likely leave you without any means of sustaining your income and is simply not a practical or desirable proposition in most cases. Otherwise, you are limited to such measures as getting your eyes tested and wearing any new glasses which are prescribed, taking extra breaks (which may mean a loss of productivity and hence of bonus payments or promotion prospects, not to mention reprimands from supervisors) or spending your leisure time attempting to undo the effects of the stresses incurred during the hours when you are paid to work. Into this last category come things like attending courses on 'coping with stress', yoga or relaxation techniques; avoiding activities which strain your eyes or wrist muscles, like reading, watching television, going to the cinema, knitting, sewing or handicrafts; or trying to get extra sleep.

Some of these might produce a greater sense of wellbeing, or a slight alleviation of symptoms, but none tackle the *causes* of VDU-related health hazards; they simply help individuals to cope with some of the worst *effects*. Such measures also share one other feature in common: in each case, it is you, the worker, who has to pay for the damage done to your body or state of mind by VDU work, either directly (for instance by paying for glasses or classes) or indirectly (by giving up unpaid time and energy or sacrificing personal entertainment or hobbies).

Clearly if VDU-related health hazards are actually to be prevented, then the job itself must be changed. For most VDU workers, this is where the problems start.

Few VDU workers have much control over their job descriptions, the equipment on which they work or their working environments. Even quite senior staff, such as computer programmers or middle-grade managers who have to work with computers and who believe themselves to be in control of their daily timetables of work are often, in practice, tightly constrained by the need to meet deadlines and may find themselves working long hours at a screen without a break. In some offices, where there are no full-time VDU workers and several staff are supposed to share a single terminal or word processor between them, constraints often come from the general pressure of work, when staff have to compete with each other to get access to the workstation. In cases like this, people taking a break are ousted from their place at the screen and have to rejoin the queue when the break is over. This creates a huge disincentive to take the breaks which their bodies may be crying out for and denies them any real control over the pace of work.

Lower down the scale, job descriptions, targets, and the order in which tasks must be carried out are often so tightly controlled that even this choice (take care of your health or complete your work) is denied. Many VDU workers are quite simply told exactly what to do and monitored closely to ensure that they do it. Any attempt by an individual worker to change this situation is regarded as a disciplinary offence. One data entry operator working for a large Midlands manufacturing company described a typical set-up:

> 'We are only allowed to take a break away from our workstations at lunchtimes, with a short break at our desks in the middle of the morning, so we're working seven and a half hours a day at the screens, and sometimes up to four hours more if there is overtime. We were getting very worried about the need to take breaks and we were advised by the VDU Workers' Rights Campaign to go to the toilet every hour – they can't stop you going to the toilet. But the machines monitor all these breaks, and they make our productivity levels go down so we can't earn a bonus. A lot of us have husbands out of work and families to support and we just can't afford to lose this money. We need every penny.'

It's a similar story when it comes to trying to make changes to office equipment and the office environment. A small minority of workers may have some say in what machines are bought, but even a decision like this will usually be limited by the amount of money which is available; by a predetermined list of requirements, based on existing job descriptions, of what the equipment must be capable of doing; and by the narrow choice of suitable hardware and software available in a market which is dominated by a handful of large transnational companies.

Within the office, some workers may be able to bring abo changes, for instance by rearranging the existing furni introducing a few potted plants, but many are denied ev freedom. At a trade union conference in Coventry in 1986 on the hazards of VDUs an officer of the CPSA (the Civil and Public Se ...es Association) described the progress of negotiations over the introduction of a new computer system into local jobcentres:

> 'We asked to have some plants in the office – not a very big demand, you'd think – but management have refused to consider it. The most they'll concede, after weeks of negotiation, is plastic plants. This completely misses the point, of course. We want plants to help keep up the oxygen levels in the air not just to look pretty. But we're determined not to give in on this one. We won't work in a plastic environment.'

If a well-organised union branch in the public sector meets with such difficulties over a relatively trivial change like this, what must the problems be for a single individual, acting alone?

According to reports which have come flooding into the London Hazards Centre, Leeds TUCRIC, Coventry Workshop, the VDU Workers' Rights Campaign and other agencies which give advice to VDU workers, they are immense.

Some have felt too insecure in their jobs and too frightened of their superiors to approach them at all. In almost every case, when VDU workers have approached their supervisors or managers, told them that they believe their health to be suffering from VDU work and asked for changes they have been met with disbelief, hostility, threats of demotion or dismissal, inaction, patronising reassurance that the dangers are purely imaginary, and abuse.

Among other things, they have been accused of being ungrateful, hysterical, hypochondriac, crackpot 'health freaks', menopausal, pre-menstrual, mentally unbalanced, just out to make trouble, communist wreckers, lazy, luddite, 'behaving like a spoilt child' and 'trying to find excuses for not doing their jobs properly'. The only response they have fairly consistently *not* received is to be taken seriously.

This is not purely accidental. Vast amounts of money have been spent in recent years on conferences and campaigns to persuade managers that VDU work is not dangerous to health. And highly paid scientists have been hired by government and industry to provide reassurance on specific hazards.

Interestingly, however, as groups of concerned VDU operators have refused to accept such assurances and produced their own alternative evidence of health damage, these arguments have subtly altered. At first, for instance, it was advised that VDUs caused no eyestrain. Now, it is argued that no harm will be done 'provided reasonable precautions are taken', and these 'reasonable precautions' have steadily increased in number and included more and more of the ergonomic features originally demanded by workers. Similarly, it was originally stated that there was no radiation from VDUs. Now, radiation is said to be 'well within recommended safety margins'.

Nevertheless, the message transmitted to managers is clear: VDUs pose no significant hazards to health. And this is a message most are only too thankful to hear, since redesigning jobs and workplaces can be expensive and their job is to save money.

This message is continuously reinforced by conferences, glossy leaflets and articles in popular newspapers and trade journals. These presentations usually have several things in common.

The first is an emphasis on the eminence and objectivity of the scientific experts who are cited, although these are often left anonymous. Their work is not explained in any detail; rather, it is suggested that it is impossibly difficult and much too technical for the lay-person to understand. Their conclusions, however, are presented as unchallengeable, often in vague phrases like, 'top scientists have concluded that . . .', 'the authorities are agreed that . . .', 'expert advice is that . . .' or 'there is no evidence that . . .'

Accompanying this elevation of one group of researchers to a position of infallibility which might be envied in the Vatican goes the denigration of those researchers who disagree with them. People who suggest that VDU work might be dangerous to health are often accused of bias, ignorance, using unscientific methods, being politically motivated and (if they are women) hysterical. It can be easy to make some of this mud stick if, as has sometimes happened, the researchers in question have lost government research funding or had their findings publicly disowned by the academic insitutions which employ them or if they work for or are involved in trade unions, women's groups or resource centres which are committed to the interests of VDU workers and can therefore be seen as 'biased'.

As well as having their intellectual integrity attacked, these researchers are also accused of causing needless anxiety to VDU workers by spreading false fears. In the case of reproductive hazards, by a neat inversion, people who have been campaigning for higher safety standards have actually become branded as the *cause* of miscarriages and birth defects because, as the Health and Safety Executive typically argues, 'anxiety can itself cause problems'[114].

Alongside this partisan attitude to researchers goes a characteristic attitude to VDU workers which, although it purports to be motivated entirely by concern for their wellbeing, consists mainly of contempt. It is the type of attitude which has given the English language such phrases as 'a little learning is a dangerous thing', 'don't you worry your pretty little head about it' and 'father knows best'. It is an attitude which states that VDU workers, *for their own good*, must be protected from any suggestion that their work may be hazardous and it implies that they are too stupid to evaluate the risks for themselves.

Such a view is, of course, very flattering to the managers to whom it is addressed. They are presented with a picture of themselves as responsible adults who can be entrusted with the important and hard-to-grasp information that VDUs are in fact safe despite some unfortunate rumours to the contrary spread by trouble-makers. Their role, they are told, is to reassure their workers without giving them any unnecessary information which would probably be misinterpreted. In contrast, VDU workers are seen as helpless, illogical, gullible creatures, likely to develop all manner of hysterical psychosomatic illnesses at the drop of a hint that there might be any cause for anxiety, rather like hens who will stop laying if flustered or disturbed. These attitudes are of course reinforced by the fact that most managers are men while most VDU workers are women, as they fall so neatly into the traditional stereotype whereby men are serious and responsible adults who provide and protect, while women are just flighty 'girls'.

With such attitudes prevailing, it is hardly surprising that VDU operators who begin behaving like responsible adults and ask for information or for changes in a situation which they believe to be harmful find themselves encountering opposition. For some, it may be the first time they have found themselves at odds with their managers. One VDU worker told us:

> 'Up to that point I thought I had a really good relationship with my boss. But when I went to him with this very real problem he more or less accused me of lying. I felt like a little schoolgirl being told off. Now I've been in that job for years, and I've always worked hard and given them my best. It really upset me that after all I've done he doesn't even have enough respect for me to believe what I say. I don't believe he gives a damn about me in actual fact. And if I pursue this thing (her complaint about health hazards) I reckon I'll be out of that door in no time.'

Others have found themselves treated as freaks when they have complained of health hazards:

> 'They can always find someone to compare you with who *doesn't* get headaches, or *doesn't* get eyestrain, and then they'll either say there's something wrong with you rather than with the job, or else they'll imply you're making it all up.'[115]

VDU workers trying as individuals to get their jobs changed do not just risk encountering disbelief and ridicule, they may also find that they have put their jobs at risk. They may find themselves faced with responses like 'if you don't like it, you can lump it' or 'there are plenty of people who'd jump at the chance of your job' or discover that by protesting they have acquired the reputation of a troublemaker. As we have seen, taking unilateral action to change the job, for instance by slowing down, or taking extra breaks, may also produce the same effect since this can be seen as not doing the job properly and therefore providing a reason for managers to take disciplinary action against the worker concerned. On their own, in fact, there is very little that most VDU workers can do.

To those who have tried these methods, it has quickly become apparent that a collective, rather than an individual, approach stands a much better chance of success. Acting together, workers are able to gather evidence that health hazards are not just individual problems, caused by neurosis, unhealthy living or a quirky constitution, but are general problems, affecting a substantial proportion of the workforce. They can also give each other support to ensure that individuals who complain are not isolated or picked on. Finally, they are in a position where they can bargain with the management, rather than simply begging for concessions.

Groups of workers who decide that a trade union offers the best structure for getting together, getting organised and negotiating with managers, tap into a number of advantages. They can draw on the advice and services of professional negotiators and researchers; they gain access to resources to help with things like holding meetings or producing leaflets; they can make contact with other groups of workers who have had similar experiences; and – in the event of a complete breakdown of negotiations – there is access to the funds and support to enable them convincingly to threaten the ultimate sanction of strike action against their employers.

It is, of course, easy to say that VDU workers should act collectively over health hazards but much harder to bring about such collective action. The obstacles are often enormous. VDU workers may be working in isolation from each other in separate offices, departments, buildings or even in different subsidisary companies owned by their employer. Many may be part-time or temporary workers, with little time even to talk to their own immediate colleagues, let alone attend meetings or meet those on different shifts. Staff turnover may be high, making it difficult to sustain continuity.

Many VDU workers are not in trade unions or are working for anti-union employers who refuse to recognise trade unions. Even where trade unions exist and are recognised, they may not necessarily represent the interests of VDU operators very well. In some cases, VDU workers may be distributed among several different unions. In others, the trade union negotiators may be drawn from senior grades, from people who not only have no direct experience of ordinary VDU work but whose jobs may in fact be connected with the management or development of new technology and who therefore have interests which are in many ways opposed to those of the VDU operators.

A majority of trade union representatives are white and male. VDU workers who are women and/or Black may have good reason to believe that their needs are misunderstood or ignored when demands for negotiation with management are being drawn up. In some cases, a fear of harassment may be added to this.

Despite these considerable difficulties there are many examples of VDU workers who have successfully organised to improve the quality of their working lives and minimise health hazards. The rest of this chapter draws on their experiences to suggest ways in which other VDU workers can organise for change.

Get together and compare notes

Informal conversations with fellow workers are the starting point for any effective organisation. Casual chat during breaks, in the canteen, in the cloakroom or waiting for the bus home can reveal a great deal about how other workers are feeling about VDU work and what symptoms they are experiencing. What are the main grievances? What do other workers think might be the best way of solving them? Has anyone attempted to get anything done about them already, and if so what happened? If not, why not? What are the main fears? And what attitudes do most people hold towards trade union organisation? As a result of such conversations it may well be possible to identify several other VDU workers who would like to do something to improve their working situation. If so, you now have a good basis for taking things a stage further.

Use your union

If you are not already a member of a trade union, this is a good time to join. In workplaces where a union is already recognised by the employer, this is a comparatively simple matter. You simply approach your shop steward or other union representative and join. If you do not know who this is, you can usually find out by looking at noticeboards or asking around amongst your fellow workers.

If there is no union recognised at your workplace, then you will have to find out which one to join. You might do this by talking to friends working for similar organisations who are in unions, by writing to your local trades council or by asking in neighbourhood advice centres, the Citizens Advice Bureau or a local resource centre. If all else fails, write to the TUC (at Congress House, Great Russell Street, London WC1) who will be able to tell you which is the appropriate union and give you a contact address. Most of the large unions have regional offices. The ones in your area will be listed in the *Yellow Pages* under 'Trade Unions'. When writing to any of these organisations, be sure to give your home address. It may not be a good idea to let your supervisor know of your interest in unions at this stage.

Once you have tracked down the appropriate trade union and joined it, you may be surprised to discover that there are already some other 'closet' trade unionists at your workplace. Whether there are or not, the next stage is to try to persuade as many of your workmates as possible to join you in the union. This can be a slow and disheartening process, which may become more difficult if your management finds out what you are up to and starts discouraging people from joining, as frequently happens. However you should be able to get help and support from your full-time trade union official and perhaps also from workers in other branches of your union or from a local resource centre. This help could include organising recruitment meetings outside the workplace (lunchtime is often the best time to ensure a good attendance – especially if it is possible to lay on sandwiches so that people don't have to miss a meal to attend), providing speakers about the hazards of VDUs and how being in a union can help, and producing recruitment leaflets, posters and other information and publicity materials.

In recruitment drives it is important not to forget the workers who are often left out of the mainstream of the trade union movement – part-time workers, temporary or short-term contract workers, evening shift workers or homeworkers who possibly need union protection more than any other group although they are less likely to get it. Taking account of their needs may involve holding meetings at different times, producing special leaflets, or focusing on different issues from those which seem important to permanent, full-time, on-site workers. Spare a thought too for groups like cleaners, who may not be eligible to join the same union as VDU operators but whose jobs are nevertheless affected by the design of your working environment and the conditions which prevail there.

It often happens in workplaces where in the past nobody has been very interested in unions, that new technology is the issue that galvanises people into action. The health hazards of VDUs have become an important recruitment issue throughout the world, drawing into the trade union movement many thousands of workers who would not have considered membership before the cathode ray tube invaded their working lives.

Fired with new-found enthusiasm, workers like these have sometimes been more successful than groups with a long history of trade unionism in winning important concessions from their managements over VDU safety.

In workplaces where unions are already well established, it is often the case that they are dominated by the groups of workers who have been the bastions of trade union strength in the past. In manual or 'craft' unions, these may be skilled apprentice-trained craftsmen. In white-collar unions they are likely to be technical or junior management staff, who are also likely to be male and white. While in the public sector, many (though by no means all) of the union activists are drawn from professional and technical workers, such as laboratory technicians, architects, social workers or computer programmers.

Many of these trade union representatives are skilled negotiators, who have given dedicated – and largely unthanked – service to the union for many years. However they cannot necessarily always be expected to have the interests of VDU operators at heart.

Because most VDU operators are women, many of them part-time, with domestic responsibilities, most are unlikely to have been able to attend many meetings in the past and may have earned themselves a reputation for apathy. When trade union representatives are men, there may be an additional feeling, quite possibly unconscious, though shared with management, that most women workers do not really know what they want, and that, in any case, their jobs are not as important as men's. As a result, female VDU workers end up feeling that they are being patronised and that their demands are not being taken seriously, which can result in their withdrawal from active involvement in the union, thereby justifying the view that they are 'apathetic', and setting up a vicious circle. A similar cycle can be set up by the conscious or unconscious racist attitudes of white trade union representatives which antagonise some Black workers, causing them to become sceptical about what the union will achieve for them. Any cynical remark they may drop can then be used by white workers to justify the view that these Black workers are not wholehearted trade unionists.

There are other, deeper, reasons why some traditional trade union representatives can be expected to have reservations about fighting for VDU workers' rights. For many skilled craft workers, new technology is seen first and foremost, quite correctly, as a direct threat to their jobs. It has been introduced by managements in many industries as part of a deliberate policy to de-skill and cheapen their labour and destroy the strength of their traditional trade union structures. The printing industry provides a particularly glaring example of this, but a similar process has gone on in many other industries. Thus the very existence of VDU operators, particularly VDU operators who are not drawn from their own ranks and did not come up through their own, union-regulated, apprenticeship systems, is evidence of defeat.

It is not surprising therefore that there is sometimes actual hostility between 'craft' workers and VDU workers, a hostility which is often carefully nurtured by management. If the two groups of workers are in different unions, it may emerge as a refusal to co-operate in negotiations, or to support each other in disputes.

Understandable though it is, this hostility can be countered if both parties are aware of it and understand how it has come about. Disunity among workers serves nobody's interests except management's, and trade unionists in many industries are becoming increasingly conscious of this, and determined to eradicate it.

One way of lessening distrust between different groups of workers is to focus on areas where it is possible to work together in harmony. Joint union safety committees can be a good forum for this. Another is to arrange educational meetings on topics like the effects of new technology, at which workers from different parts of the organisation can come together for informal learning and discussion without having to worry about the implications of what they say for particular negotiations or policies. As well as airing the issues of agreement or disagreement, such meetings can also provide a chance for people to get to know each other and help break down the stereotyped views they may have formed.

Some of these suspicions and misunderstandings can also appear in white-collar areas where new technology has been used to de-skill particular groups of workers. However the main problem in offices is usually a very different one. The difficulty most often faced by office-based VDU workers is not that their union representatives are too opposed to new technology to speak on their behalf but that they are too much in favour of it.

It is very often the case that the group of workers from whom white-collar union representatives are mostly drawn is also the group which finds new technology least threatening and often stands to gain directly from it. Junior managers may find that new technology gives them more control over information and therefore makes their working lives easier both in terms of being able to make accurate reports to higher management and in being able to control their subordinates. Workaholic young professionals with creative jobs may relish the greater productivity the new technology gives them. Others – who have some degree of control over their jobs – may simply enjoy playing with machines which they regard rather like a grown-up version of arcade computer games.

Some groups, like programmers, systems analysts, work study or organisation and management study teams (popularly known as 'O and M') may actually have jobs whose sole purpose is to introduce new technology into other people's jobs. It is not at all unusual in unions like NALGO or ASTMS, which recruit all grades of office staff, to discover that the union representative responsible for negotiating the new technology agreement with management is the same person who is designing the system or introducing it into the workplace. In fact he (it is generally a he) has quite possibly been chosen for that purpose by a group of fellow-workers who are mystified by computer jargon and feel that his knowledge of it will make him the most effective negotiator.

Needless to say, people who are themselves fascinated and excited by computers and who have a good deal of control over their own jobs are not best placed to understand the problems of workers whose relationship with the computer is that of servant rather than master, whose work contains no creative elements, who have no control over their jobs and who therefore suffer much more directly from stress and other work-related health problems.

This can sometimes lead to downright antagonism between lower-grade VDU workers and their union representatives. However it need not necessarily do so, and there are several strategies which can be adopted to generate a positive collaboration.

Perhaps the most important feature of these strategies is an insistence that *all* VDU workers in the organisation, whatever their grade or status, should have a chance to give their views and make a genuine contribution to developing the union's demands on VDU safety. This involves more than simply putting the matter on the agenda of a regular union meeting and inviting everyone to come. There are many reasons why some people cannot attend such meetings and, even if they can, feel too confused or intimidated to speak. In some workplaces, special meetings for particular groups of staff, held at times they find convenient, have been successful. Where women have found it difficult to get a word in edgeways because of dominant men, or have not liked to discuss intimate details of their health in a mixed group, women-only meetings have also been a good way of developing confidence, sharing information and devising new ideas for tackling VDU hazards.

When it comes to actual trade union representation, and the accountability of representatives to the people they are supposed to represent, specific tactics will depend very much on the particular negotiating structures at your workplace. Are you covered by a national agreement or is bargaining purely local? Is there a shop steward system, or merely a negotiating committee which is supposed to represent all workers? Is health and safety negotiated by the trade union representatives who deal with other matters too, or by specialist safety representatives? Is there a safety committee? If so, is it an independent trade union committee or a joint one in which management also participates? Are new technology issues covered by a separate new technology agreement? The most important thing is to find out where the real negotiating power of the union lies and which positions are purely advisory (i.e. toothless) or inactive.

Where VDU workers have felt themselves to be unrepresented by the union, some have elected their own union representatives from amongst themselves. One way of doing this is to elect their own safety representatives, which has been a particularly successful tactic in workplaces where the existing trade union leadership is well entrenched. Any group of workers in a recognised trade union is entitled by law to elect its own safety representatives and these safety representatives, once elected, have a number of useful rights, which are described more fully on pages 183 to 184 of this book.

Other ways of gaining direct representation include demanding that the existing union branch or shop committee, health and safety committee or negotiating team is enlarged to include direct representation of VDU workers, or getting together to outvote existing representatives and replace them with VDU workers. In some cases this has involved petitioning for a special general meeting of the union branch for the purpose. To find out about how to do this in your own union workplace group or branch, ask the chairperson or secretary for a copy of the standing orders which should explain the rules for the conduct of meetings and the election of officers.

A useful aim, though one which is not often achieved in practice, is to have a system of union representation which ensures that every major group of workers in the organisation is properly represented by people drawn from its own ranks and that the numbers of representatives are roughly proportional to the numbers of workers in each group. This is much easier to achieve where workers are in different unions (although there are also serious drawbacks to having a proliferation of different unions negotiating with one management). The reason for this is that where managers are in the same union as their subordinates, few lower grade workers are prepared to stand for election against their bosses.

Even where bosses play a relatively inactive role in the union, their very presence in a meeting can be enough to prevent the people under them from speaking up freely or putting themselves forward for office. Some workers have partly got round this problem by adding clauses to their standing orders which give them the right to exclude senior managers (often this is defined as staff 'with the right to hire and fire other workers') from any meeting by a majority vote of the members present. In other unions, there are separate branches or even separate categories of membership for senior staff.

Another method of increasing the voice of VDU workers in their union is to set up new structures specifically for dealing with the issues raised by VDUs in the workplace. This could be done by expanding the role of an existing committee, such as a women's committee, new technology committee or health and safety committee, or by setting up a new working group. What is important here is not so much the name of the group or its precise relationship to the rest of the structure, but its role in productively channelling the energy and strength of feeling of VDU workers who are on the receiving end of new technological systems into the negotiating process. What matters most is who is represented on the group and the amount of power it gives them to determine the union's demands over new technology and affect the progress of negotiations.

VDU workers who encounter open hostility, sexism or racism from their representatives may find that they can turn for help to groups within their own union nationally. Many unions now have women's committees, race committees, or equal opportunities committees at local or national level or both. Some have specialist officers in these areas, while others have action groups of women, Black people, gays and lesbians set up by members to give each other support and combat discrimination.

Harassment, prejudice and discrimination, like other oppressive practices and forms of behaviour, can be dealt with much more effectively by collective means than individually. Some workers have set up workplace women's groups or Black workers' groups and been very pleased with the results. Through participating in these groups they have developed much more confidence and have become more assertive about their rights to decent treatment and learned a great deal about how and why they have been denied these rights in the past. These groups have also provided an effective way to organise for change within the union.

Measure the problem

Once you have established a foothold in the union structure, however precarious, and a channel for communicating and negotiating with management, however obstructed, you are in a position to focus your attention on the VDU hazards themselves.

One of the most effective ways of finding out precisely what the hazards are in your workplace is to carry out a health and safety survey of VDU workers. As well as providing information which will be important for drawing up demands and making out a case for the need for change, this has several other advantages: it makes VDU workers think about the ways in which their health might be being affected by their work and, by increasing awareness, enhances their commitment to doing something about it; it provides a good way for the organisers and participants in the survey to develop their skills and confidence and get to know each other; and it provides evidence that the union is seriously taking account of the needs of VDU workers.

Needless to say, few managements will welcome the prospect of such a survey and if you want to carry it out during working hours you may find that many obstacles are put in your way. Authorised safety representatives do however have the right to carry out surveys even without management co-operation (see pages 183 to 184 for more information on the rights of safety representatives) and management opposition should not be a reason to give up the idea.

Once you have established the right to do so, organising a survey is not nearly as difficult as it might appear at first sight. The first rule is to ensure that you have the backing of your union and the participation of as many VDU workers as possible. It is a good idea to have a small committee or working group to oversee the practical management of the survey. This could be an existing union health and safety committee or new technology committee or a special group set up for the purpose. There should preferably be a majority of VDU workers in this group.

Having got the group set up, and the idea of the survey endorsed by the union branch or other representative committee, the first thing to do is to decide what questions to ask. Many trade union research departments have already drawn up model checklists or questionnaires to use for this purpose. But before running off hundreds of copies of standard checklists, it is worth stopping to examine these models in some detail.

How well do they suit the particular circumstances of your workplace? Are there some questions which are not relevant, or additional ones you would like to ask? Would VDU workers at your workplace find it easier to fill a form in themselves, or to go through the questions with an interviewer? Might some workers like an interpreter because English is not their first language or because of a physical disability? Before agreeing the final form, it is a good idea to 'pilot' it by trying it out with a range of different VDU workers, covering all the different types of VDU work carried out in your organisation and the main categories of VDU worker, and discuss it with them afterwards. This process almost invariably turns up unexpected difficulties or misunderstandings and points to issues which have been left out. The more involvement there is by VDU workers in drawing up the questionnaire and analysing its findings, the better.

The information you will want to gain from the survey falls roughly into two categories: firstly, what health problems are VDU workers suffering from? e.g. how many get headaches? Or how many are on tranquillisers? And secondly what features are there in the design of their jobs, equipment or working environment which might be contributing to these problems? e.g. how many hours a day does each worker spend at the screen? How many people have properly adjustable chairs?

When presenting your findings on health problems it may strengthen your argument with management if you have also collected information on the health of other workers who do not work with VDUs, so that a comparison can be made, and the hazards which are specific to VDU work can be highlighted. It is therefore worth considering extending your survey to cover other departments or even the whole workplace. This can only be done by agreement with management or with the cooperation of union representatives for these areas. If a health problem is found to be widespread amongst both VDU workers and non-VDU workers, that is not a reason for ignoring it. It could easily be caused by other factors in the working environment and should be investigated further and put right.

If you are in a situation where VDUs have not yet been introduced, but management are about to bring them in, then obviously you will not be able to carry out a survey of VDU workers. However it is still possible to involve workers who will be affected by them in a research process to find out about VDU hazards.

One possibility is to set up a new technology working party or similar group, with responsibility for collecting as much information as possible for distribution to the rest of the workforce. Your union research department may be able to give you help with this. Your management has a legal duty to supply information relating to health and safety, which includes information on new equipment and systems of work. The Health and Safety at Work Act also places obligations on manufacturers to supply information about the hazards of their products. You should insist on this information.

It can also be useful to locate other groups of workers who have experienced working with systems like the ones your management is proposing to introduce. This could be done through your union, through a local resource centre or hazards group, or by informal contacts through friends and acquaintances. If you find someone with this experience, you could invite them along to address a meeting of your members to alert them to the problems they might encounter.

In 1985, a local council joint union and management committee commissioned an extensive independent survey, involving 3000 employees, of the health and safety effects of working with VDUs. The survey found that in nearly every respect, VDU users reported that their health had worsened since they started to use VDUs. Heavy users suffered from more problems, more frequently, than light users. The major problem was found to be job design; recommendations

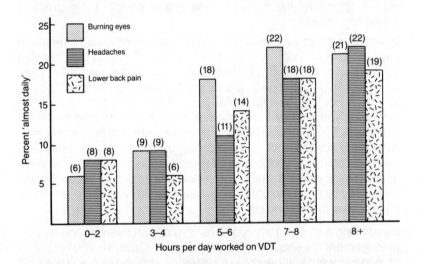

This graph shows the percentage of VDU workers who suffer particular health problems 'almost daily': when more than four hours per day are spent doing VDU work, the number of people with these symptoms doubles. The figures are from a survey of 2,330 workers in 15 different workplaces in Canada in 1982. This research also showed that working on a VDU for more than two hours without a break results in a doubling of the number of people who report these health problems 'almost daily'.

were made about redesigning jobs in such a way that they would encourage safe and satisfying methods of working with new technology[116]. If all the recommendations in the report are implemented then the outcome of the survey will have considerable benefits for all the workers involved.

Increase awareness

The very process of carrying out a health survey or setting up a research group has probably started discussions amongst VDU workers and made them more aware of health hazards. Once the research is completed, this process can be taken further.

One idea is to produce a leaflet with a summary of your findings and distribute it to all workers (including non-union members – it may encourage them to join). Meetings can then be organised to discuss them and share ideas about what can be done to alleviate the problems. This can be used as the first stage of drawing up the detailed set of demands which you will be presenting to management.

One group of workers in a Midlands tax office came up with a very effective idea for increasing awareness of the hazards of VDUs. When the PAYE system was computerised, members of the Inland Revenue Staffs Federation (IRSF) found themselves involved in intensive VDU work. Worried by the health implications, they contacted Coventry Workshop, a local resource centre, which helped them produce VDU User Check-cards, small folding cards which could be placed on each VDU worker's desk beside the machine. On one side of the card is a description of a 'mini-service' which the user can carry out to make sure the VDU is in good working order; on the other, a checklist to encourage VDU workers to monitor their own health, with advice about when to contact the union safety representative.

These cards proved so successful that they have now been adopted by another union, NALGO, in the Midlands area.

Many unions have also produced posters and audio visual materials as well as booklets and leaflets to increase awareness of VDU hazards amongst their members. You could obtain some of these through your local full-time officer or by writing to the head office of your union.

Like carrying out a survey, organising a publicity campaign can also be used as a way of involving more people in the activities of your union. Through being involved, individuals will gain confidence which might encourage them to become more vocal and active in other ways, perhaps by deciding to become a safety representative or a shop steward, or starting to participate in evening or weekend meetings run by the union. All this experience will feed back into your campaign, strengthening it and giving it a greater chance of success.

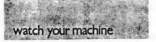

watch your machine

If your VDU is in good order any hazards involved will be cut to a minimum. But things can go wrong between its regular services.

Get into the habit of putting the machine through a weekly mini-service. If it fails on any of these checks report it to your supervisor and IRSF office secretary.

* Are electrical cables secure?
* Is the screen image sharp and clear?
* Does the brightness control work?
* Does the screen flicker?
* Is the screen clean - no smears or marks?
* Is the keyboard stable?
* Does the screen give off distracting reflections?
* Can you hear a high pitched tone?
* Does the tilt mechanism work?
* Is the regular service overdue?

watch yourself

Things can go wrong with the machine which you can't spot yourself. But your body can! Think back over the last week. If you have had any of these complaints while working REPORT IT.

* Headaches
* Problems focussing on the screen or sore eyes
* Skin rashes
* Muscular aches and pains

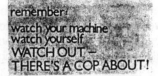

remember!
watch your machine
watch yourself
WATCH OUT –
THERE'S A COP ABOUT!

VDU user check card produced by Coventry Workshop for a branch of the Inland Revenue Staff Federation.

Draw up your demands

The most relevant demands for change, and those which stand the best chance of gaining the full backing of the workforce, are those which have been drawn up with the fullest consultation and agreement of the workers concerned. The importance of involving all VDU workers in the process of drawing them up cannot be emphasised too strongly.

It is also a very good idea to ensure where possible that your demands have the support of the other unions in your organisation, even if their members are not directly affected by the new technology. That way, you stand a better chance of getting their backing if it comes to a dispute with management.

The actual demands themselves will vary enormously from one workplace to another, depending on your own particular situation. Some of the points which you might consider covering are listed in the next few chapters (pages 125 – 173). When drawing up your demands, bear in mind the fact that the negotiating process will almost certainly result in some compromises, so it is best to ask for more than the minimum you are prepared to accept.

Depending on the size of your workplace and the structure of your union, having drawn up the basic list of conditions which the VDU workers themselves would like to see implemented in their own working situations, you may need to get this endorsed at the appropriate level higher up within your union. Check with your branch secretary or full-time official whether this is the case. If your union rules say that you must do so, it is important to follow them. If you do not, and the negotiations later founder and you need to take industrial action, you may find that it will be difficult to get the action officially endorsed, which could lead to your members being refused strike pay, or other difficulties.

If official endorsement is required at this stage, it may be necessary to make some modifications, perhaps because of unforeseen objections to some of the demands from other members of the union, or because it is the union's policy to add one or two additional points, or to change the wording slightly. Whatever changes are made, it is important that they are not agreed to without the consent of the members concerned. Any substantive change (that is, a change which substantially alters the meaning, not just the wording, of the claim) should be taken back to them in a meeting to be sure it has their approval.

Present your claim to management

The actual mechanics of negotiating your claim with management will depend on the bargaining structure which prevails in your workplace. Do most negotiations take place nationally or locally? Is health and safety negotiated separately, under a different procedure, from negotiations over other matters such as wages? Do you have or want to negotiate a new technology agreement? Or does your union prefer to respond to management's introduction of new machinery in the same way that it responds to other management attempts to change work organisation, through the normal procedural agreement? How much of your negotiating is done by ordinary members who work for the organisation, and how much by full-time officials of the union?

Whatever form the negotiations take, there are some principles which it is important to try to adhere to:

▲ Make sure that VDU workers themselves are directly represented on the negotiating team.

▲ Ensure that no agreement is reached without the affected workers having the chance to vote on it and give their consent.

▲ Ensure that no union representatives, under any circumstances, meet with management on their own.

▲ Do not let management get away with treating health and safety as an isolated issue, unconnected with job design or staffing levels.

▲ Beware of getting so bogged down in the technical details of things like screen specifications that you miss more important issues. Some managements have a deliberate policy of spinning out negotiations over ergonomics to avoid having discussions with trade union representatives about such things as staffing levels, hours, job security, grading or pay for VDU workers. Try to keep a firm grasp of the essential issues, however many distractions are presented. If there is a genuine need to agree on a lot of fiddly technical details, then it might be a good idea to set up a sub-group to sort them out, rather than involving the whole negotiating team in time-consuming discussions which are irrelevant to the main issues.

A related problem is allowing yourselves to become involved in scientific or technical discussions which neither side really understands. A classic example of this is often quoted. It concerns a trade union negotiating team which had been advised that for the operators to be comfortable the character refresh rate of a VDU screen should not be less than 60 Hz. Accordingly they asked for this, to be countered with a management offer of a screen with a refresh rate of 50 Hz. In the true tradition of collective bargaining, the two sides thrashed it out and ended up with a compromise of 56 Hz. The only problem was that no machine with this refresh rate has ever been designed!

If negotiations founder

The fact that you have asked for something does not, of course, mean that you will necessarily achieve it, and many negotiations over the safety of VDUs have been fraught with problems. The most important single factor in your success will be the strength of your organisation and the commitment of the membership to fight for the demands. The more they have been involved in drawing them up, the greater this commitment is likely to be. The whole-hearted support of other members of your own union and of other unions in your organisation can also make a great difference to your chances of success.

To put extra pressure on your management, there are a number of tactics you could try, most of which have been adopted successfully at one time or another by VDU workers fighting for improvements in their working conditions.

Boycott the new equipment

A number of good new technology agreements have been won by the simple expedient of boycotting all new equipment until an agreement satisfactory to the union has been reached. Sometimes it has been enough simply to state that the union's intention is to boycott any new equipment bought without consultation with workers' representatives. If the equipment turns out to be unsatisfactory, it is harder to oppose it if the money has already been spent.

Boycotts can be organised most easily where a large number of potential VDU users are working together. Where scattered members, such as individual secretaries, are working in isolation, this tactic can put a strain on these individuals, who may be closeted all day with an unsympathetic boss or with new machines which have been left lying around to tempt them by crafty managers. However even in situations like these a boycott can be successful where VDU workers feel involved and supported.

If the new system uses one or more large mainframe computers, then the action of a few key workers in the central data processing or computer services department may be an effective form of boycott. If selective action of this sort is being considered it is extremely important to ensure that those workers have the full support of their non-striking colleagues and cannot be victimised for their action.

Boycott all work

Members of the trade union NALGO in Strathclyde developed a novel variant of the boycott tactic in 1986, using the Health and Safety at Work Act. Section 2 of this act places an obligation on the employer to provide a safe workplace. Arguing that the VDUs which their management had installed were not safe, they reported for work each morning but refused to carry out their jobs until such time as they were made safe by the management.

Section 7 of the same act requires workers to take care of their own health and safety. This could also be used to justify boycott action.

Work to contract or job description

This tactic is a variant of the work-to-rule which has traditionally been employed with great success by manual workers. White-collar workers generally do not have 'rules', but they often have a contract or written job description which specifies the work they are supposed to do. This frequently bears little relation to what is in fact expected of them. The tactic involves doing only what is in the contract and refusing to do anything else. Contracts often fail to specify tasks like answering the phone, making tea for the managers, correcting spelling or grammatical errors, or working through the lunch-break to complete urgent tasks. It is amazing how much disruption can be caused by refusing to do these things.

Mandatory union meetings

Another tactic which falls short of all-out strike action is to hold lengthy union meetings during working hours. This is often employed in the publishing industry as means of showing management that the workers mean business. Such meetings have been known to last a day or more and have often produced a breakthrough in the negotiations.

Overtime ban

In workplaces where a lot of overtime work is expected, an overtime ban can be a convincing demonstration of strength. It can be particularly successful where the overtime is required in a short sharp burst, for instance to process monthly payments through the computer.

Strike action

Strikes are generally a last resort, and have in recent years become considerably more difficult to organise quickly because of government anti-union laws which dictate the procedures unions should use to vote for strike action and limit picketing and sympathy action. Nevertheless, it is still perfectly legal to go on strike and this can often be the most effective weapon of all. It is, however, important to have the support of the membership and to have developed a clear strategy for the conduct of the strike.

Before embarking on strike action you should make a careful assessment of its likely effect and what gains and losses are possible for both management and workers.

There are occasions when some managements actually want workers to go on strike, for instance when business is very slack. Do not allow yourself to be provoked into a strike against new technology by a management which is looking for an excuse to get rid of you. In a situation like this, a work-in, the opposite of a strike, might be a more effective tactic.

Sometimes selective strikes which involve pulling out small key groups of workers can be more effective than all-out action, but, as with boycotts, it is important to ensure that small groups required to stick their necks out in this way are well protected by the rest of the union.

Publicity

Some managements are extremely sensitive to publicity. You may find that the results of your health and safety survey are quite newsworthy and that local newspapers, radio stations or even television programmes may be interested in producing a story about the dangers to health which lurk in your workplace.

If you work in an industry which involves serving the public, then you may find it worthwhile to publicise your case to the people who use your employer's service, too. Many new systems also affect the standard of service to customers or clients, perhaps by requiring them to do unpaid work keying in their details on a remote terminal, such as a bank cash-dispensing machine, a hospital diagnostic computer or some other self-service machine. Some will prevent staff from being able to give their patients or clients personal help, even if they are old or handicapped.

Some new technology also has frightening implications for civil liberties, since it involves the storage on computer of vast amounts of personal information, often of a very intimate nature.

A well-organised publicity campaign by workers in the industry can help to break down public attitudes which see workers as obstructive bureaucrats and help to form alliances between workers and users, enabling common interests to emerge and perhaps providing a basis for a mutual campaign against the indescriminate introduction of new technology.

Such links between workers and users have been developed in the health service over privatisation and cuts in services, and in public transport over the introduction of one-person-operated buses and guardless trains. In education, parents have given teachers support in their action for better pay and conditions, knowing that their children's education will benefit. New technology could become the basis of more such campaigns in other industries.

Needless to say, all those tactics which require direct action by members are likely to be most effective if you have a strong union membership which is prepared to carry them out. Where union membership is patchy or apathetic it may be better to focus on selective tactics and those which do not involve direct action by the membership. However it is important not to underestimate the strength of feeling among members. If they have been involved in researching the health hazards of VDUs and drawing up demands which they feel are reasonable, even the most conservative members will begin to feel annoyed if management refuses to take them seriously, and they will usually want to do something to express this feeling.

A final point to remember is that the mere threat of action is often enough to bring management back to the negotiating table in a more conciliatory mood. It is one of the ironies of trade unionism that the better prepared you are for action the less likely you are to have to take it.

– 13 –

Job design

Up to now, this book has focused on the detrimental effects of VDU work on the health and safety of VDU workers. This chapter, and those which follow, looks at how some of these hazards can be overcome, drawing on the experiences of VDU workers who have already managed to bring some improvements to their working lives.

Some of the suggestions made in the next few chapters are relatively easy to achieve; some are extremely difficult, requiring a fundamental rethink of the way in which work is organised. Inevitably, these 'difficult' demands include some of the most important measures for preventing – rather than relieving the symptoms of – VDU hazards. Because prevention is better than cure, we begin with the most difficult of all, job design, even though we recognise that some groups of workers may only be in a position to achieve small changes in the way their work is organised.

Ironically, although changing job design is one of the hardest things to achieve in practice, it is probably the issue on which there is most agreement in theory. From the blandest management report to the angriest campaigning pamphlet, virtually all publications on the hazards of VDUs state somewhere that the best way to prevent the hazards of VDU work is to redesign jobs. Any rational person who has surveyed the evidence is forced to the conclusion that it is not good for anyone to have to spend a whole working day staring down the barrel of an electron gun. The logical next step is to reallocate the workload so that nobody is obliged to do this.

Accordingly, every publication on VDU safety includes a pious paragraph or two about the importance of job redesign, and some even spell out the characteristics of what they regard as a 'safe' or 'satisfying' job which includes some VDU work. A few organisations, notably the trade unions APEX and NALGO, have gone still further and produced carefully thought-out booklets with advice for trade unionists trying to negotiate job redesign. But all of these have an air of unreality about them. Despite the general agreement that it is a 'good thing', remarkably few attempts seem to have been made to put any of these ideas into practice.

It is in fact extremely difficult to find any instances where groups of workers have got together to demand a radical redesign of their jobs and succeeded in negotiating this with their management. This is not, of course, to say that jobs are never redesigned. They frequently are. However this usually comes about for different reasons. Often this is as a result of management initiatives to increase efficiency or productivity. In the private sector it is sometimes because of corporate changes, due perhaps to a merger or takeover. In the public sector, political changes may cause jobs to be redesigned, for instance if a local authoritiy decides to decentralise services, or if the central government decides to privatise them.

Jobs are also, of course, often redesigned as a direct result of introducing a complete new technology 'package'. In cases like this, the jobs have already effectively been redesigned by IBM, Wang or Rank Xerox and incorporated into the design of the hardware and software.

In none of these situations is the health, safety, job satisfaction or welfare of VDU workers the primary object of the exercise. In order to develop strategies to bring about job redesign which *is* in workers' interests, we must ask why there have been so few attempts in the past, so that the obstacles can be understood and overcome.

On examination, these obstacles turn out to be many and varied. The most obvious of these arise from the enormous gap between any abstract discussion of what an ideal job might be like and the reality of most people's everyday working lives. In the vast majority of cases, new jobs do not appear from out of the blue when new technology is brought in; they come about as the result of changes to existing jobs. These existing jobs are not an amorphous mass, capable of being moulded like putty to suit a designer's ideas, but are highly specific. They involve particular people with particular skills, experiences, expectations and degrees of confidence. Many have evolved over decades and are bounded by complex grading and pay structures and elaborate systems of demarcation. The existing job descriptions may be the result of a long history of collective negotiation between the employers and trade unions and also, on occasion, between different unions.

With most issues connected with changes to working conditions, there is a relatively straightforward difference – often an outright conflict of interest – between employers and workers. In relation to holidays, for instance, workers are trying to make sure that they are as long as possible, while employers seek to minimise them. However with job design, things are not that simple. In fact both managements and unions often find themselves having to resolve conflicting demands in order to work out what their aims are.

For employers, the main contradiction lies between two basic principles. The first of these is the drive to ensure that work is carried out as cheaply as possible. This leads to the breaking up of tasks into simple component parts which can be done by workers who are as low-skilled (and therefore as low-paid) as possible. By the same token, the jobs which are considered to need high skill-levels, and therefore to be carried out by high-paid workers, must be stripped of as many of their routine, time-consuming functions as possible, so that the efficiency of these expensive workers is maximised. It is this principle which underlay the various forms of 'scientific management' or 'Taylorism' which were developed in the past and which found their most obvious form in Ford's invention of the assembly line method of production. The existence of specialist 'word processing pools' and data entry departments is testimony to the fact that the need to break up tasks is still a very strong factor in the thinking of those who introduce information technology.

In tension with this principle, particularly in times of rapid change is another: the drive to seek maximum flexibility in the workforce. The aim of this approach is not to produce a workforce of highly efficient robots, each programmed to carry out one small repetitive task as quickly and accurately as possible, which is the logical conclusion of applying the first principle. Rather, it is to acquire a multi-skilled workforce, whose numbers can be kept to the absolute minimum, and which can be redirected to carry out whatever task is required at a moment's notice.

Such a workforce is particularly valuable to employers who are trying to introduce new technology into an industry with a strong tradition of organisation by craft unions, since it can be used to undermine the skills of craft workers (and also, of course, undermine the high wage levels their industrial muscle has won them in the past) and provide substitute labour in the event of a strike. A classic example of this strategy was the use by Rupert Murdoch in 1986 of members of the electricians' union who had been secretly trained in a broad range of skills to break the power of the craft-based print unions on the *Times*, the *Sun*, the *Sunday Times* and the *News of the World* newspapers.

During the 1980s many of the cannier employers have found a resolution to this conflict between the needs for cheapness on the one hand and adaptability on the other by adopting the Japanese model of a dual labour force. Under this system, the aim is to have a small core of multi-skilled workers and to subcontract out as many as possible of the tasks which can most profitably be carried out by specialist single-skilled workers. This effectively prevents the single-skilled workers from developing the sort of strength which 'craft' workers have won in the past because they are kept constantly insecure and can always be controlled by the simple threat not to renew the contract.

For trade unionists, the issues at stake are if anything even more complex. For a start, they have to respond to managements' attempts to deskill and cheapen their members' labour and erode traditional demarcations. Often, the way in which these management intiatives are taken leaves them with little option but to defend the status quo in whatever ways they can, even if they recognise that this status quo is inadequate. The alternative may be to lose their jobs altogether to another, cheaper group of workers.

In the past, frequently the only situation where organised workers have felt able to permit flexible working practices has been under very tightly controlled conditions, for instance under apprenticeship agreements. There are very good organisational reasons why trade unions have historically defended demarcations and job specialisation even though these often harm workers' health and safety and prevent equal opportunities. Without these schemes, they cannot control the number of new workers entering an industry, keep wage levels high or retain their bargaining power with the employers.

As well as problems in formulating defensive responses, trade unions wishing to go on the offensive over job design frequently come up against deep divisions and contradictions among their own ranks. Here, the central problem is the past division of labour, which is entrenched in existing practices. In most industries this has already produced a situation where some jobs are relatively highly skilled and desirable, while others are routine and classified as unskilled or semi-skilled.

There is, of course, a connection between these two types of job. The 'good' jobs are generally relatively interesting and pleasant to perform precisely *because* the most tedious and repetitive component parts of them have been hived off to become the basis of somebody else's 'bad' job. Being a programmer is comparative fun partly *because* it doesn't involve data entry; being an executive is stimulating *because* routine service tasks like answering the telephone and doing the typing have been taken over by others to allow more time for 'creative' work. A central problem for trade unionists seeking to improve job design for all workers is how to introduce more variety into the 'bad' jobs without reducing the quality of the 'good' ones.

The greater the division of labour in an organisation, the more difficult this is to achieve. Indeed, it can seem well-nigh impossible by the time it reaches the stage of locating different specialist functions in different departments, different cities or even within different countries.

An extreme, though by no means unusual, example of this is the specialist data-entry subcontractor. In these organisations, the vast majority of the work carried out consists of punching keys. There may be a few highly skilled data processing staff, to deal with computer operation and programming, but the only other tasks involved are supervision, dealing with clients and some administrative and clerical tasks connected with personnel functions, accounting and running the tape library. Even if all these tasks were distributed equally amongst the entire workforce, it is likely that everybody would still be spending more than half their working hours bashing a keyboard in front of a VDU terminal.

However even such a minor redistribution of tasks would be fraught with problems from the trade union point of view, let alone the management's. Skilled computer operators or programmers who have invested a considerable amount of time acquiring their training and experience would doubtless object strongly if they had to spend most of their working hours on data entry, which they would regard as unskilled (even though they would probably be simultaneously explaining that they couldn't do it nearly as fast or as accurately as specialist data entry staff!). Supervisors would also resist the prospect of a return to the shopfloor from which they probably spent many laborious years escaping. Many data entry operators would require training to develop the skills and confidence to take on other types of work. And what would happen to grading and pay structures?

This example gives some indication of the problems and complexities involved in any serious consideration of job redesign. It should not be read as a warning to trade unionists that job redesign is inevitably impracticable and should not be attempted. However it does show that careful homework is needed before launching any demands.

To make this homework effective, these are some of the main points to bear in mind:

Be aware of existing divisions in the workforce

Most forms of employment are based on a deeply entrenched division of labour. Workforces are divided sharply into separate sectors according to whether they are male or female, Black or white, old or young, skilled or unskilled, permanent or temporary, full or part-time, direct employees or contract workers, 'blue' or 'white-collar'. Any proposed job redesign should be looked at from the point of view of all the groups affected, some of whom may have conflicting interests.

The job redesign strategy should meet the needs of the workers who are currently in the worst jobs and therefore those most in need of redesign. These are also the workers most likely to be Black and female and plans to change their jobs must take account of this. It is no use to women with childcare responsibilities, for instance, if their jobs are changed in a way which requires them to work new hours, which are incompatible with these. Similarly Black workers who have missed out on good education because of discrimination in the past will not benefit if their jobs are enhanced so that there is a requirement for new skills or knowledge which they do not possess.

Simultaneously, the strategy for redesigning jobs should be sensitive to the needs of the skilled workers in the 'best' jobs. Other workers who are tempted to bring them down a peg or two will do so at their peril. In most workplaces the industrial strength of skilled workers is crucial to safeguard the interests of the workforce as a whole.

Keep your approach flexible

It is always tempting, when confronted with a complex situation, to look for hard and fast rules to help steer one through it. In the case of job design, this can be a dangerous course to follow. As we have seen, in some situations, seeking a solution by trying to achieve a multi-skilled workforce could be playing straight into the hands of a management trying to destroy the power of particular groups of skilled workers. The printing industry and many sections of the engineering industry provide examples of such situations, where defending existing demarcations seems to be the only effective way to defend jobs and enable workers to retain some control of their work.

But there are other situations where the opposite holds true, and a policy of trying to create specialist, single-skilled jobs could lead to the degradation of many types of work. In many offices, for instance, secretarial workers are used to a fair amount of variety in their daily routine. To aim for a situation where some become specialist word processor operators while others devote themselves exclusively to other duties, such as clerical or switchboard work, would simply make most of the jobs more monotonous and repetitive, and therefore more hazardous. Here, the creation of strict demarcations would act against the interests of the workers.

Each situation needs to be appraised on its own merits, with the interests of the workers affected providing the guide. Do not assume that there need always necessarily be a direct conflict of interest between union and management over job design. We were told of one data entry department in a large manufacturing company in the Midlands where there were absenteeism rates of 50 per cent due to the high levels of job dissatisfaction and stress among the staff. The shop steward pointed out that if redesigning the jobs could produce healthier and more satisfied workers who took less time off, then it would be in the interests of both management and workers.

Avoid over-dependence on outside experts

To gain an overview of a complicated situation and provide access to specialist skills and knowledge, many groups of workers find it an advantage to consult outside experts. These might be officials from their own trade union, members of a local trade union resource centre or hazards group, sympathetic academic researchers, trade union tutors or even professional consultants. However helpful and convincing their advice may be, it is vitally important to check it out with the workers affected before acting on it.

There are often hidden snags in a proposal which will be spotted only by people with an intimate knowledge of the work. For example, there are many work situations where several workers each carry out a single repetitive task. An outsider might suggest rotating these different tasks within the department to ensure variety and a change of pace and posture for everyone. But to the workers involved, this approach might have serious drawbacks, for instance:

▲ Because every worker could now do everyone else's job, each one would become more easily dispensable. This would increase job insecurity.

▲ It might make industrial action more difficult to organise by enabling each individual worker to substitute for any of the others in a strike.

▲ It might erode differentials and get rid of the promotion ladder which exists at the moment.

▲ Some workers might not have all the appropriate skills or abilities and therefore feel personally threatened with redundancy.

▲ It might make it much harder for workers to control the training of new entrants.

These difficulties are not an argument for rejecting the valuable contribution which outsiders can make to a job redesign exercise, but they do show the need for developing a creative dialogue between the outside expert and the workers concerned – a dialogue in which the workers always have the last word.

Importance of training

One possible result of making jobs more interesting and varied is to raise the standard of qualifications required for carrying them out. This can have the effect of excluding precisely those people who are most in need of them – particularly women, Black people and people with disabilities who missed out on formal education because of discrimination in the past.

The job redesign effort will thus fail to meet some of its main objectives if it doesn't include a strong training or retraining element.

The organisation which developed the most extensive range of equal opportunities training programmes for its own staff was the Greater London Council. One thing which became apprent as a result of these courses was that very often the training required is not so much in specific skills or areas of knowledge but in confidence and allowing workers to develop a sense of the value of their existing skills and experience[117]. For instance many women who believe they have no organisational ability are able to employ much more complex administrative skills than a typical manager when they organise an event like a children's birthday party, or juggle the different daily requirements of managing a household, a large family and a job.

Many trade unionists may find all these cautionary warnings very depressing. Do not allow them to deter you from trying to get the jobs of VDU workers redesigned. Difficult though this may be, it is in the long run the only way to be sure of minimising the health hazards of VDUs. Even if you only manage to achieve small changes, these could make a very big difference to the workers they affect directly, and every little improvement makes it easier for those who follow you to take things a step further.

Perhaps the ideal moment to raise the subject is before a new technological system is introduced, at a time when management is in any case looking at a reorganisation of work. This is, of course, not always possible. You may work somewhere where new technology is already in place, with systems which have been up and running for some years, or you may be in a workplace where new technology is introduced piecemeal, a few machines at a time, rather than in one fell swoop. Even if you are in a situation like this, there may still be some ideas you can pick up from the next few pages.

If a new system is being proposed, it will probably fall into one of two categories: a customised system, designed specifically for your employer, or an 'off-the-peg' package from one of the big computer companies. Sometimes it will be a hybrid of the two, perhaps with a telecommunications element (the part which links in with the telephone system) bought separately and from a different supplier than the computers themselves. Occasionally, even hardware and software will be purchased separately, but this is unusual except in very small offices where standard microcomputers are being brought in, on which a number of different software packages can be run.

With systems design costs soaring and hardware costs tumbling, an increasing number of organisations are moving towards the off-the-peg solution, although 'made-to-order' systems are still required in a number of large or specialist organisations.

If yours is to be a made-to-order system, then it will be preceded by a work study exercise. Systems analysts will need detailed information about the tasks carried out in the affected parts of the organisation in order to brief the designers and programmers who will produce the appropriate software. The number of person-hours involved in software development is colossal – programmers have been likened to the 'pyramid-builders of the 20th century'[118] – so it is important to involve the union in the design process *before* the ideas of the systems analysts and designers have crystallised into expensive computer programs. Workers should be involved from square one in any discussions which will lead to changes in the design of their jobs.

In the case of off-the-peg systems, the nature of the discussions will be different, but the basic principle of early union involvement remains the same. Here, however, it is the choice of which system to purchase which is the crucial one. Sadly, this generally offers less scope for a radical redesign of jobs than the commissioning of made-to-order systems since most standard systems are designed around a pre-existing set of ideas about job definitions. In fact some hardware manufacturers explicitly sell their customers, along with the equipment, a specific model of work organisation which they are expected to adhere to if they want to get maximum benefit from using the system.

Since most of the companies manufacturing these machines are large transnationals, with a history of anti-unionism, it is not surprising that few of their work automation packages systems are conducive to enhancing the health, safety or job satisfaction of their users. However off-the-peg systems do have one advantage from the union negotiator's point of view. It is generally possible to keep the options open for longer while negotiations continue. With made-to-measure systems, it can be difficult to reverse a decision made fairly early on in the design process without incurring great expense and delay. It is also possible that if you work for a large organisation which is seen by the hardware supplier as a major customer, some changes in the design even of standardised items can be negotiated.

Whatever the type of system, the importance of starting talks about job design *before* a final choice has been reached cannot be overemphasised. Workers' bargaining strength is normally at its highest before a new system is introduced because management needs their cooperation to introduce it. It is therefore at this stage that it is easiest to lay down the conditions on which workers will agree to implement the new technology.

Needless to say, these conditions need not – and should not – be limited only to those concerning job design. Groups of workers have successfully negotiated a range of different benefits as preconditions for the acceptance of new technology, from a four-day week (or a seven-hour day) to creche facilities, from a no-redundancies agreement to sabbatical leave, from pay rises to a better sick leave agreement. However because of the complexities of working out the details of job design, it is especially important that discussions start early, leaving plenty of time to negotiate the machinery by which new job descriptions will be agreed, and what they will consist of.

Although it is extremely complex and involves a great deal of discussion between workers, union officers and management, negotiating job design is fundamentally no different from any other type of collective bargaining. The points made in the previous chapter will therefore apply here too. The most appropriate negotiating machinery for changing job design in your workplace will depend on the history of industrial relations in the organisation, in particular whether there has been a successful experience of joint union/management committees in the negotiation of other issues or whether your bargaining tradition has been a more confrontational across-the-table one. The size and complexity of the organisation, the attitude of management, the number of jobs affected, the number of trade unions involved and the degree of unity among the membership are also important factors.

In the final analysis, of course, what is important is not how the decisions are arrived at but what they consist of and how well they meet the needs of the workers affected. The best way of achieving this is to ensure that the negotiating team, however constituted, is directly answerable to these workers, and does not reach agreements with management without referring back to them.

Perhaps the most productive technique for finding out which aspects of their existing jobs workers find most burdensome, and which changes they would most like, is the brainstorming session. For this, the most important ingredients are time and an atmosphere of trust in which participants feel relaxed enough not to worry about making idiots of themselves when they come up with unothodox suggestions. The ideal is to have workshop-style meetings with about 6-10 people in each, lasting perhaps an hour and a half to allow plenty of time for everyone to participate. Brainstorming is different from an ordinary group discussion because the object is to bring out as many new ideas as possible. The most important rule is that nobody should criticise anyone else's idea, however apparently daft.

It is a good idea to have someone, perhaps a member of the union's negotiating committee or an outside consultant, to start off the discussion with a few provocative questions and an explanation of the issues, but this is by no means essential, and it is important that such a person does not have the effect of making participants feel ignorant or inferior or inhibit the free flow of ideas in any other way. One technique is to give everyone present a sheet of paper and ask them to write down a list of ways in which they think jobs should be changed. These are then read out in turn and form the basis of further discussion. Collecting these up afterwards can help to provide a record of the meeting, but it is as well to make sure that somebody jots down the gist of the discussions which take place during these sessions so that they can be considered by the workers as a whole at a later stage[119].

In a few workplaces with progressive managements it may be possible to negotiate permission to hold such meetings during working hours, but there are many places where this will not be possible. In such cases it might be worth trying to persuade your union to hold a weekend day-school (with creche facilities) for the purpose. Failing this, you will probably have to compromise, perhaps with a series of shorter lunch-time meetings.

The idea behind such meetings is that workers themselves are the only true experts on their own jobs, and therefore best placed to work out how they could usefully be changed. However most are not used to being consulted in this way and will need some encouragement to voice their views. Some may have good reasons for initial suspicion of an approach which bears some resemblance to the 'quality circle' style of work organisation, in which workers' brains are picked for ideas which can be exploited by management to improve productivity and efficiency. In such cases, the fact that these meetings are being organised by the union in the interests of the workers should provide reassurance.

The success of the brainstorming approach is often attributed to the fact that it breaks down the rigid and hierarchical structures within which decisions are normally made and encourages a 'lateral' type of thinking which allows unconventional new ideas to emerge. In this, it is very like the 'consciousness-raising' style of organising small meetings developed by the women's movement.

Workers who have adopted this approach to thinking about work reorganisation have often come up with solutions which would never have occurred to outsiders, however 'expert' in their field. One example of this was in an office where interactive desk terminals were about to be introduced to provide an on-line information system. The staff raised a number of predictable demands including changes in the grading structure and new job descriptions. However after discussion they also asked for something which none of the union representatives had anticipated. This was that in future they should not be grouped according to what jobs they did (which was no longer necessary, since everyone could use the new system for communication) but according to who was or was not a smoker. When this was implemented, they gained a much more healthy office environment for the non-smokers, freedom from guilt for smokers, and the removal of what had been a long-standing cause of tension in the office.

Any ideas which come out of these small groups will, of course, have to be discussed with the rest of the workforce, evaluated and translated into a consistent set of demands.

Because of the enormous range of jobs and industries using VDUs, it is not possible to give specific recipes for what these demands might consist of – it is doubtful whether these could ever really be of use, in any case, since no two workplaces or groups of workers are quite the same. What we have done instead is to list some of the general principles to bear in mind when drawing them up.

▲ Each worker should have as much reponsibility and control as possible over his or her own work and the sequence in which tasks are carried out.

▲ Jobs should have as much variety as possible in terms of content and in terms of the physical movements and locations involved.

▲ Jobs should be as relevant as possible to workers' existing skills and provide opportunities to enhance them and develop new ones. Thought should be given to career progression so that new jobs do not become dead-ends in promotion terms.

▲ Wherever possible, direct human contact with fellow-workers should be retained and electronic intercommunication minimised. Co-operative, rather than competitive, work methods should be encouraged e.g. it is pleasanter, healthier and usually more efficient for copy typists to check each other's work in pairs (one reading; one checking) rather than doing it alone or having the supervisor carry out all checking.

▲ Screen contact time should be minimised. (some recommended guidelines for maximum time to be spent at the screen are listed on pages 176 – 179).

▲ Stressful visual tasks requiring a lot of concentration, for instance proof-reading, should always be done from paper print-outs rather than directly on-screen.

▲ Machine monitoring should be avoided. We have come across some situations where VDU workers have said that they would prefer to be monitored by machines than by unfair supervisors who favour some workers while victimising others. Usually these workers are not fully aware of the stress which machine monitoring can cause. Where human supervisors are racist, unfair or arbitrary, this is better tackled by other means, such as positive action programmes, making racial and sexual harassment a disciplinary offence in grievance procedures, retraining supervisors or reorganising the work so that there is a greater degree of self-monitoring.

▲ New patterns of work organisation should not give management any additional powers to move staff about from job to job or arbitrarily change their job descriptions. If an element of flexible working it required, then the union should be integrally involved in its operation.

▲ Training programmes should be designed, with union involvement, to ensure that all workers, including part-time staff, have equal access to any new skills involved in operating new machines, and the chance to develop them through their work. Where new systems are introduced into previously uncomputerised offices there should also be a chance for workers who for any reason do not wish to undergo the health risks of working with the new machines to retrain for other types of work within the organisation.

▲ Work should not be relocated outside the office without the consent of the union whether this is to homeworkers, subcontractors or branch offices where working conditions and career development prospects are likely to be inferior. The development of a pool of casual labour outside the workplace can seriously undermine trade union organisation. If you have any members of staff agitating to become homeworkers, find out why. The chances are their problems could be solved much more effectively by negotiating improvements at the workplace such as creche facilities, financial assistance with the cost of childcare, shorter or more flexible working hours or improved facilities for people with disabilities.

▲ The new job descriptions should not reflect stereotyped notions of what is appropriate work for men or women, Blacks or whites. Neither should they reinforce existing divisions in the workforce. On the contrary, the aim should be to open up new pathways into areas of work from which particular groups have been excluded in the past.

This section concludes with a discussion of two concrete examples of organisations in which jobs have been redesigned in the interests of workers.

The first is the membership department of a national trade union. Before new technology was introduced, the jobs were divided up by function. Most of the clerks in the department were working full-time on one particular aspect of the work, such as keeping track of branch contributions records, keeping records of individual members' names and addresses, dealing with membership enquiries by telephone or letter and so on.

When a new computerised system was introduced, it was decided to reorganise the work so that each staff member in the department had responsibility for a particular geographical area. This produced a much more varied pattern of work, since each worker was now involved in the full range of functions previously carried out by separate workers. It also made the service much more efficient. The workers were able to build up individual relationships with the branch secretaries in their areas and could deal with their queries without having to pass them on to other staff members within the department. The result was a much more friendly atmosphere, and less frustration all round. Since VDU work now only formed a small proportion of each individual's total workload, health hazards were also reduced to a minimum.

A similar approach could be applied to a number of different types of organisation in which work is divided by function. For instance in the sales department of a manufacturing organisation, staff currently designated as stock-keepers, order clerks, invoice clerks or whatever (perhaps including 'manual' workers such as pickers and packers) could be redeployed so that each was entirely responsible for a particular section of the product range, a particular group of customers or a particular sales area.

The second example concerns the secretariat of a large international organisation whose professional officers, drawn from all over the world, are appointed by the United Nations. When new technology was brought in, in the form of a large-scale shared-logic word processing system, there was full consultation with the workers involved and a major restructuring of work took place. What had been the typing pool was removed from its traditional home in an administrative department and placed under the management of the computer services department. The environment was extensively revamped, under the guidance of an ergonomist who consulted closely with the workers, with the result that it became the most attractive set of offices in the building, with soft lighting, comfortable furniture, carpets and so on.

To ensure that word processor operators would have the best possible chance of career development, all external recruitment was stopped other than via the central word processing pool. New entrants spent their first three months in the pool receiving a full training in the use of office technology. They were then placed on training placements in the various departments of the organisation for a further three months for half-days only (it was discovered that there was a danger of trainees being treated as skivvies if their full-time presence could be taken for granted). During the other half of the day they worked as word processor operators in the central pool, where there were frequent chances of breaks because of the system of operators checking their own work in pairs. Later, there was a chance to try out work in the departments on full-time placement and eventually to move permanently into a clerical or administrative vacancy in one of the departments.

For those who opted to remain in the central pool, there was the possibility of progressing to become a training officer, a technical officer with responsibility for liaising with the equipment supplier or a senior word processor operator/junior programmer involved in setting up new software applications.

This system brought a number of advantages to the workers concerned. It meant that nobody was obliged to work full-time on a VDU, thus producing a healthier pattern of work; it greatly enhanced promotion prospects; and it gave a traditionally weak group of workers much greater leverage within the organisation as a whole, since workers who did not like the way they were treated by the professional officers in any particular department always had the option of returning to the central pool without loss of seniority.

One side-effect was to increase the educational requirements for new recruits, since all new entrants had to be capable of filling administrative departmental posts. This might be regarded as a drawback. However an organisation wishing to adopt such a system while retaining an equal opportunities policy could solve this problem by ensuring that special training was made available for applicants who had missed out on formal education in the past because of sex, race or disability.

It could be argued that another weakness of the scheme lies in the way it leaves intact the gulf between professional officer posts and administrative support jobs. It is, however, probably asking too much to expect a divide as universal as this, and as thoroughly embedded in our national and international institutions, to be broken down completely within the confines of a single workplace.

– 14 –

Staff levels

Perhaps the greatest single source of stress at work is being overworked. However well designed your job or your working environment, if you are under constant pressure your health will begin to suffer. Staffing levels are therefore as much a health and safety issue as fire exits or electrical safety, and negotiations over staffing should form a central part of any negotiations over the introduction of new technology, all the more so because the chances are that one of your management's prime reasons for introducing new technology in the first place is to cut staffing costs.

Trade unionists negotiating over staffing levels need to bear in mind several objectives, all linked to each other. These include: minimising job loss; keeping staff numbers at a reasonable level; ensuring that no individual or group of workers is overworked; and preventing management from casualising all or parts of the workforce.

Agreeing safe staffing levels thus involves negotiation over the numbers of jobs, both overall and within each department or occupational group; over the number of hours worked, including leave provisions; and over security of employment for existing and future staff.

Many of these items will already be covered by existing agreements, so negotiations over new technology will involve reappraising these, and setting up appropriate machinery within the union and within the bargaining structure to renegotiate them.

A number of different demands are relevant here. They include:

No redundancies

In some organisations the introduction of new technology has actually brought redundancy notices, but this is in fact comparatively rare. The most usual way for managements to run down staffing levels is by 'natural wastage' – simply not replacing people who leave. This is sometimes accompanied by subtle pressures on unwanted individuals to go, by making their lives uncomfortable in various ways or making it clear that their prospects are not good. When work is being reorganised it can often be extremely difficult for trade union representatives to keep track of the number of jobs which have disappeared in this way.

Some union branches have responded to such staff run-downs by refusing to do the work of ex-colleagues who have not been replaced, and this has sometimes been successful. However if the job itself has become partly redundant because of new technology then this is obviously a difficult strategy to follow.

In many companies an initial union call for 'no redundancies' has come to seem unwinnable to union members, especially where their employers have been badly hit by the recession, and it has often been replaced by a demand for 'no compulsory redundancies'. This has shifted the emphasis away from maintaining existing staffing levels to finding ways to redeploy staff who do not want to retrain or are surplus to requirements – or worse, to collaborating with management to find ways to encourage voluntary redundancies.

It is obviously ridiculous to hold out for demands which your members are not prepared to back. Nevertheless, in negotiating staffing levels it is important too not to lose sight of the reason for such negotiations. Not only should you be trying to prevent your members being thrown onto the dole; you should also be thinking of the quality of working life for those who remain. Management estimates of the productivity savings which new technology will bring may well be unrealistically optimistic. It is important to ensure that there will be enough staff around to cope when things go wrong, to cover for absences and to allow time for people to be released for training as well as permitting everyone to take the breaks to which they are entitled. If your management has to resort to enforced overtime or the use of temporary, freelance or contract staff on a routine basis then your staffing levels are not high enough.

Negotiating staffing levels is tough. Many managements will refuse to discuss them seriously at all and others will go to great lengths to divert you onto other issues. Even when negotiations are underway they often make very poor progress and it is easy to become discouraged. Don't. Very small gains, perhaps one or two jobs in a single department, might seem hardly worth the effort, but to the individuals involved they make all the difference in the world. A single job saved does not just rescue one person from the demoralisation of unemployment but in all probability makes life a little easier for that person's workmates as well.

Permanent employee status

When negotiating staffing levels it is not enough simply to ensure that there are enough pairs of hands to do the work required. It is also important to be sure that the work is done by people with secure jobs and decent wages and conditions. This implies controlling the use of temporary staff, outworkers, freelances or casuals, and restricting the use of subcontractors for overflow work. From the point of view of your members, there are two sets of reasons for this.

The first is altruistic. No good trade unionist likes to see people being exploited, and some might also feel that 'there, but for the grace of god, go I' when they hear about the sorts of conditions under which people have to work in the 'data entry sweatshops' which have sprung up in recent years, or see the difficulties temporary workers get into when they try to book a holiday, get a mortgage or otherwise plan their future.

The second reason is a matter of direct self-interest. The existence of a pool of casual staff, desperate for work, and often prepared to accept lower wages as well as worse conditions than permanent employees, is a direct threat to the security of their own jobs. Why should management continue to employ them if they can get the same work done more cheaply by sending it outside? Why should they create a permanent job when they can get a temp in to do it without having to pay for sickness, holidays, maternity leave, pensions or any of the other overheads associated with employing someone permanently?

Ideally, you should try to get union agreements to cover these eventualities before they start happening on any scale. The first component of any such agreement should cover information and monitoring. The union should be informed of all work which is subcontracted and all use of temporary staff, perhaps on a monthly basis. If possible, try to get an agreement that union consent is required before any work can go out or be done casually. Failing this, go for an agreement that if the use of casual staff falls into any definite pattern, or exceeds a given level in any particular department, then extra permanent staff will be taken on to do it. In this way it can be limited to situations which are genuinely occasional, either because of seasonal peaks in the workflow or to deal with a one-off emergency.

Where work is being carried out by staff who are not permanent employees, then there are several provisions which can be negotiated to give them some protection:

▲ Contracts clearly setting out their terms and conditions of employment and their rights, including the right to join a trade union and the address and phone number of a union officer to contact.

▲ Hourly wages which are at least as good as those of people doing the same work on a permanent basis, and preferably higher to allow for the fringe benefits which they are not receiving. One formula which has sometimes been adopted in the publishing industry is that freelances should receive 6/5 of the equivalent staff rate.

▲ The payment of all expenses incurred in carrying out the work.

▲ The chance to apply for permanent work within the organisation should a vacancy arise.

▲ The provision of any necessary equipment and materials and information about their safety.

If outworkers are employed by a subcontractor then you should try to ensure that their wages and conditions and the safety of their workplace are as good as yours in all respects and that the employer recognises their right to be represented by an appropriate trade union. If you work for a local authority or other organisation which has set up a contracts compliance unit, then you may be able to draw on the help of staff in this unit to ensure that the employer gives fair wages and adopts equal opportunities policies.

Shorter working hours

The shorter working week is one of the oldest trade union demands in the book, though none the less topical for that. Over the years the working week for full-time workers has been steadily whittled down so that it now stands at 35 hours for many office workers, although 40 or 37½ hours are still more usual, while few manual workers have got their hours much below 40. Many unions have succeeded in linking these demands to the introduction of new technology, using arguments based on the higher productivity levels that automation brings. The result has been not just to reduce the pressure of work for everyone but also to keep up the total number of jobs, as well as making life a little easier for people with childcare responsibilities in the process.

One thing to watch out for when negotiating a reduction in hours is how the reduction should be effected. There is sometimes a conflict between women workers, who would prefer to leave half an hour earlier each day to reduce the end-of-day frenzy involved with collecting children from school or childminder and preparing tea, and men who would like to take a whole afternoon off, or even move towards a four-day week, perhaps with a slightly longer working day, in order to gain more leisure time. Some well structured flexitime systems allow for both these possibilities.

Local transport timetables are another factor to bear in mind. It is not much good negotiating a shorter working day if this simply means waiting an extra twenty minutes for the bus at the end of the afternoon. Make sure too that any shortening of the working day is not at the expense of the lunch hours and rest breaks which are so important for relaxing the tired muscles of VDU operators.

If a shift system is in operation at your workplace then reducing working hours will entail complicated negotiations over shift-length. It may be necessary to think in terms of the introduction of extra part-time shifts to ensure complete cover while shortening the length of your working week.

Part-time rights

One way to spread the available work among the greatest number of people, and to bring about a shorter working week for many workers, is to improve the quality of part-time work so that it offers a living wage and the same security and benefits as full-time working. At present, most part-timers are not only extremely badly paid compared with full-timers, but are also discriminated against by being excluded from pension schemes, having much longer qualifying periods for maternity rights, and being denied any promotion prospects, as well as lacking a number of other benefits which full-time workers take for granted.

Negotiating improvements in these can open up part-time work as an option for workers who at present cannot afford to consider it, and, by improving the security and status of part-time workers, create a more stable and cohesive workforce. By giving part-timers a reason to support the union, such action will also produce the basis for stronger trade union organisation at the workplace.

However, while supporting part-time workers' demands and improving their wages and conditions, trade union negotiators should also be aware of the dangers of an increase in part-time working on management's terms. Any attempt to substitute part-time jobs for full-time ones against the wishes of the workers involved should be resisted, especially while part-timers still have much less protection from lay-off and redundancy than full-time employees. Similarly, attempts to reduce the hours of part-time workers should be opposed, particularly when the reduction brings them below the minimum number of hours required to qualify for basic employment rights. This limit was set at 16 hours during the 1970s but at the time of writing there were Government proposals to raise it to 20 hours per week.

Leave entitlement

In addition to shortening the working week by reducing the number of hours, there are other ways to reduce the total amount of time which people spend at work, and thereby improve the quality of their lives and spread the available work out among more people.

One of the most obvious ways is to extend holidays, and this has been done with success in many new technology negotiations. However even this can sometimes turn out to be tricky to agree on. For instance, should this extra holiday entitlement be evenly distributed amongst all the staff or just among those who are producing the extra output by using the new technology? The problem was illustrated at the Greater London Council when new technology was brought in. A formula was worked out for calculating the extra productivity it was thought the new technology would bring, and it was decided to spread this evenly amongst all white-collar staff, resulting in an extra half-day's holiday all round, a half-day which was hardly noticeable to the hard-pressed data entry and word-processing staff who generated all that extra productivity. However to have given only keyboard operators additional holidays would have created an unfair precedent and brought chaos to existing structures.

The best approach would seem to be one which spreads the benefit widely, but compensates the workers bearing the brunt of the impact of new technology in other ways, perhaps through regrading or additional breaks during the course of the working day.

Greenwich NALGO set an interesting precedent in this area in 1986 when it secured a new technology agreement which limited the advantages won to union members.

As well as negotiating additional holidays, it is also possible to demand improvements to sick leave agreements, maternity, childbirth attendance and parental leave, compassionate leave, sabbaticals, training entitlements and paid study leave. Early retirement may also be suggested as a possibility for some workers, but this should be approached with caution, and only agreed to if the workers themselves really want it, and then only if pension rights are properly protected.

Compared with some other aspects of staffing level negotiations, these improvements can be relatively easy to win, and it is often

possible to come back to your members with substantial gains which will boost morale as well as improving the quality of their lives.

– 15 –

Workplace design

As many of the earlier sections of this book have shown, the design of the working environment is extremely important to the health and safety of VDU workers. There are many publications on the subject, including several which have been produced by individual trade unions for their members. Others have been published by organisations serving the trade union movement such as the Labour Research Department, the Leeds Trade Union and Community Resource and Information Centre (TUCRIC) and the London Hazards Centre, while still more have come from universities and government departments.

Although they disagree in some of their details, most are in broad agreement over the basic principles to be adopted. There are of course certain dangers in blindly following pre-set guidelines in such matters: they do not take account of new developments in the technology or new scientific research; and they do not take account of the particular characteristics of individual workplaces or groups of workers.

Nevertheless, there is a strong case for developing universally applicable standards in this area, some of which might even become legally binding at some future date. The international trade union movement is devising standards and, with this in mind, the British TUC has published its own guidelines on VDUs[120]. In this section of the book we have marked with an open triangle ($\triangle$) any recommendations which conform to these TUC standards. In most cases, you will probably find that these are very similar, if not identical, to the guidelines issued by your own trade union.

To most trade union members it is more important to understand why these guidelines are there than to follow them to the letter. Members who have a clear understanding of VDU hazards will be more likely to take preventive action before a hazard becomes serious, or report to the safety rep any inadequacies in the design of their working environment. Some may disagree with some details of the guidelines, finding that different arrangements suit them better.

In general, the wishes of the VDU workers should be the most important factor in deciding on the most suitable design. However if workers are already operating VDUs in a badly designed environment, they may very well have adapted to it, and be initially hostile to any change which involves developing new habits. This human capacity to adapt to almost anything is in fact one of the greatest causes of occupational ill-health.

Many workers quickly become so used to the peculiarities of their working situation that while they are working they cease to be aware of the aches and pains which it produces. Unconsciously they adapt themselves to avoid the worst problems, perhaps by squinting sideways, sitting at an awkward angle or placing a potted plant between the screen and the strip-light to avoid glare; propping their feet on a waste-paper bin because they have no footrest; or wedging a kleenex box under the screen to change its angle. Any traditionally designed office will reveal examples of such adaptive behaviour. Many have become so familiar that they seem almost to be extensions of workers' individual personalities and are therefore very difficult to drop.

When discussing changes to be introduced in situations like this it is important to allow plenty of time for discussion and an opportunity to try out new arrangements before making any final decision. If you have already carried out a health and safety survey among the workers, then this discussion will be much better informed. Probably there will already be some awareness of the need for change. It is also instructive to talk to workers who are new to the job, and therefore haven't yet had a chance to adapt. They may be able to give a much clearer analysis of the drawbacks of the existing set-up than those who have become used to it.

In these discussions with co-workers, and in negotiations with management, these are some of the key features of the working environment to focus on:

Space

No room should be so overcrowded as to cause risk to health. By law, each worker should have a minimum of 11.3 cubic metres of space available with 3.7 square metres of floorspace, not counting the space taken up by office machinery and furniture other than your desk and chair.

It is important that there's enough room for everyone to move around freely. Workers should have the choice of sitting away from a VDU terminal during the periods when they are not working at it. People forced to occupy the same workstation all day should have a separate area near at hand for taking rest breaks.

Vertical space can be as important as floor-space. It allows heat to disperse and provides scope for the ducting of communications cables below the floor and behind the walls and for lighting fixtures to be concealed above a false ceiling or baffles.

Many offices built during the late 1950s and early 1960s have such low ceilings that they cannot be adapted for VDU work in this way, leaving the workers trapped in a dangerous tangle of cable under the glare of naked fluorescent strip-lights. To make matters worse, this type of office often has 'curtain walls' of uninterrupted window to complete the 'dry aquarium' effect.

VDU workers have a special need for space which provides long vistas to look down, giving their eye muscles the rest which comes from focusing periodically on something further than 20 feet away.

Arrangement of furniture

It is important that furniture should be arranged to allow sufficiently wide passages for people of all sizes, including the very pregnant and wheelchair users, to move comfortably between workstations.

The arrangement of furniture is also vital in the avoidance of glare, which is one of the greatest causes of headaches and visual fatigue.

△ VDUs should be situated at right angles (90°) to windows and as far away from them as is necessary to eliminate glare.

△ VDUs must *never* be placed with a window immediately in front of them or immediately behind them.

△ The angle of view of any window should be greater than 50° from the operator, as shown in the diagram on page 151.

All VDU operators should be able, without moving from their workstation or twisting uncomfortably, to look periodically into a distance of at least 20 feet to rest tensed eye muscles.

Furnishing fabrics

△ Windows *must* be fitted with blinds or curtains which should be in neutral colours.

Similarly, all other large surfaces in the room should be as non-reflective as possible. Wall-coverings should have a matte finish, in

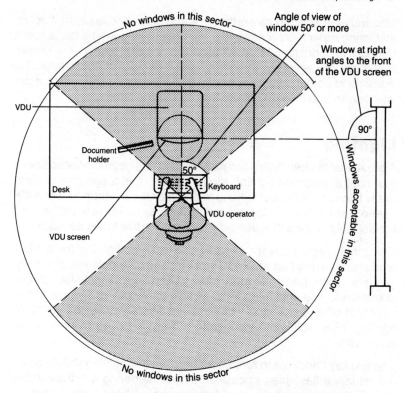

Looking down on a VDU workstation: arrangement of furniture and equipment to avoid glare. Similar rules apply to the positioning of artificial lighting.

neutral shades, and furniture should not have shiny surfaces. White should be avoided. Floors should be carpeted.

Partitions with non-reflective surfaces can be a useful way of minimising glare, and also provide a way of giving individual workers some privacy, preventing draughts and eliminating the possibility of workers being subjected to the hazard of flicker from screens at neighbouring workstations on the edge of their field of vision. However the placement of these screens should be decided in consultation with the workers involved to ensure that they don't cause isolation, block views which the workers value, or create a barrier to free movement around the office.

Carpets, partition coverings, upholstery, curtains and any other fabrics used in the VDU workplace should be made of cotton, wool or other natural fibre to minimise the build-up of static electricity. The carpet should be attached to the floor in a way which allows any accumulated static to be earthed – some glues and underlays act as insulating agents preventing this from happening. Metal tacks into a conductive flooring material will earth the carpet properly – but ensure that these are securely embedded and well clear of any cables. It is possible to obtain carpets specially designed for the job, with copper wire woven into them to ensure that earthing is effective.

Lighting

A great deal of often highly technical writing has been produced about the most appropriate lighting for VDU work. It is a complex subject partly because individual lighting requirements vary enormously. A 40-year-old may need twice as much light as a 20-year-old to see comfortably, while a 60-year-old might require five times as much.

The other major problem in designing suitable lighting for a VDU workstation is the fact that VDU work is rarely the only visual activity going on in any particular area. Most VDU workers must also refer to documents, use the telephone, check print-outs and carry out a variety of other tasks, all of which require different types and levels of lighting. Most solutions are therefore likely to be a compromise of some sort.

The two key principles to remember here are that lighting should be as individually adjustable as possible *without* interfering with the lighting of neighbouring workers. And lighting should be diffused – naked bulbs or strips are completely unacceptable in a VDU environment and should not be visible to any VDU worker[121].

There are a great many ways in which these effects can be achieved, including a variety of diffusers and baffles and various combinations of overhead and individual desk lighting. Blinds or curtains should enable workers to adjust the amount of natural light.

△ For intensive VDU work, the maximum general lighting level should be 300-500 lux, augmented by individual task lights fitted with dimmers for those jobs, such as referring to printed documents, which require higher levels. Lighting levels can be measured with an ordinary camera light meter.

Some experts recommend even lower base levels than this – 200-300 lux.

△ Like windows, lights should not be placed within a viewing angle of less than 50° from any VDU operator. (See diagram on page 151)

The positioning and shielding of overhead lighting requires great care to avoid any workstation being too brightly lit or any reflections appearing in screens.

Ventilation, temperature and humidity

Despite the off-hand way in which many managements introduce VDUs into traditional offices, the heating and air conditioning requirements are quite different from those of a non-electronic workplace. This is not because of any physical peculiarity of the VDU workers who of course have exactly the same requirements for clean fresh air, warmth and comfort as any other human beings; nor is it, as it was in the early days of computing, because of the sensitivity of the machines to extremes of temperature and dust. The air conditioning and heating requirements of electronic offices are different because of the heat, the dry atmosphere and the static electricity generated by the machines and because of the effect of these on workers whose bodies are already under considerable stress because of the nature of their work.

Office temperatures have for some time been controlled by law, under the Offices, Shops and Railway Premises Act, which sets down a minimum temperature of 16°C (60.8°F). This may be one of the reasons why a fairly high proportion of offices already have some form of central heating and air conditioning, although some other types of workplace where VDUs are found, such as warehouses and factories, do not.

Unfortunately, central heating and air conditioning systems do not always provide a healthy environment. Many have the effect of drying the air out, and therefore irritating the mucous membranes of the occupants, causing increased susceptibility to colds and flu. This dryness also affects the skin and the surface of the eyes so that they become uncomfortable. In extreme cases, a dry air conditioning system can prevent any sweating taking place and lead to itching and dermatitis[122].

The friction caused in air conditioning systems by forcing the air through ducts and fans also causes a marked increase in the number of positive ions in the atmosphere, adding to the positive charge in the air caused by emissions from the VDU itself, and hence to the precipitation of dust particles in the air. This could well be one of the factors creating what has been called the 'sick building syndrome' which has been widely reported as a feature of air-conditioned offices[123]. Its symptoms include a blocked, itchy, runny nose; itching, irritated or watering eyes; dry throat or stuffy nose; tight chest; shortness of breath or wheezing; headaches; dry skin and lethargy[124].

The obvious solution to this problem of over-dry air is to increase the humidity. In many workplaces in the UK this can be simply achieved by making sure there are enough windows which workers can open when they feel like it, letting in as much moist British air as is required. A window is in fact a worker-controlled means of adjusting lighting, ventilation, temperature and humidity all at once. However problems can sometimes arise when these different functions conflict with each other (for instance on a cold day if a worker requires greater humidity but more warmth), or when different workers have different requirements. Many workers are, of course, stuck with windows which cannot be adjusted or with no windows at all.

In such cases the use of humidifiers can be valuable. However care should be taken to ensure that these do not lead to the creation of other hazards. In some workplaces, a new occupational illness has emerged known as 'secretary's asthma' or 'humidifier fever', caused, it is believed, by bacteria breeding in the water in the humidifier. Its symptoms include intermittent chills and fever, coughing, vomiting, aching joints and tightness in the chest[125].

△   Relative humidity should be 40-50 per cent.

The trade union APEX recommends a higher standard of 65-70 per cent relative humidity.

△   Recommended temperatures for VDU operators are 19-23°C.

It is important to measure these at various times during the day when the VDUs have been switched on for some time and heat has built up to its highest levels.

Most safety representatives are by now aware that a monochrome VDU gives off a considerable amount of heat during the course of a working day. What is less well known is that the newer, full-colour VDUs give off three times as much because they use three electron guns instead of one. If there is any suggestion that your management might be considering bringing these in, or increasing the total number of VDUs in a given space, then be sure that your ventilation and cooling systems can cope.

The circulation of air should be arranged in a way that allows the air to be renewed often enough to ensure a good supply of oxygen. At the same time, it must not cause draughts.

There are several aids to keeping the air clean and unpolluted. Arrange the workspace so that smokers are in a separate environment from non-smokers. Ensure that local extraction systems are installed to remove the air from any device giving off fumes or dust, such as photocopiers, guillotines, shredders or binding machines. Negative ionisers help to clean the air by precipitating dust out of it, as can be seen by the enormous amount of dirt in the area which immediately surrounds them. If ionisers are to be installed in your workplace, make sure that proper cleaning arrangements are made. This may involve negotiating extra working time for the cleaners.

The use of negative ionisers, though controversial, does also appear to eliminate some of the undesirable effects of a high positive static electrical charge in the air. However it should be used as an addition to, not a substitute for, other means of cutting down on dust or eliminating static. These include using natural rather than synthetic materials wherever possible, avoiding highly polished surfaces and making sure that all workstations and other articles likely to build up a static charge are properly earthed.

In some workplaces, operators are asked to avoid wearing underwear made of artificial fibres to cut down on static build-up, and in others they are actually attached to their workstation by an earthing wire around the wrist. Both of these measures intrude into the individual's freedom of choice too far to be acceptable to most trade unionists. However it would be interesting to know whether managements would be prepared to pay allowances for clothing made of the more expensive natural fibres.

Minimising noise

Printers are the greatest single source of noise in most VDU environments. There may also be noise from cooling fans on computers, printers and ventilation systems, from telephones, keyboards, telex machines, filing cabinets, voices, road traffic, aircraft or neighbouring workplaces. Some of these will probably be much more irritating than others, because of their intermittent or unexpected character.

△ For VDU tasks requiring a high degree of mental effort the ambient noise level should not be more than 50-55 dBA, while for other VDU jobs noise levels of up to 60 dBA may be acceptable.

Measures which can help cut down on noise levels include:

△ Using screens or partitions to separate individual workstations (which can also help reduce glare – see page 151).

△ Ensuring that walls, floors and ceilings are covered with sound-absorbing materials.

△ Positioning printers or other noisy equipment away from VDU workstations.

△ Fitting printers and telex machines with acoustic hoods.

Information about suppliers of acoustic hoods can be found in the appendix on suppliers on page 203 of this book.

The TUC recommends that where ultrasound is a problem, the terminal casing or flyback transformer of the VDU should be padded. However it does not explain how this should be done.

– 16 –

Work station, equipment and software design

As well as ensuring that the overall working environment is friendly to the VDU operator it is also vital that the workstation itself meets recommended ergonomic standards to minimise health hazards.

Here again, the watchword is adjustability. As many features as possible should be under the direct control of the operator who should also have the opportunity to make frequent changes of posture. Where workstations are to be used by more than one person, this adjustability becomes even more crucial – it must not just cater for all the varieties of movement which one operator may wish to adopt, but must also allow for those of other workers who will be of different shapes, sizes, ages and abilities. For instance, what suits a 20-year-old 6-foot short-sighted man at 5 p.m. in the winter will be very different from the adjustments appropriate for a 45-year-old 5-foot woman with long sight on a sunny summer morning.

Desks

△ Desks for VDU work should be adjustable in height, preferably with a separate keyboard area which is also height adjustable. If there really is no alternative to a fixed height desk, then it should be approximately 700mm high, in which case it is even more important to ensure that everything else is adjustable.

Some people like to alternate between sitting and standing at their workstations, a method of working which has been seriously proposed by some ergonomists as a 'solution' to some VDU hazards. To cater for their needs it is necessary either to have a few extra workstations at standing height, or to have some desks with a greater degree of adjustability.

The surface should be matte and non-reflective, in a neutral colour, preferably made or laminated in unpolished wood, or covered in some other natural material to minimise the accumulation of static electricity.

The legs of the table and any drawers or other accessories should be situated so that they allow free movement of the operator's legs when seated. They should also allow for comfortable wheelchair access.

△ The desk should be as thin as possible, preferably no more than 20mm.

This is so that knees can move as high as possible while the hands which use the keyboard can fall as low as possible. However this thinness should not be at the expense of strength. The desk will have to carry a fair amount of weight and should be designed to do so safely.

The top of the desk should be wide enough and deep enough to allow workers to spread out everything they need without clutter, and place the screen as far back as they need to for comfortable viewing.

△ A depth of at least 900mm is recommended.

There should be enough storage space to cope with the VDU worker's personal as well as work needs. However this should be arranged so as not to interfere with movement. This is another reason for ensuring that desks are sufficiently wide.

Cables should not be allowed to trail freely up the sides or back of the desk but should be ducted and securely attached. However this should be done in a way that does not interfere with the operator's ability to move equipment around on the desk to the most convenient position. For this purpose it can be helpful to have the part of the cable which is on the surface of the desk coiled like the cable which is normally attached to a telephone handpiece.

Chairs

Any chair for VDU use must be fully adjustable *while the worker is sitting in it.* This means that you must be able to swivel it, roll it backwards and forwards, adjust the height and adjust the angle of the back easily and comfortably without getting up. However it must *not* move unintentionally. Once adjusted, it should stay that way until the worker wants to change the settings, and it must not roll of its own accord or, under any circumstances, tip. Its design should also be such that it is possible to sit comfortably in as many different positions as possible.

△ The height should be adjustable between 385 and 500 mm.

△ The back should be inclinable between the vertical and 120°.

The backrest should also support the entire trunk, with special support for the lumbar area.

△ The lumbar support should, if possible, be separately height adjustable.

The chair should have a five-arm base, for stability, with the five arms forming a circle whose diameter is at least as large as the width of the seat. It is generally advisable to have castors at the ends of these arms, to make it easier to get up and down. However these castors should be matched to the type of floor-covering so that they do not roll too easily.

△ The difference in height between the chair-seat top and the keyboard bottom should be within the range 220-300 mm.

The way in which most modern office chairs are made easily height-adjustable is by filling the central support column with nitrogen gas. Recently there have been several cases of these exploding[126].

To avoid this hazard it is particularly important to ensure that carefully made, good quality chairs are purchased and regular maintenance checks are made on them.

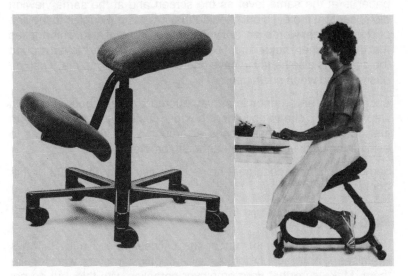

Kneelers or 'backless chairs' like the ones shown here provide an alternative form of seating for workers who find traditional chairs uncomfortable, or for those who like to vary their seating position.

Some back sufferers, and a few people anxious to avoid becoming back sufferers prefer not to use chairs at all, but to use kneelers, which provide an alternative way of supporting the body in a working posture. These should be made available for anyone who wants them. There is an argument for having a few additional kneelers available on request for people who like an occasional change of posture or who suffer intermittently from backache. Some people prefer to alternate between kneeling, sitting and standing at their workstation, which implies the need for a high degree of adjustability or a choice of workstation.

Some suppliers of VDU chairs and kneelers are listed on pages 202 – 203 of this book, in the appendix on suppliers.

Document holders

Although some VDU workers may choose not to use them sometimes, every VDU workstation should be supplied with a document holder with a retaining clip, which can be used to hold documents at an angle and distance which makes it easy for the user to refer to them, and minimises the need to refocus the eyes and turn the head.

It is usually recommended that the holder should be placed so that the paper is at the same level as the screen and at the same viewing distance from the eyes but tilted so that it is at right angles to the line of sight (in other words, so that you can look straight at it). This implies that the document holder must be adjustable and easily moved around the desk. It is also handy to have one which folds flat, so that it can be easily stored when not in use.

According to an ergonomic survey quoted by the Labour Research Department[127], cheap document holders costing about £20 perform just as well as expensive ones at around £150 when it comes to eliminating neck strain and other health problems.

Some suppliers of document holders are listed on page 203 of this book.

Footrests

It is a legal requirement, under the Offices, Shops and Railways Premises Act, to supply footrests to all office workers who require them. Make sure that your employer complies with this, but do not allow the provision of footrests to be used as a substitute for fully adjustable desks or chairs.

Keyboards

Most VDUs come with the QWERTY keyboard, which was developed in the 1870s to meet the engineering requirements of manufacturing a mechanical typewriter. The keys were arranged diagonally to make it easy to attach each to the appropriate letter arranged in a semicircle at the top of the machine.

The main drawback was the way in which these mechanical links collided with each other and jammed when two nearby keys were struck simultaneously or soon after each other, so the QWERTY inventor analysed the most common sequences of letters and arranged the keyboard in such away that they were as widely separated from each other as possible.

The result, while mechanically convenient, was not particularly convenient for the operator, involving more work for the left hand than the right (the left hand is responsible for approximately 60 per cent of the key depressions when QWERTY is used by a trained – non two-finger – typist) despite the fact that most people are right-handed. It also overuses the comparatively weak and inflexible little finger while underusing the thumb.

Now that keyboards are electronic, there is no good functional reason for staying with the QWERTY standard. Indeed, it has been made even more cumbersome by the addition of new function keys around the periphery, many of which require operators to stretch the overworked little finger even further. Nevertheless, along with the similar AZERTY keyboard used for Roman languages, it has now become so entrenched as a standard that to change it would require massive retraining and a major new investment in equipment.

Alongside it, on most computer keyboards, is a numerical keypad, mainly used for bulk data entry, derived from the format used on the old key-punch machines.

Although not well known in Britain, several alternatives to QWERTY have been developed. However with many of these the motive has been to increase the operator's speed rather than to reduce the risk of strain injuries.

One of these is the DVORAK keyboard, which has become quite popular in the United States. This basically uses the same physical layout as a QWERTY keyboard with the letters rearranged. It is claimed to be faster to learn and to produce higher speeds, but studies of world typing records reveal equally high speeds reached by QWERTY typists[128]. It is possible to obtain software packages to convert a QWERTY keyboard to DVORAK for several of the most commonly used types of computer, but it seems unlikely that this will make any great contribution to the health and safety of VDU operators.

A more radical option is a completely redesigned keyboard. Here, there are two main contenders: the Dutch Velotype, which interfaces with a number of different computers, word processors and typesetting machines; and the Maltron, a British-made keyboard specifically designed in the late 1970s with ergonomics in mind.

Both of these look quite different from the traditional keyboard. The Velotype is designed to achieve great speed and has the alphabetical keys bunched into the centre of the keyboard. It uses logic circuitry to enable the operator to press several keys at once which it will automatically sort into the right sequence. Learning to use it therefore also involves learning the 'rules' it uses for this sorting process so can take some time, although the manufacturers claim that an operator can reach a reasonable standard after a fortnight's intensive course[129]. We have been unable to discover any reports of how it compares ergonomically with QWERTY, but clearly it was not designed primarily with the operator's comfort in mind.

The Maltron looks even stranger to anyone accustomed to standard keyboards. It has several keypads, which can be on separate boards, arranged according to the shape of the hand. Each thumb has its own pad with eight keys to deal with, and most of the other keys are arranged in two curved formations, one for each hand, in such a way that only the index finger, which is the most flexible, ever has to stretch diagonally, one of the causes of muscular stress. The base of the keyboard bulges up to provide a support for the hand.

The Maltron is apparently very easy to learn, and is available in a number of different formats. It can be supplied to interface with most major computers and word processors. The letters and numbers can be assigned to any key, so it is possible to keep the QWERTY layout or use the Maltron one, which is based on an analysis of frequency. However it is fairly expensive and is reported to lack robustness. In a trial by *Practical Computing* magazine, one key fell off and an indicator light stopped working within minutes, although the operator found it extremely comfortable and straightforward to use[130]. In all probability, such problems would quickly disappear if there was sufficient demand for the keyboard to make mass production feasible.

A number of other types of keyboard and alternative inputting devices are available with special adaptations for people with disabilities.

Before making a commitment to changing over to a new type of keyboard, it is best to persuade your management to buy one or two, with the appropriate training packages, to enable people to try them out and make up their minds in the light of their own experience. A properly designed keyboard can help to prevent not just hand and wrist problems, but also those shoulder, neck and back conditions which stem from the position of the hands and the strain of supporting them.

Whatever type of keyboard you eventually adopt, it should have all the characteristics which are listed below. This is one of the areas where manufacturers have been most receptive to criticisms from users, so you will probably find that recent models of keyboard, apart from the very cheap ones designed for home use, comply with most of the standards. Nevertheless, it is always safest to check the manufacturer's specification and allow operators to try out several alternatives and state their preferences before agreeing to any particular model being introduced.

△ It should be detachable so that it can be positioned and repositioned according to the needs of the user.

△ It should be light enough to be moved easily, but not so light that it can move of its own accord when in operation.

△ The thickness of the keyboard should be less than 30mm.

△ The slope of the keyboard should be adjustable between 5° and 15° from the horizontal.

△ Both the keys and their surround should be non-reflecting (keys should have a reflectance of between 15 per cent and 75 per cent) and neutrally coloured, with clear symbol markings at least 3mm high.

△ The degree of force required to depress a key should be adjustable between 0.25N and 1.5N (25-150gm). The key should travel a distance of between 2mm and 5mm and give some sort of tactile or audible feedback, so you can be sure it has registered. It is preferable that the volume should be adjustable when audible feedback is used.

An office of any size should have available keyboards of both kinds, to cater for the needs of operators with visual and hearing disabilities.

△ Keys should be between 18 and 20mm apart (measured from centre to centre) and 12-15mm square, with concave tops.

Some suppliers of alternative keyboards are listed on page 205 of this book.

Screens

Ergonomic specifications for VDU screens are even more complex than those for keyboards. They also become out-of-date very quickly, since this is an area of rapid technological change.

Currently most of the VDUs in use are monochrome, using a cathode ray tube (CRT) to generate a display 80 characters wide and 25 lines high. However, colour VDUs are increasingly coming into use, particularly in industries where videotex (otherwise known as viewdata) terminals are widely used. Some alternatives to the CRT are being commercially developed.

The first of these alternative technologies is the light emitting diode (LED) which is a display system based on solid state devices which emit light. It was widely used on the early pocket calculators and digital watches but it has now been almost entirely replaced by liquid crystal display (LCD) technology.

LCDs have the advantage of working on reflected light, rather than needing a lot of power to emit their own. They thus have a very low energy requirement, operating on 2 volts as compared with the 16,000 or so of a CRT, which makes them intrinsically safer in several respects. As well as being easier on the eyes, LCD screens have the great advantage of being much flatter, lighter and more portable than screens with a cathode ray tube. This is why they are beginning to be used for the portable and laptop computers which are increasingly being issued to sales representatives and newspaper reporters despite their greater cost. The main disadvantage of the liquid crystal screen is that, being less bright, it is more difficult to see and needs to be precisely adjusted in angle to avoid the display being drowned out by reflected light. This can be taken care of by making it easily adjustable and ensuring that the environment is not too bright.

At the *Financial Times* the National Union of Journalists has negotiated the right for all workers, male or female, planning to become parents, to work at an LCD screen if they wish to do so.

The third alternative technology being developed is the gas plasma screen. This is also flat because it uses ionised gas between two thin layers of glass. It may pose a radiation hazard. The gas plasma screen is also very expensive. It compares favourably with the CRT in several ways, giving a very clear, high-resolution image without noticeable flicker. However brightness and contrast are not adjustable. Research is continuing into this type of screen and it is expected to become more common.

One alternative which does not appear to have been developed yet for VDUs, although it does exist as an alternative to a back-projected microfiche reader, is a system of projecting the image onto a wall or external screen, to avoid the necessity of staring straight down the tube. In theory this could provide a much safer way of retrieving data visually from a computer.

Until such alternatives are widely available and adapted for mainstream office functions, most computer-related work will still be done by means of CRT-based VDUs.

As with keyboards, screen manufacturers have taken many criticisms to heart and listened to the advice of ergonomists when designing their latest equipment. Recent models from reputable manufacturers will therefore most probably already incorporate many of the features recommended below. However this should not be taken for granted, and all specifications should be checked before accepting a particular type of machine. Operators should also have the choice of trying out several different alternatives, before deciding which they want to work with permanently.

△ The screen should be separate from the keyboard and capable of being positioned independently on the desk. It should also be adjustable both vertically (tilt) and horizontally (swivel).

△ Brightness (for which the technical term is luminance) and contrast should both be independently adjustable, to the following specifications:

△ Background luminance (i.e. the luminance of the darker part of the screen) should be at least 10 cd/m^2 (candela per square metre).

△ Character luminance (which can vary according to the size and shape of the characters) should be at least 40 cd/m^2 but no more than 150 cd/m^2.

△ If the display polarity is positive, that is if the characters are dark on light, rather than negative, when characters are light against a dark background, then these levels would be reversed.

△ Contrast ratio between background and character luminances should be adjustable within the range 3:1 and 15:1.

△ Contrast ratio between the average screen luminance and the average luminance of the surfaces immediately surrounding the screen should be no more than 3:1.

△ The operator's own preference should decide whether polarity should be positive or negative. There is some evidence that, particularly when source documents are being referred to, positive polarity produces less visual fatigue.

△ Where positive polarity is used, the refresh rate (the number of times each second the electron beam revisits each of the fluorescent phosphors which coat the back of the screen) should be at least 80 Hz to minimise flicker. For negative polarity it can be as low as 50 Hz provided the phosphors are of medium persistence (that is, provided they retain their brightness for a reasonably long time). For low persistence phosphors (those which fade quickly), the refresh rate should not be below 60 Hz. Most standard VDUs in Britain have medium persistence phosphors and a refresh rate of 50 Hz, which is the same frequency as mains electricity here.

△ Screens should not be placed where they are peripherally visible to VDU workers at other workstations, since flicker is much more noticeable at oblique angles.

△ Operators should be able to choose the colour combination they find most comfortable on monochrome VDUs. Green, yellow and orange are generally the most liked when negative polarity is used. The use of colour filters to change the colour of the display tends to make it harder to read. With colour displays, no more than six different colours should be used and no two colours should be of the same luminance.

Screens should be large enough to allow up to 30 lines of text to be displayed legibly at a comfortable distance from the viewer. When more than 30 lines are required, for instance when sub-editors need to see a lot of text in order to design a whole page, then extra large screens will be required.

△ The height of capital letters (without accents) displayed on the screen should be between 3 mm and 4.5 mm, at a viewing distance of 50 cm. Larger character sizes may be necessary if the viewing distance is greater than this. The width of characters should be approximately 75 per cent of the height and the stroke width (the width of the lines or rows of dots which make up the letters) should be approximately 15 per cent of the height.

△ Space between characters should be between 20 per cent and 50 per cent of the width and space between lines of text should be between 50 per cent and 150 per cent of the character height.

△ The dot matrix – the number of dots used to make up a character – should be at least 7 x 9. This means that a capital letter should be 7 dots high. The extra two dots allowed for in the height of the matrix are for the 'tails' of letters like p, g and y which descend below the line.

A dot matrix of 9 x 11 is even better. However, above this number there does not seem to be much improvement in legibility. Dots should be square in shape and as close to each other as possible, with as little blur as possible around the edges.

'Stroke-written' characters are preferable to those dot-matrix ones where the dots are visible or 'in-raster' characters.

Even when all these criteria are met, there is still a considerable variation in the look of differently designed screen displays and fonts (fonts are the designs of individual letters, known in the printing industry as typefaces), and in how easy they are to read. The final choice can best be made by trying them out and seeing which is the easiest to decipher. Particular attention should be given to the characters which can easily be mistaken for each other, for instance the number 1 and the letter I, the capital letters U and V, the capital letter O and the number 0, the number 5 and the capital letter S and so on.

△ To guard against the danger of implosion, the VDU should be equipped with a rim guard which exerts inward pressure on the screen and an implosion shield.

Screen shields and filters

It is sometimes recommended that anti-glare shields should be attached to the front of VDU screens to cut down on glare, although there is some dispute about their effectiveness. These shields can be curved, following the shape of the screen, or flat, and come in several different types: circular polarisers with a reflective coating, neutral density filters, notch or colour filters and directional filters. All have the effect of cutting down the brightness of the display – which means that it has to be turned up higher, thus speeding up the ageing of the CRT and increasing some hazards.

A useful side-effect of many of these shields is that they cut down the emissions of static electricity from the screen. Some also increase the contrast. Flat shields are more effective in reducing distracting reflections on the screen, simply because they can only reflect from one direction, while a curved screen is picking up reflections from a wide range of different angles. However a flat screen can distort the image, making it harder to read anything near one of the edges of the screen. Tests done in the United States comparing the effectiveness of seven different types of shield produced inconclusive findings, showing that there were wide variations depending on the brightness of the room and a number of other changeable conditions[131].

The Labour Research Department recommends that shields should be used only when all other means of reducing glare have been exhausted.

As with so many other aspects of VDU design, probably the most effective way to evaluate the usefulness of these shields for your workplace would be to persuade your management to purchase several different types and try them out on the spot, bearing in mind that some people have reported a temporary improvement, as perceived by the operators, which quickly wears off as they become used to the shields. This implies that the trials should last for several weeks before a final decision is reached. Do not expect miracles. No shield can do anything to moderate direct glare from a window or light bulb directly reflected in the screen. All it can do is cut down on diffuse glare.

A good-quality polaroid glass shield will cost about £150, compared with under £20 for some plastic shields. Some addresses of anti-glare shield suppliers are listed on page 204 of this book.

In a slightly different category comes the conductive micromesh filter. Although many of these do help to cut down on glare, several of these filters were originally designed to drain off static electrical charges. However, they may also be effective in preventing emission of ELF and VLF radiation. In Canada, Radiation Environmental Management Systems Incorporated tested three types of conductive mesh filters for radio frequency attenuation effectiveness. The tests showed that two of the filters were able to stop a 17 kHz pulsed field (of the type emitted from some VDUs and causing concern as a possible cause of birth abnormalities) from 50 to 100 times the original unshielded level of 300 V/m. A mesh filter with conductive paint around the frame reduced a screen emission from 300 V/m to 3 V/m, while a filter with a copper tape around the frame reduced this emission to 6 V/m. The least effective filter, which had a clear adhesive around the frame, reduced this emission to 24 V/m[132]. It should be noted, however, that these shields do little to block magnetic field emissions.

Bob DeMatteo, the Canadian union official who has done most to publicise the radiation hazards of VDUs, estimates that about one VDU in three emits sufficiently high VLF fields to warrant shielding in this way. However VDU workers concerned about the effects of static electricity might want to shield their machines even if VLF emissions are low. The shields are only effective if they are properly earthed. It is important when choosing one to ensure too that it does not reduce visibility or attract dust and that it is washable or removable for cleaning. DeMatteo recommends that curved shields which fit the contours of the existing screen should be chosen.

A few VDUs come with these shields fitted as standard accessories.

As far as radiation is concerned, even more important than shielding the face of a VDU screen is shielding the rear portion of the VDU, particularly the area around the flyback transformer. Padding it to muffle ultrasound emissions has already been mentioned. According to DeMatteo[133], there are also occasions when it should be completely encased in earthed copper foil, metallised cloth or nickel-based acrylic paint to prevent the emission of radio waves or static fields.

Such shielding was originally adopted for reasons quite unconnected with the health and safety of VDU workers. It was discovered in the United States that there was widespread interference to communications systems being caused by emissions from VDUs. Where banks of VDUs were being used in military applications this interference could actually cause electronically controlled weapons to be triggered by accident. Databases of politically sensitive information had also become vulnerable to electronic surveillance and espionage. Shielding thus became standard for military usage quite early on in the history of VDUs.

By 1979, new regulations made it necessary for American manufacturers to tighten up their designs to limit radio frequency emissions from all VDUs. Most recent models therefore do not require shielding in this way. DeMatteo, in his book, *Terminal Shock*, gives clear step-by-step do-it-yourself instructions for three different methods of shielding the rear and sides of a VDU.

He also gives details of how VDUs should be tested to determine the levels of radiation emitted, and therefore whether the shielding is likely to be necessary. Details of how to get access to testing equipment are given on page 205 of this book.

Other factors

In addition to screens and keyboards, many office workstations now house a range of other communications equipment and computer accessories such as disc drives, fancy telephones with mini-switchboards and built-in memories, audio playback equipment, modems, printers of various types, telex and telefax terminals.

The smaller your workplace, the more likely you are to have to operate several of these as well as your VDU. You therefore need a workstation designed to accommodate them.

There is such a variety of models on the market, and the rate of change is so rapid, that it is impossible to list all the variables here.

There are however certain basic principles which might be helpful in negotiations over their introduction:

Job design

Make sure that operators' jobs are designed so that the need to switch from one machine to another does not become stressful. For instance, having to deal with in-coming telephone calls or telex messages can make it difficult to concentrate on other tasks. On the other hand, in some jobs they can provide welcome relief. See chapter 13 (pages 125 to 140) for more information about job design.

Noise

Check out all equipment for noise. This includes the audible feedback from keyboards, the ringing tones of telephones and the cooling fans from disc drives as well as the more obvious clatter from letter-quality printers. In the case of printers, if it is impossible to locate it away from your workstation, it may be worth considering substituting a dot-matrix printer, which is likely to be much quieter, even though this may mean a less legible final product. Acoustic hoods are a great help in cutting down excess noise from printers, but even they cannot guarantee complete silence. More information about controlling noise hazards can be found on pages 155 to 156.

Electrical safety

Ensure that all equipment is designed with electrical safety in mind, properly earthed and with cables ducted so they cannot trail dangerously across any space where people move.

Size and position

Whenever any new piece of equipment is proposed, find out its dimensions and make sure that there is enough space available, in the right place, to accommodate it without crowding the operator or creating clutter.

If the operator is going to be obliged to turn from one piece of equipment to another, then *all* must be either extremely easy to reposition on the desk or positioned so that they can be operated comfortably. Occasionally, an operator is expected to work with more than one screen, with desks arranged in an L formation. In such a case, both must be arranged so that there is no glare and there is sufficient legroom, space to position a document holder correctly and so on. More commonly, a VDU worker might have to turn frequently between disc drive, disc storage area, keyboard, printer, notepad and telephone. Arranging all of these so that access is easy, without undue twisting, stretching or craning can be quite difficult. If another item, such as a switchboard or telex terminal, is added then the problem becomes really complex.

Heat

All electrical equipment generates a certain amount of heat. Find out how much is likely to be produced and make sure that your air conditioning and ventilation can cope. You should base your calculation on what might happen if everything were turned on at once for several hours on a hot day.

Performance

Make sure that the equipment actually does the job it is intended for. Machine breakdowns or errors are one of the greatest sources of stress for office workers. Inferior quality products can also sometimes damage health, for instance poor-quality dot matrix printers may produce documents which are so difficult to proof-read that they stress your eye muscles.

Software design

Although they do not always act on it, most employers and trade unionists are now aware that it is important to ensure that the hardware used by VDU workers is designed to minimise health hazards. Less well known is the contribution that software design can make to reducing, or increasing stress.

There is such an enormous variety of software in use, in such a diversity of applications, that it would be impracticable to attempt an exhaustive set of guidelines for negotiators. What follows is a summary of some of the main points to look out for, which should be used in combination with a detailed examination of the software your employer is proposing to adopt and practical try-outs by the workers who will be expected to use it.

In general, the software should not include a capability of monitoring workers' performance either individually or collectively. Where some element of monitoring is unavoidable, then the parameters should be decided in negotiation with the union and strict rules drawn up about how the results can be used and who has access to them. This may involve revising your grievance and disciplinary procedures to ensure that computer-collected data cannot be used to dismiss someone.

△ No VDU-based system should be used to collect or store individually identifiable data on arrival and departure times, work breaks, keyboard speeds, error corrections made or other performance-related data. No individually identifiable data of any type should be collected unless the prior agreement of the union representatives is reached on the prinicple of collecting it and on the type of data collected and the use to which it is to be put.

△ Any information collected by these means should be made available to the employee concerned as well as to his or her union or works council representatives. Agreements should include provision for the erasure of all personal information collected after a period of time to be jointly agreed by the employer and union representatives.

Software should not be designed so that it gives management new access to individual workers' skills or knowledge, thus making them more dispensible and making it easy for substitute labour to be introduced, for instance when industrial action is taken.

The Canadian Telecommunications Workers Union managed to get an agreement with British Columbia Telephone which limited management use of VDUs by assigning managers passwords which gave them access only to computer applications consistent with management tasks. This prevented executives from carrying out work normally done by the union's members[134].

△ No VDU operator should be paid wholly or partly by means of incentive payment schemes based on keystroking or error-free operation. Such schemes encourage excessive work speeds with greatly increased stress on the workers involved, For the same reasons keyboard speed competitions with prizes should not be permitted.

The software should be designed to avoid long or unpredictable delays, for instance when searching databases or retrieving files. Study after study has shown that one of the greatest causes of stress among VDU workers is being forced to wait, eyes on the screen and fingers poised for action, without knowing exactly when the required information will appear. It is, however, equally stressful to have prompts which appear so fast that they result in a speed-up of work outside the operator's control. All VDU workers should be in control of their own pace of work.

△ A maximum response time of 3-5 seconds is recommended.

Menus and other displays should be clearly legible and unambiguous, displayed near the centre of the screen and with sufficient space between lines to distinguish them easily. Where colour is used, the different colours should be limited to the number which genuinely makes it easier to understand the display. Colour which is added purely for decoration can cause confusion and therefore increase the stress on the operator. The language used should be as simple, self-explanatory and jargon-free as possible.

Error messages should be friendly and avoid suggesting that the operator is stupid or incompetent. Any potentially 'fatal' error should be preceded by a clear warning of what might happen.

The software should be well documented with an easy-to-follow training package.

All software should be appropriate both for the job it is intended for and for the level of training and ability of the operators.

– 17 –

VDU workers' rights

The four previous chapters have dealt with staffing levels and the design of jobs, of the working environment and of the hardware and software used by VDU workers. These are all important for preventing VDU hazards, but no health and safety policy is complete unless it also considers the workers themselves, and their individual rights to such things as training, time away from the screen and regular health checks. This chapter covers the rights of VDU workers which can be covered in a new technology agreement. Legal rights are discussed in the next chapter. As in previous chapters, recommendations which are made by the Trades Union Congress are marked with a triangle ($\triangle$).

Training

All too often, when new technology is introduced, the training is limited to a few hours snatched between other tasks and consists of self-training from a manual or training disc provided by the software supplier, perhaps supported by a short demonstration by the company's sales representative. In fact, of course, a much wider range of training is required. The TUC recommends the following:

$\triangle$ Employers should, under conditions negotiated with the union, provide finance and give time off for adequate training for employees involved in work with VDUs. Such training should include:

a) an overall appreciation of the system of which the VDU forms a part

b) phased training over an extended period of time in system principles and operation techniques, including training away from the workplace at least in the initial stages

c) general principles of ergonomics including the optimum adjustment of furniture, screen, keyboard, lighting etc.

d) skill development training to enable workers to benefit from enhanced job design

e) trade union training

f) training for workers and union representatives in the early identification of health problems and the development of health and safety programmes

g) training for managers in ergonomic and health and safety principles so as to enable them to better implement the standards established by the regulations and/or collective agreements

h) continuous retraining for older workers whose jobs are affected by technological change

To these, we would add:

i) equal opportunities training for managers to ensure that they do not consciously or unconsciously discriminate against disadvantaged groups when redesigning jobs or selecting workers to fill the redesigned posts

j) skills training for women, Black workers and people with disabilities to help them enter types of work from which they have been traditionally excluded but which may have been potentially opened up to them by the development of new technology, and assertiveness training to help them build up the confidence to develop their careers

k) training for managers in the types of aids which are available to enable people with disabilities to carry out information processing tasks

l) training for the colleagues of workers with disabilities to enable them to understand their special needs and communicate effectively with them e.g. training in the use of specially adapted keyboards or in sign language

m) the creation of training placements for the young unemployed, for women who have been out of the workforce caring for their families and who wish to return, and for people with disabilities, to give them access to VDU skills

n) the provision of extended study leave for workers who wish to transfer away from VDU work or develop new skills or knowledge

o) the provision of career counselling for workers whose jobs have become dead-end as the result of the introduction of new technology

Screen contact time

As already noted in chapter 13, when discussing job design, if stress is to be avoided it is essential that continuous time spent working at the screen is minimised.

△ As a general principle, intensive VDU work should be limited to 50 per cent of the working day.

Trade unions have succeeded in a number of workplaces in negotiating a top limit of four hours per day for continuous VDU work, and, according to a survey carried out in 1985 by the Labour Research Department[135], some have even bettered this, with reports from three workplaces of a three-hour maximum and another three of a two-hour limit.

Where such agreements exist it is important that they do not become a pretext for management to convert full-time jobs into part-time ones. Expressing the number of hours as a percentage of the working day is one way of avoiding this. Despite the existence of some extremely good trade union agreements, the majority of workers engaged in concentrated VDU work still spend considerably more than half their working lives at a screen. What it is possible to negotiate will depend on the tradition in your industry and the strength of your union organisation. Do not be discouraged if you can only negotiate a much more modest reduction. Every little helps, and your members will be grateful for any improvement. Besides, you may be able to achieve a little more next year and slowly work towards a healthier working pattern in the future.

As well as limiting the total number of VDU contact hours it is also advisable for operators to take frequent rest breaks. Here again, there is great variety in the agreements which have been negotiated by trade unions around the country. The Labour Research Department survey found some agreements where rests were taken for 10 minutes in every hour, for 20 minutes in every two hours, for 15 minutes in every hour and – the best agreement in this respect – for 15 minutes in every 45 as well as many examples where rest breaks were shorter or less frequent.

△ The TUC recommends breaks of 15 minutes per hour of intensive VDU work and 15 minutes every two hours for less intensive work. However these breaks should be more frequent if the job or workstation design is below ergonomic standards in other respects. A break which is shorter than 15 minutes does not allow enough time for the eye muscles to recover from the visual effort of reading the screen.

There are two difficulties involved in working out the best ways for VDU operators to take their breaks. One is allowing for the extremely wide variation in tasks carried out at VDUs and the differing personal needs of their operators, and the other is ensuring that breaks will actually be taken at the specified intervals. The two problems are in practice closely connected.

To have a system controlled by supervisors, on the 'Right, everybody stop work now' model creates a situation which does not allow for individual variations, which may be inconvenient from the point of view of the task in hand and which is likely to be resented by the VDU workers themselves who would prefer more control over their working rhythms. On the other hand to leave it up to operators to determine their own breaks often leads to a situation where the breaks are not taken at all. There are many reasons for this, including the general pressure of work, fear of falling short of productivity targets, fear of being seen as a skiver and lack of anything else to do or anywhere else to go during break periods.

Many VDU workers will testify to the compulsive nature of some aspects of the work. Software is often designed in a way which eliminates the natural breaks offered by most traditional tasks, perhaps at the end of a page, or a batch of orders. It usually has the effect of taking the user automatically onto the next stage after the completion of each task, by presenting a screen which seems to say 'What next?'.

VDU workers also frequently become so tense and hyped up that it is difficult to force themselves to relax and do nothing for a while, particularly if they are women whose non-working hours are taken up with a frenetic round of household tasks. As one word processor operator working in a large pool told us:

> 'We're told to take 10 minutes break every hour, but I can't stand sitting there at my desk doing nothing, knowing there's work to be done and seeing the others hard at it. Sometimes you have to stop keying while there's a document being printed and I nearly go mad waiting for it to finish. I know it's destroying my health, but I just can't seem to stop myself.'[136]

A different sort of pressure arises where one VDU has to be shared by several workers and taking a break involves having to rejoin the queue at the back to regain one's place. Other workers find that they are penalised financially if they take their breaks because they are paid by results.

Avoiding problems like these involves implementing a package of measures of which the actual agreed length and frequency of breaks is only one component.

Ideally, jobs should be designed so that the breaks occur naturally because of the mix of different tasks involved. Failing this, there are several measures which should be adopted to ensure adequate rest:

▲ No VDU operator should be paid by results (see also the section on software design on pages 171 – 173).

▲ No individual's workload should be so heavy that targets will not be met if rests are taken (see section on staffing levels on pages 141 – 147).

▲ A separate area should be provided away from the screen for breaks to be taken. If the jobs are well designed with less than 50 per cent screen work, then this can be another work area where different tasks are carried out. If operators are spending more than half their time at the screen and engaged in intensive VDU work, then these should be rest areas, equipped with comfortable chairs, decorated in soothing colours and with long vistas to look at to assist with defocusing the eyes. Drink-making facilities and potted plants are an advantage.

▲ Where operators are expected to do other work during their breaks from the screen then this should not be intensive visual work, such as proof-reading.

▲ Where operators are taking breaks which involve complete rest then they should be permitted to take them in groups, rather than individually, to replace some of the social contact which VDU work removes from everyday office life, and to allow the social interaction to assist relaxation. If entirely alone, many VDU workers will, out of boredom, spend their time reading or watching television, in effect replacing one intensive visual activity with another.

▲ All VDU operators should receive training to give them an understanding of the health hazards of prolonged screen work and the principles lying behind the agreement on rest breaks. They should be taught to take their breaks *before* any adverse health effects are felt. Waiting until you already have aching wrists, a headache or trouble in focusing is leaving it too late. Once things have reached this stage you will need more than a short break to put things right. Indeed, in the case of some strain injuries, permanent damage may already have been done.

▲ All VDU workers should not only be clearly informed of their rights to take breaks but should also be continually reminded of them. Posters on the wall or cards or stickers on individual workstations are ways of doing this.

▲ It should be a serious disciplinary offence for a supervisor to discourage VDU operators from taking the breaks to which they are entitled.

If all these recommendations are put into effect, and an atmosphere created in the workplace in which the taking of breaks is positively encouraged as sensible behaviour, not just reluctantly tolerated or, worse, actively discouraged, then it should be possible to implement a system in most workplaces in which the timing of breaks can be left up to the operators themselves, thus enhancing their control over their work.

Health and safety monitoring

However well designed you think your workplace environment is, and however carefully selected the equipment, the only way you can be sure that health hazards do not exist is by monitoring the health of the workforce. Some information about conducting a health and safety survey of VDU workers has already been given on pages 114 – 117. A one-off preliminary survey is certainly extremely useful. However it needs to be followed up periodically either by further surveys or by good information systems which will ensure that improvements can be monitored and any new hazards are brought to light.

All VDU workers should be made aware of the importance of health monitoring, and encouraged to report any symptoms they experience to their safety rep. Short questionnaires or checklists can be designed for the purpose if necessary.

In addition, union representatives should have full access to staff medical and absence records (to ensure confidentiality, this can be provided as a summary of the statistics for each department or occupational group without any individual names being mentioned).

Trade union safety representatives should not be hindered from taking up their legal rights to paid time off and the appropriate facilities to attend and run training courses and to carry out regular surveys.

△ At the commencement of the job and at annual intervals thereafter, all VDU workers should be given a thorough eye examination by a qualified ophthalmologist. In addition, more regular eye tests may be given at the workplace by people qualified to operate eye testing equipment.

△ At a minimum, such tests should include:

near visual acuity

distance visual acuity

colour vision

oculomotor coordination

a slit lamp ocular examination of the lens and retina to detect cataracts and other defects

△ The employees concerned, their doctors and their union representatives should receive a copy of the results. Any employee who complains of eyesight problems should be referred for an additional examination. Any costs associated with these examinations should be borne by the employer.

Where workers prefer to consult their own ophthalmologist or need to visit an optician, then they should be given paid time off to do so.

All VDU operators required to work regularly from dictation on audio tapes or from information supplied by telephone should similarly be given audiometric hearing tests at the commencement of their employment and annually thereafter. Tests should be done at the beginning of a working week or immediately after a holiday, *before* the worker has been exposed to any sound which could cause temporary hearing impairment.

Because audiometric tests are not always accurate, especially if the person is tense, workers should be tested several times in succession. Audiometers used for testing hearing should be regularly checked to ensure that the calibration is accurate.

Copies of the audiograms, the results of these hearing tests, should be given to the workers concerned, their trade union representatives and, where necessary, their doctors.

△ Vision and hearing tests should not under any circumstances be used to screen workers out of a job.

If any workers are found to be suffering from visual defects which make VDU work unsuitable, then they should be found other jobs within the organisation with no loss of salary, grade, seniority or responsibility.

Similarly, if there is a hearing defect, the worker concerned should be given alternative employment which does not involve intensive listening, on the same conditions.

Adapting the worker

One of the themes which runs through this book is that with VDU work, as with other types of job, the way to ensure safety is not to adapt the worker but to adapt the job. In our experience, where there is a will there is nearly always a way to achieve this, avoiding the unpleasant and potentially dangerous consequences of a policy which seeks to adapt workers to a hazardous environment by swathing them in protective clothing or relying on other shielding devices.

One partial exception to this is the prescription of special lenses for VDU workers who wear spectacles. It is believed by some that 'VDU glasses' are a universal solution to the eye problems caused by VDU work. This is complete nonsense. There is no such thing as a pair of 'VDU glasses' and the tinted lenses which many VDU workers are advised to wear are positively dangerous because they cut down on visibility, causing extra eyestrain, and encourage operators to turn the brightness and contrast controls higher than they need be.

Anything wrong with the brightness, contrast or colour of the display on a VDU should be dealt with by adjusting the set, not the worker's eyes. However it may well be that a VDU operator is already suffering from a slight visual defect, unnoticed before she or he began to work with a screen, which requires correction to make it possible to work without strain. Again, some VDU operators may already be wearing spectacles with lenses, such as bifocal lenses, which are unsuitable for VDU use because they force the worker to adopt an unsuitable posture in order to see the screen through the right part of the lens. In other cases, contact lens wearers may find that their eyes become dry and irritated during VDU use, so they would prefer to wear spectacles when at work. In these and other instances, it is important that the correct lenses are prescribed and worn for VDU work.

△ In such cases, the cost of any visual correction which is necessary in order to work on VDUs should be borne by the employer. This is particularly important where existing spectacles are unsuitable for viewing at a typical VDU viewing distance of 50-60cm.

Some employers are prepared to pay for lenses but not for frames in these circumstances. This is, of course, better than nothing but strikes us as mean and petty. Several trade unions have already successfully negotiated agreements in which the total cost of visual correction is paid for by the employer and there seems no reason why others could not do so as well.

Other forms of correction or protection for the VDU operator are more contentious. Some manufacturers have cashed in on the fears of pregnant VDU operators for the safety of their unborn children and produced protective aprons or pinafores, some of which contain lead or nickel, to guard against radiation. There is no evidence that these do any good and some that they can actually do the opposite, because their weight may force the operator to adopt an unsuitable posture. Lead is also a substance which can cause harm to both mother and foetus. We do not recommend the use of these aprons.

Alternative work for would-be parents

△ Until more research has been done on the effects of prolonged exposure to VDUs on conception, pregnancy and foetal development, it is advisable to ensure that your new technology agreement gives would-be parents the option of working in a non-VDU environment while they are trying to conceive or are pregnant. This transfer should take place without loss of pay, status or career prospects and should apply to men trying to become fathers as well as women trying to become mothers. Wording which would cover this eventuality has already been negotiated in the United States, in an agreement made in New York in February 1983 between the Newspaper Guild of America and Time inc, publishers of *Time* and many other magazines[137].

Provided the alternative work does not itself entail other hazards to the survival or health of the unborn child, such a switch of employment should be effective regardless of whether the hazard to pregnancy turns out to be radiation, static electricity, stress, poor posture or some combination of these.

– 18 –

VDU workers and the law

British law offers no specific protection to VDU workers. However they are covered in a general way by the provisions of the Health and Safety at Work Act 1974 which places a statutory duty on employers to ensure the health and safety of their employees at work as far as is reasonably practicable.

This act, together with the Safety Representatives and Safety Committees Regulations 1977 also gives workers a number of specific rights:

To elect trade union safety representatives

In any workplace with more than two employees, where a union is recognised, the workers can appoint as many safety representatives as they like to represent their interests on health and safety issues.

To carry out inspections

Safety representatives have the right to inspect the workplace at least once every three months and more often by negotiation or if there is a change in working conditions (such as the introduction of new equipment or working methods), a notifiable accident, disease or dangerous occurrence or new official information about a hazard. If management agrees, they can call in independent technical advisers.

To investigate

There is also a right to investigate hazards between formal inspections.

To obtain information

Management must make available to safety representatives information about health hazards or potential health hazards at the workplace. The Health and Safety Executive and local authority

Environmental Health Officers are also required to make certain information available to safety representatives.

To time off

Safety representatives have the right to carry out their trade union business during working hours without loss of pay.

To training

They also have the right to attend health and safety training courses during working hours without loss of pay. Details of the TUC's 10-day courses for safety representatives can be obtained by writing to the TUC at Congress House, Great Russell Street, London WCl.

To facilities

The employer must provide adequate facilities for safety representatives to function effectively. These might include meeting rooms, office equipment including a desk, a typewriter or word processor and a lockable filing cabinet, use of noticeboards and access to a photocopier and a private telephone.

To call in a health and safety inspector

Where workers believe there is a health hazard or need information, they have the right to call in an inspector from the Health and Safety Executive or from the local authority's environmental health department to make an investigation on their behalf and, if necessary, instruct their employer to make changes.

Some VDU workers have successfully used the existence of the legislation as a tactic in organising action to obtain a safer VDU environment at work. We have already described on page 122 how, as part of their campaign for a new technology agreement, NALGO members in Strathclyde reported for work each morning but refused to sit at their desks, on the grounds that their management was failing in its legal obligation to provide them with a safe workplace.

At Morrison's supermarket in Leeds, a group of workers who developed strain injuries called in the environmental health officer who instructed their employer to make substantial changes to reduce the risk of further injury.

Generally speaking, however, it is a mistake to place too much reliance on the Health and Safety Executive as a source of support for VDU workers. The Executive's published guidelines on VDUs[138] are very complacent about many VDU hazards, including stress and reproductive hazards. The document does, however, lay down useful guidelines on the design of equipment and workstations to minimise problems of vision and posture, and recommends varied job design and frequent rest breaks for VDU operators. This provides some good arguments for negotiators and could perhaps become a means of bringing some of the more obstinate employers to heel.

The Health and Safety Executive's leaflets aimed at VDU workers themselves are not to be recommended. They are extremely patronising, adopting a reassuring tone which has the effect of making operators feel that any health problems they suffer are more likely to be the result of their own neurosis than of hazardous working conditions.

There are other ways in which the law can sometimes be used by VDU workers. However these are not ways to *prevent* damage being done to their health and safety, but ways of getting some redress *after* damage or injustice has already been done.

The first of these concerns the situation where VDU workers are dismissed for insisting on protecting their own health or that of their unborn children. There have now been two cases of the kind in Britain. The first, described in greater detail on page 73, concerned Hazel Johnston, a library assistant who was found by an industrial tribunal in September 1984 to have been unfairly dismissed by Inverness Highland Regional Council for asking to be transferred to other work when she was pregnant. Interestingly enough, the Council had been advised by the Employment Medical Advisory Service, a branch of the Health and Safety Executive, that there was no risk to the foetus. To collect evidence in support of her case, which rested on the argument that her fears were justified, Ms Johnston carried out a considerable amount of research in local libraries to establish that there was a body of literature which suggested that VDUs might be hazardous to the foetus[139].

In the second case, Lesley Bradley, a secretary with Addleshaw Sons and Hatham, a Manchester firm of solicitors, was dismissed when she asked for rest breaks from her VDU after suffering two miscarriages when operating it without a break for up to seven hours at a stretch. Her employers, who admitted unfair dismissal, were ordered by an industrial tribunal in March 1986 to reinstate her and pay her salary for the period since her dismissal[140].

These precedents are useful ones, which might be worth following if you or one of your members has been dismissed and it has proved impossible to gain reinstatment by straightforward collective bargaining methods. It is worth emphasising, however, that the use of the law in such situations should be regarded as a last resort. Going to a tribunal can be an extremely upsetting and stressful experience for the worker concerned, as well as being time-consuming and inconvenient, all problems which are multiplied if she is pregnant or has recently given birth. Tribunals are also uncertain, in that you can never be sure of winning, or that the tribunal's decision may not be overturned at appeal. It helps to be a trade union member, so you can call on expert advice and support from specialist union officials.

The other way in which the law can be useful to VDU workers is in claiming compensation for industrial injuries. In the United States, a number of VDU-related health compensation claims have been taken through the courts. These include cases of tendinitis, carpal tunnel syndrome, cervicobrachial strain, generalised muscle impairment, visual disorders including cataracts, stress-related psychological damage, general nervous system disorder and a nervous breakdown[141].

There is not such an extensive tradition of suing for compensation in Britain. However some groups of workers have been successful in claiming compensation from their employers after developing tenosynovitis, which is a prescribed industrial disease. In order to do so, they have had to prove that the disease was actually caused by the job and that a 'good employer' would have prevented it. Successful claims include an assembly-line worker at Thorn Electronics in Newhaven who was awarded £11,000, six workers at Dunlop in Barnsley, and four women who received damages ranging from £750 to £4,260 from MK Electrics of St Leonards-on-Sea.

As can be seen, the amounts which can be claimed are not enormous. In a typical tenosynovitis case in 1986, for instance, it was estimated that a five per cent loss of faculty for life would have been worth a once-and-for-all payment of £1,245.

Before embarking on any legal adventures, it is a good idea to seek expert advice. This can be obtained from your trade union, from a local hazards group, trade union resource centre or law centre, from the VDU Workers' Rights Campaign or, failing these, your local Citizens Advice Bureau. Addresses of some of these organisations can be found on pages 206 – 208.

Needless to say, even if you win a compensation claim, it will not bring back your health. The best way to ensure that you stay fit and healthy is to ensure that the injury does not happen in the first place. As in all things, prevention is better than cure, and, in the case of VDU hazards, prevention lies in good design of the job, the environment and the equipment.

Tenosynovitis and 'writer's cramp' (described in greater detail in chapter 7 on pages 52 to 55), are both prescribed diseases, which means that VDU workers who suffer from them are eligible for disablement benefit from 15 weeks after they have been disabled by the disease. The amount of benefit depends on the severity of the disability and the extent to which it prevents you from living a normal life. You cannot claim disablement benefit compensation unless you have at least a 14 per cent degree of disability.

Until recently, the rules which were operated were highly discriminatory against women, requiring them to prove that they could not do housework, whereas men were simply obliged to prove that they could not go out to work. This practice has recently been outlawed by the European Court, and a new benefit was introduced in 1986, with new methods of assessing how serious an injury is considered to be. It remains to be seen whether these will be unbiased against women in practice.

If you want to claim this benefit, it is important that your musculoskeletal problems are diagnosed either as tenosynovitis, bursitis or writer's cramp. Other strain injuries, such as carpal tunnel syndrome or tendinitis, are not eligible. Further information about claiming can be obtained from the leaflet, *Prescribed Industrial Disease*, NI 2, available from your local social security office. Many trade unions, local hazards groups and resource centres also keep copies of this leaflet.

In recent years there have been campaigns in Canada, several states in the United States and some Scandinavian countries to gain greater legal protection for VDU workers. In 1985, a campaign was launched in Britain, co-ordinated by the City Centre, a resource centre for office workers in the City of London. The VDU Workers' Rights Campaign, as it is called, has the support of about 50 MPs and of leading trade unions representing VDU workers including the NCU (National Communications Union), SCPS (Society of Civil and Public Servants), NGA (National Graphical Association), and CPSA (Civil and Public Services Association) as well as a number of other organisations and women's groups concerned for the safety of VDU workers.

The campaign is demanding: an Act of Parliament which will limit the amount of time VDU workers spend at the screen to four hours a day or half of their total working time; safe design of equipment, including the compulsory shielding of VDUs to eliminate all non-visible electro-magnetic radiation; and the right for people plannning to become pregnant to be transferred to other work. The address of the campaign is given on page 208.

Campaigns like this one perform a very valuable function in making people aware of the hazards of VDUs and publicising what can be done to prevent them. If the campaign were successful, and these provisions became the law of the land, then it would undoubtedly become easier for VDU workers, particularly those who are not in trade unions (and therefore have no other way to defend themselves), to win safe working conditions.

However legislation can never provide a complete substitute for trade union organisation. Since the first Factories Acts of the early 19th century, British industrial history has provided many examples of laws designed to protect workers' health and safety. There have also been laws governing such things as the minimum wages which employers can pay in certain industries. But the overwhelming experience of workers has been that these laws are simply not implemented unless there is a powerful workers' organisation prepared to enforce them. In 1985, for instance, over a third (34.6 per cent) of employers visited by wages inspectors were found to be paying below the minimum rates of pay laid down by the Wages Councils[142].

In the past few years we have seen a steady erosion of existing rights, with some abolished altogether, and drastic cutbacks in the numbers of factory and wages inspectors. This makes it more important than ever to ensure that workers' rights are laid out in trade union agreements, with negotiated procedures to make sure that they are implemented.

– 19 –

Conclusion

After reading through the first draft of this book, one of the workers at the London Hazards Centre commented, 'It's rather depressing, isn't it? Haven't you got anything positive to say about the new technology?'. The simple answer to this question is that hazards are by definition negative, and any book which focuses on the hazards of VDUs is bound to bring out all their worst features while ignoring any benefits they might bring.

There is, however, a more profound aspect to it. Critics of new technology, or indeed of any aspect of modern science, are frequently presented as naive romantics, hankering for some lost golden age when everything was 'natural' and work was unalienated, carried out by dedicated craftspeople, perhaps to the leisurely strains of a rustic worksong. Forced onto the defensive when new and potentially dangerous techniques and practices are brought in, they become cast in the role of Luddites or conservative defenders of the status quo, and are rarely able to develop radical, positive alternative programmes which look forward to the future.

This view is, of course, a distortion which serves only the interests of those who want to bring in new technologies regardless of the social cost. Nevertheless, some of the mud usually sticks, often fast enough to become a real deterrent to taking action over the negative features of new technology.

VDU workers must remind themselves that to be critical of some aspects of new technology is not necessarily to be against progress. Indeed, those who are most aware of present-day work hazards are often also those who know most about the horrors which workers have had to face in the past and are most active in opposing them where they remain.

Nobody with any knowledge of history could seriously advocate a return to the working conditions which prevailed in the 18th and 19th centuries, or even the earlier parts of this one. On the contrary, most would complain, not that things have changed but that they haven't changed enough. The differences of opinion emerge only when there is an attempt to define exactly what these new changes should consist of.

In analysing the effects of new technology, it is tempting to divide the world into 'pessimists' and 'optimists' and the various features of the technology into 'good' or 'bad' ones. This approach is in fact one of the central obstacles to producing a useful strategy for the future, since it ignores the questions 'good for whom?' or 'bad for whom?'. A more useful approach is to recognise that many of the effects of new technology are in fact *contradictory*, that is, they are capable simultaneously of bringing benefits to some, and disadvantages to others. Some are even capable of producing both positive and negative effects on the same person.

We must remember too that these effects are being superimposed onto a status quo which itself has both positive and negative features.

To take one example, the status quo for many office workers is that they are required to work in city centres, in a polluted landscape dominated by skyscrapers where the sun rarely reaches the pavements and all other forms of life have been driven out. Apart from a few stationers, sandwich bars and pubs, the streets are devoid of services, and of children, old people, people with disabilities, animals or anyone else who is not an able-bodied, employed office worker. To get there, they have to endure hours of travelling in cramped and uncomfortable public transport, or crawling along in traffic jams. They may not see their families for ten or more hours a day and may, in addition, have the worry of knowing that their children are in precarious and inadequate childcare arrangements. Compensating for this, they may enjoy the advantages of working in a 'social office' with a wide range of people to interact with, of being able to arrange lunchtime get-togethers with colleagues working for different employers in the area, of being able to stay on in town after work to enjoy the cultural pleasures of the big city, and of feeling at the centre of things, well placed to pick up gossip and assess the possibilities of new jobs with rival employers.

Onto this scenario comes a technology which is capable of radically reorganising the location of employment. Suddenly, using a remote terminal and telecommunications links, it becomes possible to relocate work out of the city centre, perhaps to a suburb or small town, perhaps to individual workers' homes. Is this a positive or a negative development? Surely the answer must be that it depends. It depends on who you are and what your personal needs are, on where you live, and where you'd like to live, and on what the employer is proposing.

If you are a parent living in a small town outside the city, you might welcome the chance to work locally, somewhere near the schools and shops. If you are a childless culture-vulture living in the inner city, you would probably thoroughly resent such a change. If you are a confident professional, living in a collective household with plenty of adult company during the day, you might delight in the opportunity to work at home; if you are a low-paid single parent trapped in a small flat, it might be your idea of purgatory.

The great advantage of the new technology in this context, surely, is that it potentially allows for a much greater degree of choice in the location of work than has been possible in the past. However this is only an advantage to those who are in a position to exercise that choice. If someone else's choice is imposed on you against your will, then this advantage quickly becomes its opposite, a disadvantage which could bring about something considerably worse than the status quo, by scattering workers away from the centres where at the very least they have each other's company, and the possibility of organising together to defend their interests.

To take another example, the new technology makes it possible to store and quickly retrieve vast amounts of information in central data banks. This could be seen as positive, enabling everyone to have access to much more information than would have been conceivable in the past and, because knowledge is power, strengthening democracy and creating an articulate and well-informed population capable of demanding its rights much more effectively than at present. However if the information flow is imagined to run in the opposite direction, we can conceive of an equally plausible scenario where democracy is eroded, with a hierarchical central state apparatus capable of a degree of control which up to now has only existed in the books of writers like George Orwell, a control which is made possible by the central collection and correlation of detailed information on every aspect of people's lives. This second vision is as frightening as the first is attractive.

Such examples could be multiplied. In each case there are positive and negative features, and in each case these vary depending on who you are. There is, however, one feature they all share. In each case, the crucial determinant, the factor which decides who benefits and who stands to lose, is the same: it is control. To use a well-worn analogy, the new technology is like a car. If you are in the driver's seat, the chances are it is taking you where you want to go. If you are a pedestrian, it is simply a threat.

The greater the control you have over any feature of the technology, the greater the range of choices available to you and the more likely it is to enhance your life. If you are in control of your job, and have a computer to help you, it can relieve you of drudgery, improve the quality of the services you can provide, increase your accuracy, enable you to communicate more effectively and shorten your working day. If you are not in control, it can become an alien, threatening force, bringing compulsory speed-up, insecurity, stress, the atrophy of your skills and the health hazards this book has discussed. The difference lies not in the technology itself but in your relationship to it.

The tragedy in Britain today is not that new technology is being brought in, but that so few people have control over their jobs. This fact has itself influenced the design of the technology, creating a vicious circle in which employers who want more control over their workforce order machines which will give it to them, creating a situation where it is difficult to find equipment which can be used in a worker-centred way, and thus depriving workers of the chance to demonstrate how things could be done differently.

VDU workers are at the sharp end of this development, the guinea pigs for the new experiments in working methods. But this can be a source of strength as well as of weakness. It means that we are uniquely placed to develop an alternative vision of how the new technology could be used creatively to improve all our lives in the future. Knowing the worst features of the present systems, we have also caught glimpses of the best and can see their potential.

It is an enormous task, but we can begin now to construct an alternative programme for releasing the liberating potential of the new technology, beginning in our own workplaces, with our own demands. The details will vary according to what type of work we do, but many of the essential features will be the same. Some of the things we should insist on include:

▲ Technology which increases choice, rather than limiting it

▲ Technology which decentralises decision-making rather than centralising it

▲ Technology which is controlled by its users

▲ Technology which enhances skills instead of limiting them

▲ Technology which improves the quality of services to their users, perhaps by improving the quality of information provided or by releasing people to give personal help to the needy

▲ Technology which is accessible to all citizens, not just to those who can afford to pay for it

▲ Technology which improves the quality of life for people with disabilities and helps them to become mobile, to communicate and to become more integrated with the rest of society

▲ Technology which benefits all people in the developing countries as well as the industrialised ones

▲ Technology which is safe to manufacture and to use

▲ Technology which is developed for peace, not destruction

As we develop these and other demands, and their scope broadens, new alliances can be forged with others who share some of the same interests: with people concerned about their children's education for life in a high-tech world, with groups of women, pensioners, Black people and people with disabilities, with consumer groups, civil liberties campaigns and peace groups, with workers in other industries and occupations, here and in the developing world. All these lives are touched by the effects of the new technology, and all stand to gain from bringing it out of the control of transnational companies and warmongering governments and into the control of the people who now experience its worst effects.

References

[1] *Women and Micro-Electronics in Japan*, Committee for the Protection of Women in the Computer World, Japan (1983)

[2] *Condition of the Working Class in England*, Engels F, Penguin Modern Classics (1987)

[3] *The Impact of New Technology on the Working Lives of Women in West Yorkshire*, Leeds Trade Union and Community Resource and Information Centre (1980)

[4] Quoted in *New Technology in Banking and Insurance*, Banking, Insurance and Finance Union (1983)

[5] From the proceedings of a conference on office automation organised by the *Financial Times* (1979), quoted in Huws U, *Your Job in the Eighties*, Pluto Press (1982)

[6] *The New Homeworkers: The Changing Location of White-Collar Work*, Huws U, Low Pay Unit (1984)

[7] **The Runaway Office Jobs**, Huws U, in *International Labour Reports* No 2 (February 1984)

[8] *Jobs for the Girls? The Impact of Automation on Women's Jobs in the Finance Industry*, Banking, Insurance and Finance Union (1985)

[9] *Politics is for People*, Williams S, Penguin Books (1981)

[10] Willis J, Vice-chairman Housing Associations Charitable Trust, in the invitation to the conference, *Planning for Homework*, London (May 1984)

[11] *Videotex: Key to the Wired City*, Aldrich M, Quiller Press (1982)

[12] *The Human Factor in Innovation and Productivity*, Gregory J, Working Women, National Association of Office Workers, Cleveland (1981)

[13] *Keying in to Careers*, Huws U, Phillips E, and Griffiths F, GLC Equal Opportunities Group (1985)

[14] *Information Technology and the New International Division of Labour in Office Services*, Posthuma A C, unpublished MSc dissertation, Science Policy Research Unit, Sussex University (September 1985)

[15] **Le Teletravail**, Clavaud R, in *Telesoft* No 1 (December 1981/January 1982)

[16] *Women and Micro-Electronics in Japan*, Committee for the Protection of Women in the Computer World, Japan (1983)

[17] *Women and Micro-Electronics in Japan*, Committee for the Protection of Women in the Computer World, Japan (1983)

[18] **The Health Hazards of Video Display Terminals**, Bertell R, in *Environmental Health Review*, Canada (March 1982)

[19] *Journalists and the New Technology*, National Union of Journalists (1976)

[20] **Electric Field Exposure of Persons using Video Display Terminals**, Harvey S M, in *Bioelectromagnetics*, Vol 5, No 1 (1984)

[21] *New Technology: A Health and Safety Report*, Association of Professional, Executive, Clerical and Computer Staff, London and Home Counties Area Technology Sub-Committee (1985)

[22] *The State of Knowledge Concerning Radiation from VDTs*, Marha K, Canadian Centre for Occupational Health and Safety (1982)

[23] *Currently at risk* Directed by Richard Belfield for Channel 4 (1982) and *Microwave News* (numerous reports)

[24] **Review of the Soviet Literature**, Byrd E, in *Proceedings of the International Forum on Low-level Radiation*, Ottawa (June 1982)

[25] **VDT Radiation: New Research Suggests Biological Effects Possible**, *VDT News*, Vol 1, No 5 (September/October 1984)

[26] *Health Hazards Assessment of Radiofrequency Electromagnetic Fields Emitted by Video Display Terminals*, Guy B, University of Washington, Seattle, Washington (undated)

[27] *Electromagnetism, Man and the Environment*, Battocletti J H, Environmental Studies Series (eds Rose J and Weidner E W) No 3, Elek Books (1976)

[28] *VDUs: The Shocking Truth*, Cleary, London Ioniser Centre (1985)

[29] *The Ion Effect*, Soyka F and Edmonds A, Bantam Books (1978)

[30] *Video Displays, Work and Vision*, Panel on Impact of Video Viewing on Vision of Workers, National Academy Press, Washington DC (1983)

[31] **VDU operators display health problems**, Evans J, in *Health and Safety at Work* (November 1985)

[32] *Video Displays, Work and Vision*, Panel on Impact of Video Viewing on Vision of Workers, National Academy Press, Washington DC (1983)

[33] Information from users of the London Hazards Centre

[34] *Women and Micro-Electronics in Japan*, Committee for the Protection of Women in the Computer World, Japan (1983)

[35] *Video Displays, Work and Vision*, Panel on Impact of Video Viewing on Vision of Workers, pp154-170, National Academy Press, Washington DC (1983)

[36] *The Hazards of VDUs*, Leeds Trade Union and Community Resource and Information Centre (1985)

[37] **The Hazards of VDUs**, Ontario Public Service Employees Union, Canada, quoted in *New Technology: A Health and Safety Report*, Association of Professional, Executive, Clerical and Computer Staff, London and Home Counties Area Technology Sub-Committee (1985)

[38] **Cataracts and Visual Display Units**, Zaret M M, in *Health Hazards of Visual Display Units?*, ed Pearce B, John Wiley (1984)

[39] *Electromagnetism, Man and the Environment*, Battocletti J H, Environmental Studies Series (eds Rose J and Weidner E W) No 3, Elek Books (1976)

[40] *Visual Display Units*, Health and Safety Executive, HMSO (1983)

[41] *Women and Micro-Electronics in Japan*, Committee for the Protection of Women in the Computer World, Japan (1983)

[42] **Beat Conditions and Tenosynovitis**, Health and Safety Executive Guidance Note MS10 quoted in *Repetition Strain Injuries: Hidden Harm from Overuse*, London Hazards Centre [to be published 1987]

[43] *VDUs, Health and Jobs*, Labour Research Department, LRD Publications (1985)

[44] **Guidelines for the Prevention of Repetitive Strain Injury (RSI)**, Australian Council of Trade Unions, *Health and Safety Bulletin* No 18 (August 1982)

[45] **Guidelines for the Prevention of Repetitive Strain Injury (RSI)**, Australian Council of Trade Unions, *Health and Safety Bulletin* No 18 (August 1982)

[46] *Repetition Strain Injuries: Hidden Harm from Overuse*, London Hazards Centre [to be published 1987]

[47] **Guidelines for the Prevention of Repetitive Strain Injury (RSI)**, Australian Council of Trade Unions, *Health and Safety Bulletin* No 18 (August 1982)

[48] Interview with the author (1986)

[49] Quoted in **Women Suffering RSI: An Examination of the Hidden Relations of Gender, the Labour Process and Medicine**, Meekosha H and Jakubowicz A, a paper presented to the *Behavioural Medicine Conference*, Sydney (16th May 1985)

[50] *New Technology Bulletin* No 3, Civil and Public Services Association, Research Department (September 1984)

[51] *Keying into Careers*, Huws U, Phillips E, Griffiths F, GLC Equal Opportunities Group (1985)

[52] *Information Management*, The Journal of ROCC Computers Limited (Spring/ Summer 1986)

[53] **Batch scores over online**, in *Information Management*, The Journal of ROCC Computers Limited (Autumn 1986)

[54] **An Outbreak of Rosacea-like Skin Rash in VDT Operators**, Stenberg B, Department of Dermatology, University of Umea, quoted in *VDT News*, Vol III, No 4 (July/ August 1986)

[55] **Report of Facial Rashes Among VDU Operators in Norway**, Tjonn H H, in *Health Hazards of VDTs?*, ed Pearce B, John Wiley (1984)

[56] **Facial Particle Exposure in the VDT Environment: The Role of Static Electricity**, Olsen W C, Christian Michaelson Institute, Bergen, quoted in *VDT News*, Vol III, No 4 (July/August 1986)

[57] Quoted in **Video Display Terminals: Health and Safety**, Slesin L and Zybko M, in *Microwave News* (1983), from *International Archives of Occupational and Environmental Health*, Digernes V and Astrup E, Vol 49, p193 (1982)

[58] **Melanoma, Fluorescent Lights and Polychlorinated Biphenyls**, Jenson A A, *Lancet*, Vol II, No 8304, p935 (23rd October 1982)

[59] *VDUs: The Shocking Truth*, Cleary, London Ioniser Centre (1985)

[60] *New Technology: A Health and Safety Report*, Association of Professional, Executive, Clerical and Computer Staff, London and Home Counties Area Technology Sub-committee (1985)

[61] *Health and Safety for White-Collar Workers*, FIET Handbook No 1, International Federation of Commercial, Clerical, Professional and Technical Employees, Geneva (1983)

[62] *Code of Practice for reducing the exposure of employed persons to noise*, Health and Safety Executive, HMSO (1972) [reprinted unchanged 1978]

[63] **Effects of Ultrasound Emissions** in *VDT News*, Vol 1, No 3 (May/June 1984)

[64] Cases 1-8 reported in **Video Display Terminals: Health and Safety**, Slesin L and Zybko M, *Microwave News* (1983)

[65] Cases 9-10 reported in *VDT News*, Vol 1, No 2 (March/April 1984)

[66] *VDT News*, Vol 1, No 3 (May/June 1984)

[67] Cases 12-15 reported in *VDUs, Health and Jobs*, Labour Research Department, LRD Publications (1985)

[68] *VDUs and Pregnancy*, City Centre, London (1985)

[69] **Japanese miscarriages blamed on computer terminals**, *New Scientist* (23rd May 1985)

[70] **Pregnancy Outcome and VDT Work in a Cohort of Insurance Clerks**, Westerholme P and Ericson A, Swedish Confederation of Trade Unions (1986), quoted in *VDT News*, Vol III, No 4 (July/August 1986)

[71] **Birth Defects and Video Display Terminals: A Finnish Case-Referent Study**, Kurrpa K and others, Department of Epidemiology and Biostatistics, Institute of Occupational Health, Helsinki (1986), quoted in *VDT News*, Vol III, No 4 (July/August 1986) and **Birth Defects and Exposure to Video Display Terminals during Pregnancy**, *Scandinavian Journal of Work, Environment, and Health*, Vol II, pp 353-356 (1985)

[72] Cited in *Adverse Pregnancy Outcomes Associated with VDUs: Interpreting the Evidence of Case Clusters*, Roberts R S, Evidence submitted to the Task Force exploring the impact of video display terminals on the health and working conditions of Canadian office workers (1984)

[73] *VDUs, Health and Jobs*, Labour Research Department, LRD Publications, (1985)

[74] *No Immediate Danger: Prognosis for a Radioactive Earth*, Bertell R, The Women's Press (1985)

[75] Cited in *Adverse Pregnancy Outcomes Associated with VDUs: Interpreting the Evidence of Case Clusters*, Roberts R S, Evidence submitted to the Task Force exploring the impact of video display terminals on the health and working conditions of Canadian office workers (1984)

[76] quoted in **Occupational Radiation Exposure of Women Workers** Hunt R V, in *Preventative Medicine* 7, pp294-310 (1978)

[77] Cited in *Adverse Pregnancy Outcomes Associated with VDUs: Interpreting the Evidence of Case Clusters*, Roberts R S, Evidence submitted to the Task Force exploring the impact of video display terminals on the health and working conditions of Canadian office workers (1984)

[78] **A Statistical Comment on the paper by Lee B V and McNamee R, 'Reproduction and Work with Visual Display Units'** [based on the 1982 survey of women data processors at the Department of Employment, Runcorn] SCS Division, HMT (undated)

[79] *Biological Effects and Health Hazards of Microwave Radiation*, ed Czerski P and others, Proceedings of an International Symposium, Warsaw (15-18th October 1973), Polish Medical Publishers, Warsaw

[80] Quoted in *New Technology: A Health and Safety Report*, Association of Professional, Executive, Clerical and Computer Staff, London and Home Counties Area Technology Sub-committee (1985)

[81] **Gonadic Function in Workmen with Longterm Exposure to Microwaves**, Lancranjon I and others, *Health Physics* (1985), quoted in *New Technology: A Health and Safety Report*, Association of Professional, Executive, Clerical and Computer Staff, London and Home Counties Area Technology Sub-committee (1985)

[82] Quoted in *New Technology: A Health and Safety Report*, Association of Professional, Executive, Clerical and Computer Staff, London and Home Counties Area Technology Sub-committee (1985)

[83] Quoted in *Reproductive Hazards of Work*, Fletcher A C, Equal Opportunities Commission (1985)

[84] **Review of the Soviet Literature** Byrd E, in *Proceedings of the International Forum on Low-level Radiation*, Ottawa (June 1982)

[85] **VDT Radiation: New Research Suggests Biological Effects Possible**, *VDT News*, Vol 1, No 5 (September/October 1984)

[86] **VDT Radiation: New Research Suggests Biological Effects Possible**, *VDT News*, Vol 1, No 5 (September/October 1984)

[87] **Miscarriages in Pregnant Women Employed at VDTs and Effects of TV Radiation on Experimental Animals**, Mikolajczyk H and others, quoted in *VDT News*, Vol III, No 2 (March/April 1986) and *VDT News* Vol III, No 4 (July/August 1986)

[88] **Effects of Low Frequency Magnetic Fields on the Development of Chick Embryos**, Juutliainen J and Saali K, Department of Environmental Hygiene, University of Kuopio, Finland, quoted in *VDT News*, Vol III, No 4 (July/August 1986)

[89] **A snoop around the City**, David Allen, *The Guardian* (20th November 1986)

[90] **The Role of Serotonin in Gynaecology and Obstetrics**, Sulman F G, *The Hebrew Pharmacist*, Vol 14 (undated)

[91] **Aeroionotherapy**, Gualterotti R, Carlo Elba Foundation, Milan (1968), quoted in *The Ion Effect*, Soyka F and Edmonds A, Bantam Books (1978)

[92] *New Technology: A Health and Safety Report*, Association of Professional, Executive, Clerical and Computer Staff, London and Home Counties Area Technology Sub-committee (1985)

[93] *Stress at Work*, Transport and General Workers Union, 9/12 Branch (March 1981)

[94] London Hazards Centre records (1986)

[95] *The Penguin Medical Encyclopaedia*, Wingate P, Penguin (1976)

[96] *Super-mind*, Brown B B, Harper and Row (1980)

[97] **Stress Reactions in Computerised Administrative Work**, Johansson G and Aronsson G, Reports from the Department of Psychology, Supplement 50, University of Stockholm (November 1980)

[98] Quoted in *VDT News*, Vol 1, No 5 (September/October 1984)

[99]   Quoted in **Operator Stress: The Impact of Computer Monitoring** in *VDT News*, Vol 1, No 4 (July/August 1984)

[100]   Quoted in *Office Workers' Survival Handbook*, Craig M, BSSRS Publications (1981)

[101]   **Pot Bellies, Video Displays and Heart Disease**, Anderson I, in *New Scientist* (31st January 1985)

[102]   **Social, Psychological and Neuroendocrine Stress Reactions in Highly Mechanised Work**, Johansson G, Aronsson G and Lindstrom B O, in *Ergonomics*, Vol 21, No 8, pp 583-599 (1978)

[103]   **Stress Reactions in Computerised Administrative Work**, Johansson G and Aronsson G, Reports from the Department of Psychology, Supplement 50, University of Stockholm (November 1980)

[104]   *Keying into Careers*, Huws U, Phillips E and Griffiths F, GLC Equal Opportunities Group (1985)

[105]   *The Stagnant Pool and other Habitats: Word Processing Operators in the Public Service*, Manchee J, Office of the Coordinator, Status of Women, Canada (January 1982)

[106]   **Studies in Working Women's Nervous Systems**, Sumioka T, quoted in *Women and Micro-electronics In Japan*, Committee for the Protection of Women in the Computer World, Japan (1983)

[107]   **Stress link with breast cancer** *Guardian* (24th February 1986)

[108]   **Women's Place in the Integrated Circuit**, Grossman R, in *Changing Role of SE Asian Women*, Southeast Asia Chronicle (January-February 1979) and Pacific Research, Vol 9, No 5-6 (July-October 1978) joint issue

[109]   **Sources and Effects of Ionising Radiation**, UN Scientific Committee on the Effects of Atomic Radiation, Report to the General Assembly, nos 90-91 (1977) quoted in *No Immediate Danger: Prognosis for a Radioactive Earth*, Bertell R, The Women's Press (1985)

[110]   *No Immediate Danger: Prognosis for a Radioactive Earth*, Bertell R, The Women's Press (1985)

[111]   All the research referred to in this section on low frequency radiation is described in *Electromagnetism, Man and the Environment*, Battocletti J H, Environmental Studies Series (eds Rose J and Weidner E W), No 3, Elek Books (1976)

[112]   **The Possible Benefit of Negative-Ion Generators**, Hawkins L H, in *Health Hazards of VDTs?*, ed Pearce B, John Wiley (1984)

[113]   *The Ion Effect*, Soyka F and Edmonds A Bantam Books (1978)

[114]   *Working With VDUs*, Health and Safety Executive leaflet 360M, 1/86 (1986)

[115]   This quote is taken from a conversation between the author and a group of VDU workers in Coventry (1986)

[116]   *Visual Display Units. Health and Safety Survey*, prepared for the London Borough of Newham and Newham NALGO by Albury D, Butler T and Craig M, on behalf of North East London Polytechnic (September 1986)

[117]   *Training for Change*, Campbell F, GLC Equal Opportunities Group (1986)

[118]   Jones J C, [Author, *Technology Changes*, Princelet Editions (1985)] in conversation with the author (1986)

[119] *Design Methods*, Jones J C, John Wiley (1970 and 1981)

[120] *TUC Guidelines on VDUs*, Trades Union Congress (December 1985)

[121] *Fluorescent Lighting - A Health Hazard Overhead*, London Hazards Centre (March 1987)

[122] Quoted from *British Journal of Dermatology*, Vol 105, supp 21, pp29-33 (August 1981) in *Hazards Bulletin*, No 28 (November 1981)

[123] **The sick building syndrome: prevalence studies**, Finnegan and others, *British Medical Journal*, Vol 289, pp 1573-1575 (8th December 1984)

[124] *VDUs, Health and Jobs*, Labour Research Department, LRD Publications (1985)

[125] *The Office Workers' Survival Handbook*, Craig M, BSSRS Publications (1981)

[126] **Exploding chairs a pain in the office**, Andrew Moncur in *The Guardian* (9th August 1986)

[127] *VDUs, Health and Jobs*, Labour Research Department, LRD Publications (1985)

[128] **Alternative Keyboards: Goodbye to QWERTY?**, Stobie I, in *Practical Computing*, Vol 9, Issue 6 (June 1986)

[129] **Alternative Keyboards: Goodbye to QWERTY?**, Stobie I, in *Practical Computing*, Vol 9, Issue 6 (June 1986)

[130] **Alternative Keyboards: Goodbye to QWERTY?**, Stobie I, in *Practical Computing*, Vol 9, Issue 6 (June 1986)

[131] *Video Displays, Work and Vision*, Panel on Impact of Video Viewing on Vision of Workers, National Academy Press, Washington DC (1983)

[132] *Terminal Shock: The Health Hazards of Visual Display Terminals*, DeMatteo B, NC Press (1985)

[133] *Terminal Shock: The Health Hazards of Visual Display Terminals*, DeMatteo B, NC Press (1985)

[134] **Terminal Limits**, in *Global Electronics*, No 61 (January 1986)

[135] *VDUs, Health and Jobs*, Labour Research Department, LRD Publications (1985)

[136] Unpublished interview with VDU worker by the author (1984)

[137] *VDT News*, Vol 1, No 2 (March/April 1984)

[138] *Visual Display Units*, Health and Safety Executive, HMSO (1983)

[139] Reported in *VDUs, Health and Jobs*, Labour Research Department, LRD Publications (1985)

[140] **VDU fear typist wins back job**, *Times* (15th March 1986)

[141] *Terminal Shock: The Health Hazards of Visual Display Terminals*, DeMatteo B, NC Press (1985)

[142] *Hansard*, 493-498 (1985)

– Appendix 1 –

Suppliers

We know that many VDU operators and their employers have had trouble tracking down some items of equipment recommended by ergonomists as suitable for VDU work and have therefore included the names and addresses of some suppliers.

We must emphasise, however, firstly that this list is not complete, and secondly, that inclusion here does not constitute a recommendation. We can take no responsibility for the quality of any items of equipment which are supplied by any of these firms.

The addresses of all suppliers listed here apart from those marked with a * are taken from the excellent Labour Research Department booklet, *VDUs, Health and Jobs*, which also includes addresses of ergonomists and other specialists who can advise on the design of VDU workstations and working environments.

Chairs and desks

Project Office Furniture
Haverhill
Suffolk CB9 8QJ tel 0440 705 411

NKR Office Furniture Systems
73 Welbeck Street
London W1M 7HA tel 01 486 7051

Mines and West
Downley
High Wycombe
Bucks HP13 5TX tel 0494 34411

*Ericsson Information Systems
14 Old Park Lane
London SW1

Kneelers

Kneelers can be purchased by mail order from:

*Quorum Ltd
McIntyre House
Canning Place
Liverpool L70 1AX tel 051 708 5050

Document holders

Luxo Superholders
Malt Keyboards Ltd
262 Woodstock Road
Oxford OX2 7NW tel 0865 510043

Advanced Media Ltd
Media House
6 Knolls Way
Clifton
Beds SG17 5QZ tel 0462 811817

Willis computer and word processing supplies
PO Box No 10
Southmill Road
Bishops Stortford
Herts CM23 3DN tel 0279 506491

Acoustic hoods

Commercial Acoustics Ltd
Vincent Walk
South Street
Dorking RH4 2HA tel 0306 886464

Power Equipment Ltd
Kingsbury Works
Kingsbury Road
London NW9 8UU tel 01 205 0033

Lynnem Computer Products
277 London Road
Burgess Hill
Sussex
RH15 9QU tel 0446 3377/6632

Monarch Acoustics
Unit 12, Highview Avenue
Keyworth
Nottinghamshire NG12 5EL tel 0607 76606

Anti-glare filters

Promar
6A Church Street
Romsey
Hampshire SO5 8BU tel 0794 522434
(some Promar screens incorporate an anti-static component)

Romag Safety Glass Ltd
Patterson Street
Blaydon-on-Tyne
Tyne and Wear NE21 5SG tel 091 414 5511

CW Cave and Tab Ltd
5 Tenter Road
Moulton Park
Northampton NN3 1PZ tel 0604 43677

Sericol Group Ltd
24 Parsons Green Lane
London SW6 4HT tel 01 736 3388

Power Equipment Ltd
Kingsbury Works
Kingsbury Road
London NW9 8UU tel 01 205 0033

Negative ionisers

*London Ioniser Centre
65 Endell Street
London WC2H 9AJ tel 01 836 0251

*Leek Electrical Domestic Appliances Ltd
Dairy House
Ford
Near Leek
Staffordshire ST13 7RW tel 0538 8300

*Astrid Ltd
61 Laburnam Avenue
Hornchurch
Essex RM12 4HF tel 04024 48368

*Sidha Technology Ltd
Peel House
Peel Road
West Pimbo
Skelmersdale
Lancs WN8 9PT tel 0695 21155

Alternative keyboards

*PCD Maltron Ltd
15 Orchard Lane
East Molesley
Surrey KT8 0BN tel 01 398 3265

*Velotype
Special Systems Industry BV
Lange Voorhout 45a
2514 EC Den Haag
Holland tel 010 31 70 659912/3

*Ceratech Electronics
Lenten House
20 Lenten Street
Alton
Hampshire GU34 1HG tel 0420 88674

Information about keyboards specially adapted for people with disabilities can be obtained from the Disablement Resettlement Officer at your nearest Department of Employment Office who may refer you to a specialist adviser. A useful booklet which summarises the aids available is *With a Little Help from the Chip*, BBC Publications (1985)

Radiation testing and shielding

*Promar
6A Church Street
Romsey
Hampshire SO5 8BU tel 0794 522434
[manufacture simple (not quantitative) VLF meters and anti-radiation screens]

– Appendix 2 –

Useful addresses

Information about trade unions

Trades Union Congress
Congress House
Great Russell Street
London WC1B 3LS tel 01 636 4030

The Trade Union Directory - A Guide to all TUC Unions, Eaton J and
Gill C, Pluto Press (1981)

HSE area office information services

Area	Address	Telephone number	Local authorities in each area
1 SOUTH WEST	Inter City House, Mitchell Lane, Bristol BS1 6AN	0272 290681	Avon, Cornwall, Devon, Gloucestershire, Somerset, Isles of Scilly
2 SOUTH	Priestley House, Priestley Road, Basingstoke RG24 9NW	0256 473181	Berkshire, Dorset, Hampshire, Isle of Wight, Wiltshire
3 SOUTH EAST	3 East Grinstead House, London Road East Grinstead, West Sussex RH19 1RR	0342 26922	Kent, Surrey, East Sussex, West Sussex
5 LONDON N (Merger of AOs 4 & 5)	Maritime House, 1 Linton Road Barking, Essex 1G11 8HF	01-594 5522	Barking and Dagenham, Barnet, Brent, Camden, Ealing, Enfield, Hackney, Haringey, Harrow, Havering, Islington, Newham, Redbridge, Tower Hamlets, Waltham Forest
6 LONDON S	1 Long Lane, London SE1 4PG	01-407 8911	Bexley, Bromley, City of London, Croydon, Greenwich, Hammersmith & Fulham, Hillingdon, Hounslow, Kensington & Chelsea, Kingston, Lambeth, Lewisham, Merton, Richmond, Southwark, Sutton, Wandsworth, Westminster
7 EAST ANGLIA	39 Baddow Road, Chelmsford, Essex CM2 0HL	0245 84661	Essex except the London Borough in Essex covered by Area 5; Norfolk, Suffolk
8 NORTHERN HOME COUNTIES	14 Cardiff Road, Luton, Beds LU1 1PP	0582 34121	Bedfordshire, Buckinghamshire, Cambridgeshire, Hertfordshire
9 EAST MIDLANDS	Belgrave House, 1 Greyfriars, Northampton NN1 2BS	604 21233	Leicestershire, Northamptonshire, Oxfordshire, Warwickshire
10 WEST MIDLANDS	McLaren Bldg, 2 Masshouse Circ., Queensway, Birmingham B4 8NP	021-236 5080	West Midlands

Area	Address	Telephone number	Local authorities in each area
11 WALES	Brunel House, 2 Fitzalan Road, Cardiff CF2 1SH	0222 497777	Clwyd, Dyfed, Gwent, Gwynedd, Mid Glamorgan, Powys, South Glamorgan, West Glamorgan
12 MARCHES	The Marches House, Midway, Newcastle-under-Lyme, Staffs ST5 1DT	0782 610181	Hereford & Worcester, Shropshire, Staffordshire
13 NORTH MIDLANDS	Birbeck House, Trinity Square, Nottingham NG1 1AU	0602 470712	Derbyshire, Lincolnshire, Nottinghamshire
14 SOUTH YORKSHIRE	Sovereign House, 40 Silver Street, Sheffield S1 2ES	0742 739081	Humberside, South Yorkshire
15 W & N YORKS	8 St Pauls Street, Leeds LS1 2LE	0532 446191	North Yorkshire, West Yorkshire
16 GREATER MANCHESTER	Quay House, Quay Street, Manchester M3 3JB	061-831 7111	Greater Manchester
17 MERSEYSIDE	The Triad, Stanley Road, Bootle L20 3PG	051-922 7211	Cheshire, Merseyside
18 NORTH WEST	Victoria House, Ormskirk Road, Preston PR1 1HH	0772 59321	Cumbria, Lancashire
19 NORTH EAST	Arden House, Regent Centre, Regent Farm Road, Gosforth, Newcastle-upon-Tyne NE3 3JN	091-284 8448	Cleveland, Durham, Northumberland, Tyne & Wear
20 SCOTLAND EAST	Belford House, 59 Belford Road, Edinburgh EH4 3UE	031-225 1313	Borders, Central, Fife, Grampian, Highland, Lothian, Tayside and the island areas of Orkney & Shetland
21 SCOTLAND WEST	314 St Vincent Street, Glasgow G3 8XG	041-204 2646	Dumfries & Galloway, Strathclyde and the Western Isles

Local TU Health and Safety Groups

Birmingham Region Union Safety and Health Campaign, Tommy Harte, 68 St Joseph's Avenue, Northfield, Birmingham B31 2XQ. Tel: 021-475 4739.

Blackburn District Environmental Protection Group, 16 Woodbine Road, Blackburn, Lancs.

Community and Occupational Safety and Health in Tyneside (COSH-IT) Secretary Dave Dodds c/o TUSIU.

Coventry Workshop, 38 Binley Road, Coventry CV3 1JA. Tel: 0203 27772/3.

Cumbrians Opposed to Radioactive Environment, 98 Church Street, Barrow-in-Furness, Cumbria LA14 2HJ. Tel: 0229 33851.

Hull Action on Safety and Health, 31 Ferens Avenue, Cottingham Road, Hull HU6 7SY. Tel: 0482 49768.

Isle of Wight Trade Union Safety Group, Bob Davies, 12 Winston Road, Newport, IOW PO30 1RF.

Leeds Trade Union and Community Resource and Information Centre, 1st Floor, Market Buildings, Vicar Lane, Leeds LS2 7JF. Tel: 0532 439633.

Merseyside Trades Council Health and Safety Committee. Tel: 051-709 4398.

Merseyside Trades Union Resources, 24 Hardman Street, Liverpool L1 9AX. Tel: 051-709 3995.

People's Asbestos Action Campaign, c/o SCAT, 31 Clerkenwell Close, London EC1. Tel: 01-253 3627.

Portsmouth Area Health and Safety Group, Norman Harvey, 32 Rowner Close, Gosport, Hants PO13 0LY. Tel: 0329 281898.

Potteries Action for Safety and Health, Bill Edmundson, 16 Fieldway, Longton, Stoke-on-Trent ST3 2AN. Tel: 0782 327144.

Scotland South East Hazards Group, Alan Beard, 10 Fountainhall Road, Edinburgh. Tel: Dave Smith 031-557 0616.

Sheffield Area Trade Union Safety Committee, Seb Schmoller, 312 Albert Road, Heeley, Sheffield S8 9RD. Tel: 0742 584559.

Sheffield Occupational Health Project, Birley Moor Health Centre, 2 Eastgate Crescent, Sheffield S12 4QN. Tel: 0742 392541 Mon, Tue.

Sunderland Community and Occupational Health and Safety Group, Jimmy Harrison, 48 Wearmouth Drive, Sunderland. Tel: 0783 494482.

Walsall Action for Safety and Health, 7 Edinburgh Drive, Rushall, Walsall WS4 1HW. Tel: 0922 25860.

Wiltshire Hazards Action Group, 33 Milton Road, Swindon SN1 5JA. Tel: 0793 486926.

West Yorkshire Hazards Group, c/o Bradford Resource Centre, 31 Manor Row, Bradford, West Yorkshire BD1 4PS. Tel: 0274 725046.

Wolverhampton, The Law Centre, 2/3 Bell Street, Wolverhampton. Tel: 0902 772250.

Work Hazards Groups
Resource Centres

Health and Safety Advice Centre, Unit 304, The Argent Centre, 60 Frederick Street, Birmingham B1 3HS. Tel: 021-236 0801.

London Asbestos Action Campaign, c/o London Hazards Centre. Tel: 01-833 2487.

London Hazards Centre, 3rd Floor, Headland House, 308 Gray's Inn Road, London WC1X 8DS. Tel: 01-837 5605.

North East Work Hazards Group, c/o TUSIU.

Scotland South East Hazards Group, Alan Beard, 10 Fountainhall Road, Edinburgh.

TUSIU, Trade Union Studies Information Unit, Southern Fernwood Road, Jesmond, Newcastle NE2 1TJ. Tel: 0632 816087.

VDU Workers' Rights Campaign, c/o City Centre, 32–35 Featherstone Street, London EC1. Tel: 01-608 1338.

Women and Work Hazards Group, c/o A Woman's Place, Victoria Embankment, London WC2N 6PA.

Index

About the London Hazards Centre

Fighting for health and safety at work and in the community

▲ **Information on hazards**

▲ **The law and how to use it**

▲ **Organising and helping build campaigns**

A vital resource for London's trade unions, community groups and tenants' associations

The London Hazards Centre was set up in 1984 to provide people in London with the resources to fight hazards at work and in the community. We can supply information on thousands of different hazards, from asbestos in the home to noise and chemical pollution in the workplace. We try to present technical information in plain language. We advise on the law and how to use it. We help people to organise effective campaigns, and work mainly with groups such as trade union branches and tenants' associations.

Getting involved

In order to make sure the work of the Centre reflects people's needs, we have set up working groups which draw in users of the Centre. There are working groups for Black people, for tenants and others organising around community issues, for women, for trade unionists, and for people interested in the collection and exchange of information.

Fighting racism

In our racist society, Black people end up in the most dangerous jobs and polluted workplaces, doing more than their share of shiftwork and homework, and running a higher risk of unemployment. Black people are also more likely to be allocated the worst available housing. The London Hazards Centre has made a positive commitment to work with Black organisations and to develop the resources they need to fight hazards.

Women and hazards

Because of discrimination and domestic commitments, women often have jobs where the law offers little protection. Deregulation in employment law means that more and more women find themselves in workplaces where organising together is the only way to improve working conditions. New technology is enabling employers to create a new generation of sweatshops and new risks to workers' health in offices and countless other workplaces. The Hazards Centre works with women organising at work and in the community against dangers such as asbestos, damp, pest infestations, chemicals at work and hazards to reproduction.

Resources

We have a large and ever-growing library of hazards information to help us respond appropriately to people who contact us, seeking the most effective strategy and putting people in contact with others who have been fighting similar hazards. Sometimes an inspection is appropriate, and we may use our monitoring equipment or help groups to organise a survey by an outside agency.

Other publications from the London Hazards Centre

▲ **Fluorescent Lighting – A Health Hazard Overhead**
£5.00 (£2.00 to trade union and community groups)
March 1987 ISBN 0 948974 01 X

▲ **Repetition Strain Injuries – Hidden Harm from Overuse**
£6.00 (£3.00 to trade union and community groups)
(to be published) 1987 ISBN 0 948974 03 6

Affiliate!

We welcome affiliations from individuals and groups committed to the fight against hazards at work and in the community. Affiliation shows support for the Centre, brings you a year's supply (five issues) of our newsletter, the *Daily Hazard*, and news of the Centre's other publications and activities.

▲ **Contact the London Hazards Centre for further details and affiliation rates**